The Swedish story

From extreme experiment to normal nation

Jan Sjunnesson

Table of Contents

CHAPTER 4:
Humiliation 1970 - 2000 81

CHAPTER 5:
Hope 2000 - 133

CHAPTER 6:
Contemporary extremes 161

CHAPTER 7

Normal Sweden 231

Afterword by an extreme Swede 237

Acknowledgements: 245

Governments in Sweden 1876 - 2014 246

Parties 2010 - 2014 247

References 249

CHAPTER 1

Land of extremes

The title *The Swedish Story: From extreme experiment to normal nation* needs some explanation. There is an abundance of stories and details and many heroes and villains in the following pages. Scandals, sex and bodily fluids will occur as well as Soviet submarines, phallic trumpets, film, fiction and welfare art tricksters. Everything happened as written. No exaggeration is needed in the land of extremes.

The first part of the subtitle, extreme experiment, comes from economist Assar Lindbeck's 1997 article "The Swedish Experiment"[1] in which he wrote:

> "Why should foreign observers be interested in economic and social conditions in Sweden? The best answer is probably that institutions and policies in Sweden have been rather experimental, and that some of these experiments may also be relevant for other developed countries. Sweden may therefore be seen not only as a small country on the periphery of Europe, but also as a large ('full-scale') economic and social laboratory."

Note here that professor Lindbeck claims in a scientific article that Sweden is a pre-existing social laboratory in which planners can try out new utopian and extreme policies with real human beings as guinea pigs. The results revealed in this book are as bewildering as the staggering costs.

The second part of the subtitle is from German writer Hans-Magnus Enzensberger's 1992 collection of essays *In defence of the normal*[2]. He states that the normal has gotten a bad reputation and has been overtaken by

---

[1]   Lindbeck 1997.

[2]   Enzensberger 1992. See also Stjernfelt and Thomsen 2007.

the abnormal. But by the time, being abnormal becomes the new normal, épater le bourgeois the everyday routine. The Swedish kind of welfare art tricksters will appear with their tiresome provocations that have become routine rather than the exception in Swedish art and politics. All attitude, no content. Ideology not art. All left.

The two sources from which the terms in the subtitle are drawn, an article on welfare economics and an essay on European decency, cover the areas of intellectual curiosity that make up the arguments in chapters that follow. On the one hand, politics, business, economy and law, on the other ethnology, stories, culture and morals. Together with stories so strange that they will surprise most people, the story of Sweden will be told from the point of view of an outsider, a normal person trying to inhabit an extreme nation. Sweden is not a normal country but it could once again be. Only through reading this book can this fact be understood and appreciated and possibly prompt people to act. You as a non-Swedish reader have an important role to play.

Every country needs to have its self-image critiqued every now and then. What was normal in apartheid South Africa seemed extreme to the rest of the world after 1960. Today North Koreans live what they believe are normal lives, which for all the planet's other thinking and feeling people seems maddening. During the Balkan crisis, what had been normal divisions between ethnic groups erupted into extremes. Sweden is far from any of these regions but there is a Swedish normality which is extreme by all standards. Some good, some bad. Taken together, Sweden is an extreme country which makes questioning Swedes like me and most visitors question whether it is us that are extreme in trying to uphold sanity and normality or the country? For me there is no question. We are not extreme but Sweden is. We are normal and Sweden is not. *The Swedish story* will give some clues, but it is not a scholarly work. It is written with a fervour that comes from living and thinking a double life. One life of extremes which is normal in Sweden and another life trying to stay normal by global standards which is extreme in Sweden. Lives that are extreme by any global and sane standards are normal in Sweden and vice versa. National schizophrenia is rampant but it has remained undiagnosed until now.

The aim of this book is threefold, with two lesser goals and one gigantic one:

1. To expose the shortcomings of a large welfare state and high taxation.
2. To show the conformist and silent nature of the Swedish national character.
3. To remake Sweden into a normal country, getting rid of the extreme

The first has been the topic of debate of welfare economics and clientelism for many decades. In some OECD countries, Sweden has been used as a textbook example of wanting to tax and spend a country into a sclerotic, dull welfare state with totalitarian tendencies. Others, including leading economists and newspapers in USA and UK, praise Sweden for what is considered its clever and stable economic policy. A critique of large welfare states from a center-right political perspective will surface in the forthcoming pages, but these conservative or libertarian critical comments will not be the sole focus here. Instead, the focus will be the ongoing Swedish support for the welfare state from all political areas, including the political parties to the right. The historical roots for this broad support are much deeper than is usually appreciated when blaming socialist and ambitions welfare state policies. National traits run much deeper than politics, and the Swedes like their state take care of them. They willingly pay high taxes and get something in return, even if they never completely understand how much they pay and what they get back. Still Sweden functions well, even if lower taxes and a smaller government will become essential in coming decades. The current changes of welfare economics go in the right direction, so there is less to worry about, in contrast to the second aim for this book.

The second topic, the dull, conformist and totalitarian streaks within the smooth welfare state, has also been the topic of studies and stories over the years. However, this book gives an updated version of the Swedish conformism and correctness in media, education and policy, among citizens and undemocratic repression of free thought. The last decades

of identity politics and dominance from the cultural left play a large
role building on earlier traits of rural awkwardness and welfare state social engineering, resulting in self-censorship, learned helplessness and a
pathological need for security. While the first aim, to change Swedish
welfare state foundations is both unwanted and not yet immediate, the
second aim, to stop repression of free thought and open debate is something this book supports strongly. Paying high taxes might do, but silence
not. The combination of the two is maddening, to simply pay and shut
up, which is what most Swedes do. The dominance of political conformism and the citizens' fear to speak their mind are becoming even more
stifling, and heading in the wrong direction, especially after the racially
and right-wing politically motivated Norwegian massacre of 2011.

The last megalomaniac ambition of writing this book is my conviction
that Swedes are unable to change their extreme country into a normal
Western democracy. Help must come from immigrants and foreign readers who do not take Swedish extremes for granted. The last chapter will
explain how that change may come about.

This chapter is divided into three parts. First, the most common image of the Swedish, or sometimes called the Scandinavian (or sometimes
named Nordic) welfare state Model is presented. Then the strange concept of state individualism is presented; it is a key to understanding the
extreme Swedish identity. Lastly there is a story from the perceptive of
a Polish writer living in Sweden on his first encounter with the welfare
services in the land of extremes.

THE CAPITALIST WELFARE STATE

To the world, Sweden wants to be known for its naturalness, innovation, compassion and openness, which can be reduced to the single
term of being progressive[3]. A slick modern market economy yet car-

---

[3]   Svenska Institutet 2010. Interestingly, the left leaning political interpretation of be-
        ing progressive is not noted at the national image building Swedish Institute. Being
        Swedish is being progressive which leads to a welfare state liberal and mostly socialist

ing and equal, the Swedish Model has been described in many ways as stemming from a mixture of economic, political, and nationalist lines of thought. A common way to analyze the model is to view the successful economic story over a century. Then it is obvious that Sweden had successful economic growth from 1870 -1970 based on a model of:

> **Mixed economy** - capitalism and a planned economy with strong national control over capital flows, credit and interest rates
> **Corporatism** – good independent relations between employers' federations and labour unions, organized interest groups and popular movements supported by government
> **General welfare state policy** – universal welfare programs that also benefit the middle class
> **Rehn - Meidner model** – unions support structural changes and a fair wage policy (wages are paid according to agreements, not business' ability to pay) [4]

The role of institutions in the economy is crucial to explain the emergence of poor and isolated 19th century Sweden into the rich Sweden of the 20th century. Due to a homogenous population of equals, political mobilization, free trade and an emerging -corruption-free government administration after 1850, trust evolved in the emerging popular institutions that became foundations of the welfare state from 1900.

Sweden is split into two sectors, government and private, in ways that are more accentuated than elsewhere. The combination of the two makes up the capitalist welfare state. Without technologically advanced exporting industries, the welfare state would not obtain enough taxes. But the welfare state also contributes to providing good conditions for innovation, social services and infrastructure. The two sectors work in tandem and

---

ideology. Swedes finds it very hard to imagine being progressive without these features.

[4]   From Bergh 2009, p. 14. The Rehn-Meidner model will be explored more in chapter 3.. See also Eklund 2011 for overview of the Nordic model in English.

complement each other well. The sectors below describe the two.

THE WELFARE SECTOR

The modern Swedish welfare state, which some view critically, others with admiration, has some extreme economic and social features:

- Government spending comes to 55 % of GDP (vs. an EU/OECD average 45 %).
- Taxes total more than 50% of income (vs. EU/OECD average 45 %).
- For 65 years of last 80 years, the social democratic labour party has been in power.
- Almost 20 % of all citizens aged 20 - 64 are wholly supported by welfare benefits
- More than 20 % of all single mothers depend on welfare benefits in full or in part
- 25% of the employees in the work force are in the public sector (vs. an OECD average of 15%)
- Sweden ranks 9 out of 169 in the UN Human development index.

One might conclude from these figures that being an expensive welfare state may be burdensome, but it attracts good UN ratings. But this is not the case; more credit is due to the private sector. Here are the global market rankings of same Sweden as a —highly functional, capitalist high-tech country[5]:

THE PRIVATE SECTOR

Position

4/167   Global Democracy Index, *The Economist*

4/178   Corruption Perception, Transparency International

2/50   Country reputation, Reputation Institute

3/ 142 Global competitiveness, World Economic Forum

---

[5]   International indexes available at Swedish Institute web, Sept 2012.

2/125   Innovation index, INSEAD
2/134   Knowledge economy, World Bank
1/131   Innovation capacity, European Business School

Sweden is viewed as an ideal for capitalism and innovation, even if indexes of economic freedom are less impressive. The *Economic freedom of the world 2012 index* (Fraser Institute) ranks Sweden as number 30 of the 141 countries measured[6]. *The Economist* looked up to the 'North star of Sweden' with 'The New Model' as the best student in the tough EU financial class and Stockholm as world's number 6 best city to live in. *The Financial Times* followed suit by selecting moderate (former conservative) Anders Borg as best finance minister in EU 2011.

A growing proportion of Swedes have come to accept the welfare state since neo-liberalism appeared in early 1990s. 75 % of polled Swedes in 2010 imagined proclaimed themselves even willing to pay more taxes if the money went to government health services. In 1997, only 67 % had held that view[7]. Since 2006 when center-right coalition took power, support has risen for government-run welfare services, especially among middle class voters. This is a paradox since this non-socialist coalition traditionally had stood for smaller government, but won by changing their election campaign to promise better government, not smaller.

Critics of large welfare stateism could argue that the reformed and slimmed down welfare state of the post-1990s has gotten its renewed support because of these changes and liberalizations (school vouchers, health choices, deregulation of government corporations, topping up with private alternatives etc.). Paradoxes emerge. A properly reformed, if socialist-initiated, welfare state can work if run by center-right or market oriented socialist governments dedicated to piecemeal social engineering with no red or blue utopias getting in the way. Historical precedents include the a kind of low key politics of the European 18th century rational

---

[6]   The Heritage Foundation Economic Freedom 2012 index ranks Sweden at 21, Denmark at 11th.

[7]   Svallfors 2011.

enlightenment, the 19th century romantic ideals of equality, and 20th century democratic reformism. Capitalism and welfare seem to join hands in their belief in technology, individualism and secular rationality, resulting in a specifically Swedish modernity. But there is a price to pay, even if few Swedes recognize it.

Regular Swedes contribute to the large welfare state through their daily spending and monthly wages. Welfare state technocrats are clever in making new taxes invisible. Of the total of 46 % of GDP going to taxes, 25 percentage points come from invisible taxes. The smaller part of 21 percentage points is seen on pay cheques and is often lamented yet tolerated. Few even know about the major invisible part. Suppose the total payroll cost of an employee is SEK 100/hour., which means that within the 100 Swedish Crowns, all expenses for this particular employee are included. The table below shows how visible and invisible taxes reduce disposable income:

100	Net salary paid from employer but not seen by employee
-32	Deducted as payroll tax by employer to various governmental social insurance schemes incl. 18 % for pensions but also 9 % to government with no specifications (löneavgift)
68	Salary seen by employee and agreed to in the union contract
-20, 4	Municipal income tax for low and medium salaries, but higher for higher salaries
47, 6	Money available to spend on services and goods
-11, 9	Value added tax (VAT, at 25 %, the second highest in the EU)
35.7 =	Available to spend out of a total of 100 SEK

The 32 SEK in payroll tax is absolute minimum. Usually the employer and union have agreed on higher levels, 40 – 50 SEK in voluntary agreements but done under pressure from unions. These agreements are collective and for all, whether union members or not. The payroll taxes for social benefits and agreed minimum salaries are protected by unions, which may interfere in industrial disputes outside their union

domain. On top of that, 20 % of all citizens pay a supplemental national tax if their salaries are higher than average. This national tax is progressive, so the more you earn the higher the tax. With these additions, the sum of disposable income is more often $3 out of $10, or even less if you use tobacco, petrol, alcohol and other highly taxed goods. Thus Swedes are drawn into collective agreements on salaries and benefits without their knowledge. To volunteer to work for a lower salary or with lesser social benefits than agreed collectively is not possible, not even in theory.

The secret way to tax Swedes, using governmentally administered and mandatory social benefits for pension, sick leave support and other benefits as shown above leaves them no option to use that part of salaries for private pension schemes or save or spend as they may wish. With progressively higher taxes on higher wages, incentives for careers and higher education are small. Professionals who chose Sweden for work may come for the welfare services and maybe because their work was relocated, but they seldom come to start a career, work hard and amass some money. They might voice their thoughts about how high taxes or how the political system represses any dissent, but they will be excused. Dissenting Swedes on the contrary face all kinds of repression of thought and silence themselves. Only with the arrival of more non- Swedes will anything happen as the Swedes themselves are afraid to act, I will argue in the last chapters.

EXTREME VALUES, LEFT POLITICS AND "STATE INDIVIDUALISM"

Sweden has been compared to all other nations as being the most self-expressive, rational and secular country in the world according to the cultural map of the world done by *World Values Survey* in 2008[8]. Sweden is the absolutely most modern and most lonely country in the world, as there is no country quite like it in its extreme position. Befitting image as it pictures both the extreme and solitary position of the nation and its

---

[8]   www.worldvaluessurvey.org

citizens.

©Inglehart & Welzel. www.worldvaluessurvey.org

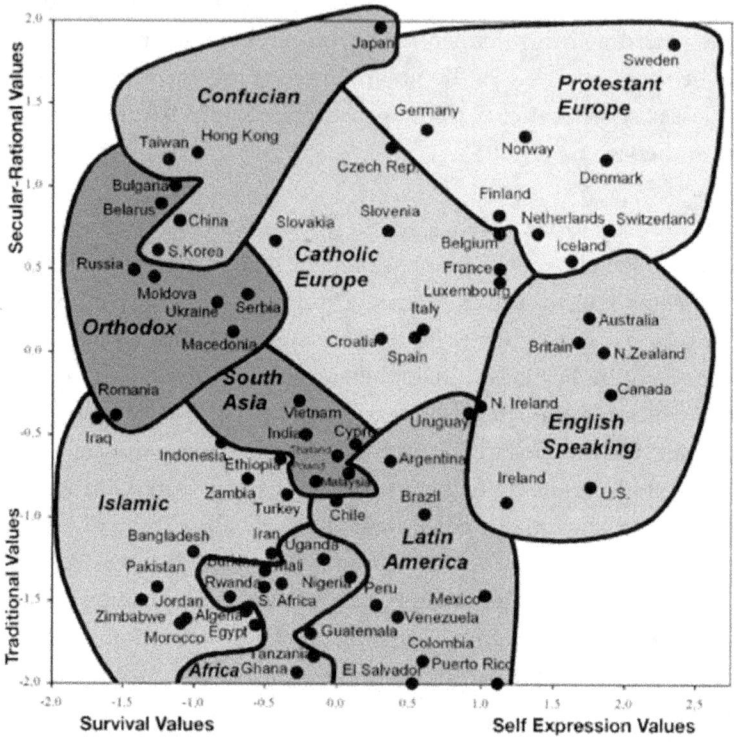

The diagram should be read as follows: Traditional on the vertical axis values emphasize the importance of religion, parent-child ties, deference to authority and traditional family values. People who embrace these values also reject divorce, abortion, euthanasia and suicide. These societies have high levels of national pride and a nationalistic outlook. Secular-rational values have the opposite preferences to the traditional values. These societies place less emphasis on religion, traditional family values and authority. Divorce, abortion, euthanasia and suicide are seen as relatively acceptable. Self-expression values on the horizontal axis show the ability and tolerance to stand out from the survival values of the collective, usually family and society. Swedes are then the most self-expressive people in the world. The particular Swedish interpretation of expression is rather independence from family and society, not necessarily expression any certain individual values[9].

In the upper right corner, Sweden reigns in splendid isolation, way apart from Norway and Denmark. Post-materialist values are more important than careers and material wealth. Organized religion plays little role, but government's is huge. Developing countries and other industrialized nations in the might go in the direction of Sweden, but it has its drawbacks[10]. If other countries could get richer but not develop these disadvantages, the world would see more semi- Swedish, but better functioning, leaner and more tolerant welfare states. This book is a tale of caution for those countries.

There are correlations between being more rational and self- expressive and economic growth but not all rich countries are as extreme as Sweden Japan, Australia, USA, Germany and Belgium for example. Some of these have smaller governments, and lower taxes but same or better living standards. The usual defence of a rich welfare state by Swedes does not hold up well, as the country has declined rapidly in wealth rapidly over the last four decades. No longer the richest, not receiving the same welfare benefits, alone and extreme is rather the current Swedish predicament.

Another view of Swedish extremes can be seen in the political arena. Policies that are common across developed nations within the OECD and considered normal, mainstream, are usually framed as reactionary, anti-women and ethnic minorities and right-wing by Swedish political standards. If current Prime Minister Fredrik Reinfeldt, or any Swedish minister from any party, were to go to Washington or London to give a

---

[9]   See Gustavsson 2009 for a defence of tolerance of individual expression among Swedes rather than expressing non-conformist values in reply to Svanberg 2009 who states that young Swedes paradoxically have a conformist pressure to not conform, at least emotionally.

[10]   See forecasts by Swedish professor Hans Rosling at www.gapminder.org

description of some basic and shared policies of his center-right leaning cabinet, he would be depicted as a pinko-liberal or old labour. Why that is so can be seen in this table of political parties from USA and UK:

Letters in italics describe the Swedish Social democrats, Center party and

LEFT	CENTER		RIGHT
	"BBC/NYT"		
SOCD CEN MOD			
	LAB	TORY	
	DEM		REP

Moderates (formerly the conservative Right party), capitalized the British Labour party and Conservative Tories, and underscored the two American parties, Democratic and Republican. This figure is not scientific at all and has no reference scale, but gives a reasonable view of the global political spectrum that is widely shared by news agencies and newspapers. To read *New York Times* or watch BBC news will hopefully be from a political center, mainstream or even slightly left of center standpoint but still sane and normal. The bold and capital headlines on top are supposed to state an imagined political scale with the two established Western news media almost at center.

If these news bureaus and papers would cover some topic which is normal in Sweden, that story would come out extreme, as anything from the political center, mainstream or at best neutral by Swedish standards, is quite on the left in the world. To be politically center in Sweden is left in the world, and to be right or even liberal in Sweden is center in the world. To be right of center in the world, as a Tory or Republican is considered mad, reactionary and extreme. To state views that are normal in other parts of the world becomes impossible, both in content but also in form as the Swedish establishment and media know what is best for everyone everywhere. The American interpretation of being liberal which means left leaning Democrat in favour of big government is the normal Swedish center-right position. But being liberal in the Swedish interpretation is mostly considered politically right. In this book the Swedish center-right interpretation of liberalism will be used even if it confuses Americans. And of course it is confusing if liberals talk of mandatory preschool for

all children from 3 years, which some do, and of outlawing home schooling, which happened. The extreme in the world is normal in Sweden; the
normal in the world is extreme in Sweden. Spend an hour or two on the
website *The Local* for news of Sweden in English and read what foreigners
think of Swedish news and politics is enough to understand the differences between the land of extremes and normal countries[11].

If one sums up all the above-mentioned features about Sweden, one can
arrive at a new concept which sums up all extremes:

> High taxation and a large welfare state
> Silent conformism and thought repression
> Extreme secular rationalism and self-expression
> + Leftist politics
> = state individualism

The strange concept of "state individualism" is used in the book *Is the
Swede a human being?* (Är svensken människa?) from 2006, co-authored
by historians Henrik Berggren and Lars Trägårdh.[12] The concept is not
well known to ordinary Swedes, but they recognize it when explained,
mostly nodding shyly in the affirmative. State individualism sounds partly egotistic, partly repressive and nothing to be proud of. To be human is
to belong to some human community they state, but the modern Swede
does not need to nor wants to belong. The welfare state takes care of
all needs from the cradle to the grave so the citizens can concentrate of
working and paying high taxes. Individualism does not imply voicing
individual opinions, but is the same freedom of self-expression that the
World Values Survey found was common in Sweden. Individuals make
decisions on their own and with little regard to community, civil society
or public sphere. An example is the proportion of single-households.
Sweden has the highest number of men and women preferring to live
alone, Stockholm the highest in Sweden and Kungsholmen island the
highest in Stockholm areas. Yet Stockholm is ranked among the six best

---

[11]   www.thelocal.se

[12]   Berggren and Trägårdh 2006

cities to live in. How can the extreme also be the best? This book will not answer this question but gives a perspective on how the best and the extreme go together in Sweden with its national features.

Berggren and Trägårdh are quite fond of their vague concept of state individualism that gives room for interpretation; they defend this extreme position. With roots in Swedish history before the welfare state of early 20th century, they show that Sweden has fostered independent citizens that lack ability and interest in undertaking common purposes outside their small world of friends. The concept of Swedish (and Nordic, among which Sweden is the most extreme) state individualism was presented in 2012 by Swedish think tank Global Utmaning at the World Economic Forum in Davos. This positive message of state individualism is what the authors Berggren and Trägårdh proudly stated to the world of international business and governments, as having found the Holy Grail of modern welfare governance[13]:

> "While much has been written about the institutionalized aspects of the Nordic welfare state, few have paid much attention to its underlying moral logic. Though the path hasn't always been straight, one can discern over the course of the twentieth century an overarching ambition in the Nordic countries not to socialize the economy but to liberate the individual citizen from all forms of subordination and dependency within the family and in civil society: the poor from charity, the workers from their employers, wives from their husbands, children from parents – and vice versa when the parents become elderly / ... /
>
> The Nordic countries [are] the least family-dependent and most individualized societies on the face of the earth. To be sure, the family remains a central social institution in the Nordic countries, but it too is infused with the same mor-

---

[13]   Berggren and Trägårdh 2012. Available in English at www.globalutmaning.se. See also Trägårdh 2012.

al logic stressing autonomy and equality. The ideal family is made up of adults who work and are not financially dependent on the other, and children who are encouraged to be as independent as early as possible. / . . . /

Less tied down by legal and moral obligations within the family, yet still protected from extreme risk by a universal safety net, they become more flexible on the labour market, while as individual consumers they have developed far-reaching needs of products and services that previously were satisfied within the traditional family /. . . / Economic policies that cater both to our desire for individual autonomy and our need of community and security can be remarkably successful".

Applauds from at the 2012 Davos audience yet confusion. Most be some hidden costs, social or cultural if not economic. "Remarkably successful" seems too good to be true in 2012 . . .

The state individualist credo continues with the hardest calculation of all human acts, love. Love should not be based on practical needs or family obligations but romance born out of the feelings of two independent individuals. Children should not be born due to accidents, needs or to satisfy parental desires, but should be planned and welcomed for who they are as individuals. The utopian dream of a perfect society seems to have been realized in Sweden, these authors maintain but they do not tell the whole story as this book tries to do. The Davos crowd should invite me next time or at least grab this book. You are lucky to be reading it.

The two authors asked 'Are Swedes really humans' in their 2006 book title *Is the Swede a human being?* Do Swedes understand the value of human dignity? What is going on when the welfare state is responsible and not the human beings in it? That's the topic of next story.

A STORY FROM WELFARE LAND

In 1969 Maciej Zaremba had to leave communist, Catholic Poland and a good Jewish family for secular, safe Sweden and work at Beckomberga hospital in Stockholm[14]. He started working as a hospital orderly with elderly people in need of daily care. He had three duties; clean the rooms, feed the patients, and help with toilet visits. Nothing else. Patients were fed for 5 minutes apiece. If there was not enough time, too bad. Many newcomers lost both weight and appetite, in which case a nutritious gruel was quickly pushed down their throats.

Morning visits to the toilet were done with movable toilet seats on which old women sat naked as they were rolled openly through the ward corridor down to the collective bathroom. There they were all splashed with water from a hose, sometimes lukewarm, sometimes not, by a young man. The women sat all in a row like pigeons. Some cried but were quickly silenced with a slap from a towel. Zaremba protested saying that people cannot be treated like this. No one reacted or seemed to understand his reasoning. None of his colleagues, nor did the head nurse or doctors understand what the strange Pole talked about. Human dignity? This was properly administered welfare services.

Zaremba understood that what happened each morning to the naked women being run through the corridor was not extraordinary but common procedure, sometimes even in the presence of relatives. He had left a totalitarian state where he witnessed protesting pregnant women being kicked in their bellies by the military police. To be in a democracy and witness old people being treated as barn animals was bewildering, as was the lack of dignity, empathy and self-respect. The inability of the old to keep their bodily functions private was made worse by the inhuman treatment, one would expect among only primitive oafs and unkind louts (*cham* in Polish). Zaremba was guided by his family upbringing and sense of duty. For him there was no question as to whether the hospital staff should spend more time and energy to make the lives of the elderly better, more respectful and easier. It was one's pure duty to human dignity

---

[14]   Zaremba 1992.

and to older people. Period. Impractical yes, even undemocratic (which he was called by people when the embarrassing topic was mentioned), but necessary to remain human oneself he thought. The Swedish idea of rationality led the staff to demand rational justifications for Zaremba's insistence of respect, duty and dignity and he had none.

Later when he became a celebrated writer in Sweden, he held a speech in 2003 called *When will Sweden be European*[15]? The ambition of this book is similar in its search for *when will Sweden be normal*. In early medieval ages, Sweden was probably most normal and European, as will be shown in the next chapter on the history of Sweden from around AD 1000 to 1930.

---

[15]   Zaremba 2003. See also Zaremba and Malmström 2003.

CHAPTER 2

History from 1000 to 1930

Sweden is on the Scandinavian Peninsula, well north and isolated from continental Europe. Due to kilometres of thick ice from the North Pole lingering until around 10 000 BC, a harsh climate and its remoteness, Sweden was populated later and more sparsely than the rest of Europe. Not until the Viking age 800–1100 AD did international contacts by trade and plundering become frequent. Neither a part of the Roman Empire nor Christian until 1103 AD, the kingdom of Sweden formed by 1200 was a weak nation-state. Not until 1397 under the Scandinavian Kalmar Union treaty did Sweden have almost full reign over what would become the country. The southern tip remained Danish, the northern tip Sami/Finnish and to the west were the borders to Norway always changing. The southern and western coasts of Finland were under Swedish sovereignty from early 13th century. Culturally, scientifically and intellectually Sweden was on the sidelines during the great changes in European civilization from the middle ages. Imitating European customs and using Latin, German, French and English at royal court, civil service and in trade did not make Sweden into an ordinary European power with national confidence in its culture and nationhood. What became specifically Swedish were its peasantry, central planning and fascination for technology. The harsh climate needed rational and foresighted people that could survive four to eight months of severe cold on stored food with few human contacts and little sunlight. Even today the shy and blunt Swedes are marked by their common rural roots as they navigate a sophisticated cosmopolitan world.

DEMOCRATIC ORIGINS

Unlike continental Europe and the British Isles, Scandinavia had few feudal institutions with repressed serfs and civil strife among medieval fiefdoms, but was strong in its belief in laws for all men and in peace. One of the first laws stated in 1296 that "land shall with laws be built and

not with violent actions" (Upplandslagens Byalagsbalk)[16]. In 1319 when
the three year heir to the throne, Magnus Eriksson, was selected at Mora
ting outside Uppsala, four farmers from each parish were present. The
young king had to respect the voices of the "men of Sweden" in taxation
matters. Men selected their own representatives in each parish to decide
in tax matters[17]. 400 years before the young republic of the United States
of America claimed the right to be represented when taxed by colonial
British kingdom, Swedes had a rudimentary democratic system for taxation and representation.

Swedish peasants and farmers had a voice in the Estates of the Swedish
Realm (Ståndsriksdagen), a rare democratic institution in medieval Europe. The four Estates were Nobility, Clergy, Burghers and Farmers. No
universal suffrage existed of course, but each rural ward chose their own
representative to become member of the Estates in Stockholm with functions as to those of members of parliament. Swedish democracy defined
broadly and generously, can thus be said to exist for almost six centuries.
Not perfect but with deeper traditions than elsewhere. Roots of early
popular rebellions, labour movements and welfare state building built
on these old democratic traditions. The Estate of Farmers, consisting of
common farmers, was unique in Europe at the time. Only Switzerland
and a few German states had similar representative bodies for common
land-owning men outside churches, courts and noble houses.

In 1436 the first council of all Estates was gathered in the city of Uppsala
to give advice to the then king, Eric of Pomerania. He, like other kings,
pitted farmers and burghers against the other Estates or vice versa to
gain a balance of power. But now King Eric was in dire straits. Some
farmers had, together with miners, fought the king, had him deposed
and restored under severe conditions, that he respect their demands. A
song of freedom from this time, The Bishop Thomas' Freedom song
(Frihetsvisa), recalled the rebel leader Engelbrekt and hailed freedom as
the best thing there is. King Eric could continue to rule with the condi-

---

16   Hirschfeldt 2011.

17   Rojas 2005, p. 8- 9 and Berggren and Trägårdh 2006, p. 42.

tional support of farmers. These farmers were self-respecting men with their own lands, unlike serfs in middle and southern Europe.

The urban middle class of burghers, traders and tradesmen with some education, was weak in the start of the 15th century, but gained some strength in late 19th century along with other groups outside the Estates, such as manual labourers. Landless peasants and urban workers were outside all representative groups but since almost all delegates to the Estates came from the countryside, workers and farm hands were acquainted with elections, discussions and decisions by parishes, wards and at farmers' local assemblies. These structures were not without powers as the main part of property was in the hands of free farmers. Land ownership was split four ways by the early 16th century: 50 % owned by farmers, 22 % each by church and nobility and the state around 6 %. This would change soon when church and nobility would lose quickly to the state. Enter the founder of the modern Swedish state, King Gustav Vasa I.

NATION BUILDING 1500

King Gustav I Vasa reigned from 1521 to 1560 and is considered the father of Sweden. Vasa disengaged from the Roman Catholic Church and favoured the Protestant Luther in order to control his subjects better. Few opposed the new Lutheran religious order and the reformation process went quite fast and peacefully. With no pope involved to support the church and almost all noblemen slaughtered in 1521 by his Danish predecessor, Christian King Gustav I reigned with all the Royal might possible at the time and built an impressive national administration not equalled in Europe until Napoleonic France three centuries later.

Submission and acquiescence rather than fighting for ideas and principles characterized Swedish mentality even then. The first Swedish university in Uppsala, founded in 1477, declined and king Vasa fought the clergy and academics there, which were used to Catholicism and opposed the new rule. Taxes increased and nobility and clergy lost many privileges. Rebellions were brutally crushed like the southern Dacke uprising 1543, the largest peasant rebellion in Scandinavia ever. Farmers' support was used by king Vasa to extend his powers. The bonds between a strong state lead by a ruthless but also kind king and poor but supportive farmers was important to weaken the strength of nobility, church and whatever small urban classes existed. This alliance would later be the foundation for the concept of state individualism with the ruthless but kind king replaced with a bureaucratic but kind welfare state establishment.

Parallel to the strong state were parishes that by a royal decree in 1571 became responsible for the poor, elderly without families and the sick. Under Catholic rule everybody was threatened with purgatory and hell if they did not pay enough to support church run charities that cared for the weak in each parish. By late 16th century the now Protestant Swedish subjects had quit paying, since God's grace was assured to them anyway by the teachings of Luther. Thus the church had no powers over men. When the church could not rule to support the poor, the state stepped in with legislation. This early national responsibility to care for less fortunate members of society given to local institutions is important when discussing how medieval origins of welfare state building grew alongside a centralized civil service and a loyal church administration that effectuated population registry for taxation and conscriptions. But the church would not be entirely without powers. As the only country outside Israel of ancient Judaic times, Sweden enforced the Mosaic laws from the Old Testament in 1608. These laws lead to capital punishment for adultery, swearing and opposition to parents. The Lutheran church could be as fearful as the Catholic.

The ensuing century consolidated the power of the state and its capital Stockholm. The Swedish Empire lasted from 1561 to 1721. Sweden occupied parts of Germany, Denmark, Russia, Finland and the Baltic states, leading to a militarization of the country and royal autocracy. The expansion was not to find new markets for Swedish goods but to occupy land and to plunder. Royal propaganda told the people that the wars were a special mission for Sweden to spread protestant Christianity in the region. During 17th century national pride seemed to have no bounds. The most famous philosopher in Europe, Frenchman René Descartes, was called to the royal court to entertain and educate Queen Christina I, with fatal results. Her early hour to discuss philosophy was at 5 am in the cold Stockholm castle. The distinguished philosopher caught pneumonia and died in 1660, a few months after arrival. But there were more chances to display Swedish fame to the world. The royal chaplain, professor of medicine and rector magnificus of Uppsala University, Olaus Rudbeck, proposed in his treatise *Atlantica* by 1679 that Sweden was in fact the source of the ancient lost paradise island of Atlantis and the glimmering hope for Western civilization since Plato. Further in Rudbeck's national megalomania, Swedish was the original language of the biblical Adam's divine language and the linguistic roots of Latin and Hebrew. Sweden had not only a royal and religious prophetic mission to save the world, but was also the origin of all wealth and truth. This self- proclaimed mission to the world would be reiterated over the centuries[18].

The war economy led to much misery, as men were drafted and farms abandoned. Unlike in England and Holland, no pre-capitalist culture or urban bourgeois class of any measure existed. Instead ironworks in mill towns flourished in the countryside. These hamlets were dominated by patriarchs who knew how to manage furnaces and people. Housing, schooling, insurance, health, food, and transports were taken care of by export oriented owners who often were foreigners themselves, often from Wallonia in present Belgium. The close connection to global markets has ever since been a feature of Swedish industrial life along with safe and good living conditions granted by benevolent rulers for their workers. The first signs of a capitalist welfare state had started.

After a strategically insane march towards Russia under madcap king Charles XII, the royal Swedish army was defeated in Poltava in Ukraine and fled to Turkey. At home the country was virtually bankrupt and territories were lost. After its defeat in the Great Northern War (1700– 1721) against the combined forces of Denmark, Poland and Russia and a (possibly Swedish) bullet killing king Charles XII in 1718, Sweden lost most of its provinces on the other side of the Baltic Sea. The Swedish Empire was reduced to essentially the same frontiers as present day Sweden and

---

[18]   Edwardsson 2010, p. 46 and Andersson and Hilson 2009.

Finland. And a century later during the Napoleonic Wars, Finland was surrendered to Russia.

AGE OF LIBERTY 1700

The Age of liberty (Frihetstiden) in mid-18th century Sweden that followed the miserable years of drafts, deaths and hard times was nothing compared to the renaissance or enlightment periods in continental Europe or on the British Isles. Liberty here meant liberation from royal autocracy as the Realm of the four Estates took power for half a century. Sweden had few noblemen and Stockholm had only around 50 000 inhabitants so the resources and networks for exchange of new ideas were quite restricted. But liberal ideas were not totally unknown to small educated circles and even at government itself. *Two treatises of government* by John Locke were translated in 1726 into Swedish on assignment by the Swedish cabinet[19]. Natural law was well established in Sweden already in mid 17th century by the German political philosopher Samuel von Pufendorf who was professor of law at Lund University in southern Sweden and later became royal historiographer in Stockholm. Later developments in legal traditions would go in the opposite direction towards legal positivism which was more useful to royal autocrats and 20th century social democrats and welfare state liberals more in need of malleable citizens for efficient welfare purposes than defence of civil liberties as in Anglo-Saxon and French legal traditions.

Pamphlets were printed in these free spirited decades that espoused physiocratic economic policies against stagnant mercantilism and for civil liberties for all citizens. Peter Forsskål wrote 1759 a treatise with thoughts about civil liberties in which a catalogue of liberties was listed. First was the "right to live according to one's own wish" (lefwa efter egit behag). The pamphlet was forbidden and Peter Forsskål had to leave the country which led to much discussions. The authorities realized that banning undesirable printings gave them more attention. Better to ignore irritat-

---

[19]   Norberg 1999b, p. 21. The Swedish title was *Oföregripliga tankar om werldslig regerings rätta ursprung, gräntsor och ändamål.*

ing pamphlets altogether. Another important reformer was the prolific parliament member Anders Chydenius. He used this freedom to express his economic vision of how all citizens on free market contribute to the good of all, even if all pursue their own interests. 11 years later Adam Smith would repeat the idea of the invisible hand with a greater depth of analysis in his economic treatise *The wealth of nations* 1776.

In 1766 the Swedish regime introduced freedom of the press for the first time in the world on the initiative of Chydenius. His writings were influenced by natural law and threatened the privileges of nobility and guilds. But he also criticized when authorities forced citizens to act for their own good, as if citizens could not take care of themselves and be responsible even for their own bad decisions. Chydenius believed that regulations that forced farmers to keep storages of grain or to pay a village doctor were unnecessary. People can mind their own business and the state should keep out, especially out of business. Further subsidies to manufacturers and farmers were unproductive and led to inefficiency as these trades could not sustain themselves on a market without government support[20].

Another important event in Swedish history in mid 1700s was the agrarian redistribution reform that led to better use of lands but also to more isolated villages and farms. This reform would be followed by two more land reforms until the Swedish countryside was totally transformed and rationalized by 19th century. Popular movements for democracy, temperance, sports and free evangelical churches would fill the needs for these abandoned rural men and women. Peasants and land labourers started to leave villages towards the growing cities, when they became replaced by simple machinery and later by tractors.

Scientific discoveries and early industries from 18th century and onwards were also important to make way for modernization, technology and wealth. Important Swedish world renowned scientists and innovators from the 17th - 19th centuries included Christopher Polhem, Carl von Lin-

---

[20]   Norberg 1999b, p. 39-41. State protection of unsound industries and trades would live on to 1980s.

né, CW Scheele and Olof Celcius[21]. Sweden during the 1800s became an innovative centre due to strong belief and investments in technology and entrepreneurship. By 1885 Stockholm had the highest number of telephones in the world. The successful welfare state could never have been built without these technical and scientific innovations and the natural resources in fields, forests and mountains.

Along with free men from self governing farms since medieval times, these traditions established a poor but proud exceptionalism of Sweden as being better than other countries. All did not agree, but dissenters were in minority, among them Sweden's most famous author, August Strindberg, who later made an unpatriotic outburst [22]. Most people were hard working and proud of their innovations. International fame from innovations that were used all over the world, like dynamite, adjustable spanners, ball bearings, packaging for liquids, propellers, milk separators, telephones, refrigerators and pacemakers contributed to this self image[23]. 19th century nationalism enhanced national features all over Europe but in Sweden the national self image took a popular turn, less royal and more democratic, built on hard work, conformism and innovative technology[24].

---

[21]   Later industrial innovators like John Ericsson, LM Ericsson, Albert Nobel, Gustaf Dahlén, JO Johansson, Ruben Rausing and Gustav de Laval completed the success under the 20th century. 17 Nobel laureates in science have come from its own country since the inception of the Nobel Prize in 1901.

[22]   August Strindberg wrote that he "needed to travel abroad in order to purge Sweden and Swedish stupidity from his body with a laxative".

[23]   Braw 2009 views this exceptionalism in school text books. Almqvist and Glans eds. 2001, ch II argues that the exceptionalism is overstated. See also Ohlsson 1994 and Lifvendahl 2011.

[24]   Said ruthlessly: "Sweden is a country in which modern institutions have been grafted onto a medieval frame of mind/.../ they have preserved their medieval core intact, where Western man is heir to the Renaissance. In this lies the fundamental difference between Sweden and the West", Huntford 1971, p.34 - 35. Swedish political culture is characterized historically by concentration of power, conformism and democracy, Berggren and Trädgårdh 2006 argues less despitefully, p. 42.

The Farmers' Estate represented around a third of all farm owning men which was much more democratic representation than in the other estates. The farming political representatives campaigned in their parishes and mixed liberal ideas with technological innovations, fervent religion and popular demands, much like the popular American politicians who had astonished Alexander Tocqueville at the same time in mid 19th century USA. Farming and labouring classes wanted lower taxes, right to open business everywhere, elementary schools, freedom of speech and spoke loudly of their high principles and feared only God. These harsh but easy going Swedish farmers have more in common with contemporary down-to-earth American politicians, especially Texans like President Bush and candidate Ron Paul. 19th century rural and popular democrats on both sides of the Atlantic were the target of sneers from the aristocrat Tocqueville and the rigid Swedish establishment, much along the same lines as today's US and European cultural left ridicule popular demands coming from hearts of unheard voices and parties critical to welfare state building and political conformism[25].

ECONOMIC FREEDOM 1800

The liberal nobleman Johan A Gripenstedt changed Sweden profoundly during his reign as finance minister 1856 - 1866. Economic freedom, deregulation of banks and interest rates, women attaining the age of majority at 25, establishing railways and telegraphs, abolition of punishment of household members, free immigration and emigration took place during this short decade. Most important for economic freedom was of course free trade. Gripenstedt delivered speeches in parliament portraying how the backward country in Europe, Sweden, could make a difference if its resources in transport, modern banks and freedom of business were well used. He did not trust the conservative and protectionist parliament enough when it would vote on the free trade bill in 1865. He had settled an international agreement months before the bill came up in parliament. After heated debate, with Gripenstedt sick at home, sending dispatches

---

25   See Lasch 1994 for same contempt from today's cultural cosmopolitan urban left and his earlier books on 19th century American populist politics.

with replies to parliament, the bill was carried by the Swedish parliament.[26] Swedes deserved to be proud when their isolated underdeveloped country on the periphery, plagued by famines and receiving aid as late as the 1860s from Europe, became one of the richest in the next century. The ugly duckling had become a swan.

Three features gave rise to Sweden in the 19th century. First, modernization processes towards industry and innovation originated among the popular base, not the elite. Unlike in Europe where farmers were more conservative, the Farmers Estate was driving the country forward toward modernity. Second, the emerging working class did not lead to pauperism as in Europe but was employed in new commercial and more efficient agrarian and urban activities[27]. Third, trust in institutions was built through reforming the aristocratic networks, replacing rent seeking, corrupt traditions and groups with neutral transparent administration and self- respecting civil servants[28]. These changes generated a certain trust but built also on earlier democratic and communal rural traditions. Levels of trust have always been high in North European nations, especially Scandinavia. This trust would be essential when universal welfare services were introduced which did not inspect every beneficiary but rather trusted all.

Behind these crucial changes were many years of struggle and sometimes despair. Kings and conservative groups of clergy and most noblemen did not give away much at the start of the 19th century to aspiring entrepreneurs and free spirited Swedes, more often farmers than burghers, i.e., the urban dwellers, artisans, professionals and tradesmen, being at the forefront. But time and numbers were on the side of liberty and prosperity. A new urban class, the merchant and professional bourgeoisie, started to make itself better known than the earlier burghers of guilds and artisan descent. Together with farmers who never fully had succumbed to the state nor to noble mas-

---

[26]   Edwardsson 2010, p.70 h

[27]   Rojas 2005, p. 14

[28]   Rothstein 2011b, p. 112- 118 on successful anti-corruption methods in 19th century Swedish civil service.

ters, but governed themselves and educated themselves, liberal ideas had rooted and spread in the Swedish countryside as much as in townships[29]. The democratic reforms of 1809-1921 were the fruits of early campaigning primarily by liberals alone and only later together with social democrats. An example is that the social insurances for sick, old and injured workers were jointly proposed by the liberal party leader Karl Staaff and his social democratic counterpart, Hjalmar Branting.

WELFARE STATE BUILDING 1900

From 1870 to 1970, Sweden had a unique long period of practically un-interrupted growth unparalleled in world economic history with higher growth rates than every other industrialized country besides Japan. The birth of Sweden's welfare state is a topic that historians still debate. Social democrats pride themselves and have written the national history in a way that gives them the credit for creating the welfare state. But others outside the socialist camp know that non-socialist movements organized workers long before the social democratic party was founded. The birth of the Swedish welfare state can be traced to these self-help associations in mid 19th century and the earlier medieval parishes run hospitals and poorhouses for the needy in 16th century legislation.

Sweden became more free and tolerant in the latter part of 19th century with social charities for the poor and self-help organizations for common people. Liberal leaders understood early that charities could lead to dependence and condescending attitudes towards the poor. Thus liberals formed self-governed alternatives partially with public funding. In 1884 the first parliamentary commission on a universal welfare policy started to plan for a pension system for all[30]. Evangelical Christian movements, along with temperance, labour, athletic and educational popular reform-ist movements with their warm optimism became popular opponents to the fearsome hell preaching state church of Sweden. Many of these were labelled *associationer* in Swedish, and functioned as voluntary welfare

---

[29]   Ådahl 2009.

[30]   Bergh and Erlingsson 2008, p. 83.

systems for mutual aid. Small savings accounts pooled together by members helped poor workers and peasants when sick, in need of housing, to learn crafts and handle weapons, organize education, or to buy daily groceries in low budget cooperative stores. These associations were neither social democratic (as many of them are now), nor directed towards class struggle, but in favour of free markets and self-support[31]. A democratic and liberal proposal from business leaders was to introduce shares for the workers in their companies. This would foster responsibility for the company and an understanding of how a market economy works among the workers, so the leaders claimed. A similar but much more sinister idea would surface later in 1970s as the socialist wage earners funds initiative.

Liberals and social democrats both took part in these popular movements. Not all social democrats were workers and not all workers were social democrats. Not all workers were sober either. Farmers defended their home distilleries and sales, though they met resistance. The temperance movement was the largest popular movement by the mid 1800s counting over one hundred thousand members. By the year 1900 one tenth of all adult Swedes and a majority of parliament members participated in, or supported abstinence to keep themselves and others off alcohol. Without that effort Sweden could have gone the Russian way.

Liberal, temperance and evangelical movements were behind many social reforms but were soon to face competition from the rising social democrats in the last decades of 1800s. Liberal minded charity and popular associations welcomed workers into society, albeit not with a socialist class warfare ideology. The mid 19th century Swedish establishment worked hard to integrate the rising proletariat into mainstream society, but in the end lost to the social democrats for more than half a century. A hand was stretched out to help workers and the poor to organize themselves, which some did on their own, disregarding middle class help. These workers formed socialist working class struggles, outside well-meaning middle class charities and strict associations. But the religious attitudes and ethics of altruism, broth-

---

[31]   Norberg 1999b, p. 184. Many influences for liberal associations came from pioneers and economists in Europe like Herman Schultze – Delitzsch and Frédéric Bastiat.

erhood and longing for a shared communal Christianity inspired these early socialists with emotional and moral authority. In this way non-socialist
human values continued inside the working class movement.

The Swedish Social Democratic Labour party (Arbetarepartiet- Socialdemokraterna) was constituted in 1889. Its open radicalism was in
strong opposition to the liberal leaning and pragmatic leadership. The
first major party leader, Hjalmar Branting, was elected to parliament by
1896 on a liberal ballot. Socialist reformism became the main ideology
along with Marxist rhetoric[32]. Many historians view the Swedish labour
movement, and its success, as products of avoiding radical ideologies.
They claim that the lack of direction from Marxists and other socialists
was useful when navigating the emerging welfare state.

Nobel laureate, economist and social democratic minister Gunnar Myrdal stated almost a century later looking back at the origins of the social
democratic Swedish welfare, that it was never planned in any ideological framework but made in small incremental steps[33]. Historians Sten O
Karlsson and Timothy Tilton claim the opposite and point to available
ideologies at the turn of last century by year 1900. They state that Swedish social democracy was influenced by many 19th century ideologies:
Fabianism from England, the German historical school of economics,
American progressivism (Dewey), idealist organic and communitarian
social philosophy (Hegel, TH Green), reformist socialism like that of
Fernand Lasalle, and domestic political theoretical thought by promi-

---

[32] Branting was from solid high class family and went to school with prince Gustav,
later king Gustav V (reigning 1907 – 1950).

[33] Myrdal in 1960 quoted in Ljunggren 1994, p. 30. Andersson and Hilson 2009 supporting this writes: "In other words, Swedish modernity was not the construction of
a particular socio-economic model, but the product of national instinct and psyche,
a frame of mind which meant that the Swedes were more prone to modernity than
other peoples. This instinct is associated with the values of reformism and pragmatism, the practical application of rational principles to social problems . . . ", p 220.
The term "national instinct" leave much to discuss which will be done in the last two
chapters.

nent national leaders like the finance minister Wigforss [34]. However one views ideology vs. practice, the pragmatic streak in Swedish socialism is undeniable and has led many international viewers and admirers of Swedish welfare policies later to claim its specific nature. By pragmatism or principles, Sweden's system had features that many inside and outside the country view as unique.

The social democratic party gained more influence through the foundation of the national trade union confederation of workers, LO (Landsorganisation) in 1898. The union confederation decided early to align itself to the German model of union and party organizations. The German Social Democratic Party (SPD) had, unlike the British Labour Party, direct links to the union which led to an enormous power to enlist whole trades to a political view and party by collective membership enlisting. In Sweden this powerful legal method of forced yet invisible membership with a party existed from the start of LO in 1898 until 1987. This fact of concentrated union power is absolutely necessary to understand the Swedish social state and political life. Unlike in other countries, unions were not tools of organized crime even if some union sections and employees behaved both badly and illegally, as will be seen later.

Another important principle of the welfare state that was established early was the level of allowance for leave due to injury at work. Instead of awarding a small and equal amount to all, this principle stated that the injured was to be paid in proportion to his wage (with a maximum of 2/3). Later this principle, initiated by liberals, to cover lost income together with the general payment to all pensioners formed the cornerstone of the Swedish welfare state policy.

INDUSTRIAL PEACE 1906

The compromise between capital and labour, leading to better benefits for workers and workplace peace for employers, is another important mechanism of the Swedish welfare state. The compromise started in

---

[34]   Karlsson 2001.

1905 when 18,000 metal workers were locked out for five months from 97 workplaces by the employers in Swedish Metal Manufacturers Organization (Sveriges Verkstadsförening). Employers did not want collective bargaining with the unions and were aiming to destroy radical union members by depriving them of work and support. In the end, a compromise was established in 1906 that led to peaceful negotiations for many decades of calm industrial relations ahead.

Two principles were acknowledged by both parties:
1. The right to organize. Employers respected the right for workers to organize in unions.
2. Management rights. Unions respected managers' rights to hire and fire employees, even non-unionized workers.

Minimum wages were granted as well as mutual respect for negotiated deals. By giving employers managerial rights and acknowledged respect for union contracts, unions could organize larger sections of workers. Employers found a counterparty to negotiate with instead of having to deal with thousands of unruly individual workers. Unions saw that collective bargaining was useful and kept wildcat strikes at a minimum. This rationalized workplace peace was useful when Swedish firms were fighting in the global market and could be less worried about sudden strikes.

During the long lockout of 1905, the cabinet headed by the liberal Karl Staaff did not get into the contest between workers' rights and employers' powers. Prime Minister Staaff had himself earlier defended workers in High Court as lawyer, but held the view that as long as workers did not have voting rights, laws must not be applied to union-employers matters. By remaining unaffected by governmental and legal interference, conflicting unions and employers were able to resolve their rivalries themselves and came out stronger and with more mutual respect after the 1906 agreement. Collective laissez-faire was the result, something that was rare elsewhere at the time. Swedish employers and unions shaped the rules of the game, not the government and courts as in US and internationally.

All leftist leaders were not of same reformist mind at the time. Vladimir Lenin passed through Stockholm 13 April 1917, on his way to Moscow to support the communist revolution. The German secret police had bought him a one way ticket to Sweden in the hope of getting rid of him and that he would continue on his way to Germany's enemy Russia to make trouble. Lenin was broke upon arrival, but on that the same day a fundraising was quickly organized. The right party chairman Arvid Lindman contributed $ 400 in today's value for a ticket, maybe hoping as the Germans did to get rid of the revolutionary quickly. Social democrat leader Branting missed the transiting revolutionary but was nevertheless excited and wrote a few days later that "there is no socialist that for a moment has doubted the honest interests of Lenin"[35]. Agitation spread quickly and a few months later, rulers witnessed rebellions all over the country, often caused by hunger and strife but also radical opposition among soldiers. A nationalist militia was being formed by rightist forces to secure law and order during May 1st demonstrations, but when social democrats replied by organizing red guards, the militia initiative was shut down by the conservative led cabinet. A Bolshevik revolution was averted in Sweden, a few months before the October coup d' état in Moscow 1917.

The events of 1917 radicalized and split the socialist movement. A new party broke off in May 1917, the Swedish Leftist Social Democratic Party (Sveriges Socialdemokratiska Vänsterparti), which again changed its name in 1921 to Swedish Communist Party (section of the Third International, directed from Soviet Union). The larger reformist Social Democratic Party (*Sveriges socialdemokratiska arbetareparti)* continued with parliamentary advances. The first social democratic cabinet led by Prime Minister Hjalmar Branting in 1920 lasted seven months, but a threshold had been passed. For the first time the Swedish king, who still selected Prime ministers, accepted a social democratic led cabinet. Revolutionary ideas stirred still. To calm them, Branting initiated a parliamentary committee to investigate the idea of industrial democracy, i.e. socialized economy, but few unions were interested and he did not gain support in parliament for further socialization of property.

---

[35]   Edwardsson 2010, p. 147

This process would be repeated in 1928, 1948 and 1976 when radical social democratic party initiatives and tactics would be voted down in public elections.

DEMOCRACY 1921

The majority of workers were still liberal minded and ensuing socialist victories in the next century were not granted[36]. What gave the social democratic party its first surge into the Swedish debate was its total dedication to immediate adaptation of the universal right to vote? The liberal and conservative parties were also in favour of one man - one vote, but wanted general elections introduced through reforms. These reforms could include restrictions of wealth, or paid taxes or voters not being sentenced to jail etc. All parties agreed that universal suffrage was important, not the least for calming socialist agitation and uprisings, but also to include fair and rational demands for democracy and freedom. In 1897, the social democrats had stated in their program that all goods-the forests, mines, transportation, machines, and lands-should become collective property[37]. But all peasants and workers were not happy to give up dreaming of owning farms or workshops of their own. Only a few Marxists, party rabble rousers and radical scholars would support this rhetoric. To win over the poor working masses, the social democrats needed another more realistic goal - common men's democratic influence through elections. Universal suffrage fit that need well.

The liberal leader Karl Staaff who earlier had founded Swedish National Suffrage Union (Sveriges Allmänna rösträttsförbund) did not accept

---

[36]   Ibid., p.118

[37]   "Social democracy wants therefore also to implement the political organisation of the working class, claim public power and by and by transform all means of production – transport, forests, mines, mill works, machinery, factories and land – into collective property" [Socialdemokratin vill därför genomföra även arbetarklassens politiska organisation, sätta sig i besittning av den offentliga makten och efter hand förvandla till samhällelig egendom alla produktionsmedlen - transportmedlen, skogarna, gruvorna, bruken, maskinerna, fabrikerna, jorden."], Socialdemokratins partiprogram 2001, p.14.

strikes that disrupted negotiations on suffrage and parliamentary democracy. But disturbances were used by socialist interests, for instance during the 1902 rebellion in central Stockholm leading only to police repression and little progress as Branting himself tried to calm the masses. Strikes were initiated through fighting for better wages and socialist agitation as well as for electoral reforms. The labour market was affected by a general dissatisfaction among workers and underpinned by social democrats for their own more vested interests. The view that strikes, uprisings and even assassinations, openly advocated by social democrat turned anarchist Hinke Bergegren, could lead to progress, was by then a not uncommon part of socialist thought at the time in Sweden and elsewhere in turbulent Europe. Strikes were met by opposite forces when employers used their own weapon, lockouts of striking workers from their jobs. Few at that time believed a reasonable and accepted social policy could emerge from such social discord. Other consequences were that the political center-right parties pushed the welfare state forward as an alternative to the leftist idea of class struggle leading to socialism and communism. Inspired by Otto von Bismarck in late 19th century German Prussia, social conservatives and liberals proposed reforms of social welfare insurances that could rival the socialist ideas. This was a delicate matter for socialist reformers and revolutionaries. Why bother repairing capitalism? Socialists had time on their side, as Marx had prophesized in his deterministic scientific materialism: Why bother with more reforms when class society was going down soon anyway? Welfare benefits would only dampen class consciousness revolutionaries argued.

The following decades saw more social reforms and deepened democracy as victories for reformist social democrats. With half of the population participating in the general election in 1921, the first democratically elected Swedish government was elected. Men had gained the right to vote in 1909 and women in 1921. Social democratic party leader Hjalmar Branting led a minority cabinet for two years, succeeded by liberal Prime ministers. But a campaign for the abolition of all alcohol sales and production threatened to divide the liberal party agenda. Within the liberal party, a social conservative section consisting of a rural evangelical fraction wanted to abolish drinking while still keeping to a free market liberal ideology. The urban liberal party fraction resisted abolition along with parts of the labour movement and conservatives. After being defeated in a referendum 1922 on total ban of alcohol, abolitionists formed their own party and did not to cooperate with any other party. Since there was neither left nor right majority in parliament, the period from 1921–1932 was fraught with parliamentary crises and fragile minority cabinets. Decisions were made outside of democratic influence. Nevertheless equality reigned. A comparison of historical rates of income inequality in Sweden, United States, Canada, France and the Netherlands shows that already by 1920, well before the existence of a welfare state, Sweden was among those with the lowest levels of inequality[38].

ENGLISH – AMERICAN INFLUENCES 1920

English life and culture replaced the power of the losing German nation in World War I, which had dominated Swedish culture since 1300s, apart from a thin French influence in court and aristocracy in 18th century. It would take another decade until English was made the mandatory second language instead of German in primary education, but the public already favoured Anglo – American culture. Jazz music was heard in Stockholm by 1920. Through the large migration to USA of 1,300 000 Swedes from mid-19th century to early 20th, influences in technology and popular culture reached even this periphery of Europe. Against the influence from American mass culture of workers and rising middle classes stood the established values and traditions from German political philosophy, Swedish conservatism and puritan Protestant religion. These institutions were defending old traditions, but lost against the fascination of popular entertainment and new mores from the New World. Opposition to the old hierarchies and traditions were mixed with regard to drinking and dancing. Hard liquor was rationed from 1917 to 1955, leading to widespread sobriety yet also to practical troubles and the romanticizing of drinking as a subversive act. Two factors explain the strange relation Swedes have to alcohol: Shyness and rationing system. Through drinking people could behave badly and loosen up, while the opposite happened

---

[38]   Sanandaji 2011, p. 23

at the government liquor store, hiding rationed bottles in paper bags and awkwardly, secretly stealing away. This social awkwardness was relieved by alcohol, which gave rise to a drinking culture that is closer to Russian and Finnish vodka binge drinking than Danish and German socializing over beer and Mediterranean wine sipping.

A positive outcome of the lack of government power, with short-lived minority cabinets and exhaustion with the regulations imposed in WW1, was that free market ideas and non-interventionist politics flourished. Parties of social liberalism, social conservatism and social democracy all had prospered and enjoyed government economic powers during World War I, but gained less support during the roaring 1920s. The mood was definitely liberal *laissez-faire* and for a return to classical liberalism. Academic economists like Eli F. Heckscher and Gustaf Cassel argued in the press in favour of lower taxes and deregulation[39]. Even within the social democratic camp voices rose in favour of private property, personal freedom, free competition on markets and even workers' associations outside trade unions and party. Nils Karleby and Anders Örne were among those libertarian socialists inspired by British guild socialism who feared state interventionism and welfare schemes, claiming such thinking leading to irresponsibility and state repression[40].

Being in power was harmful for social democrats as they could not affect policies much different than the liberals in their three short minority cabinets between 1920 and 1930. From their communist rivals, they got much critique for being reformist. But the social democratic party did not close borders to the left as there was still hope to unify the two ri-

---

[39]   Cassel inspired the Austrian school of economics, Edwarsson 2010, p. 176.

[40]   "Better roads in Norrland [harsh northern areas] mean more for Sweden than all of socialism", Karleby wrote 1926 (in Berggren and Trägårdh 2006, p. 202). Karleby was instrumental in the late 1920s when socialists almost had become a party without an ideology, since the hard core socialist agenda had been scrapped. Workers' participation in society together with the bourgeoisie and middle class, rather than nationalisation of property was Karleby's mild message. Hamilton 2012 recommended re-reading Karleby to revive the social democratic party.

val socialist parties, in vain though and at a high price. Hopes from the two left parties which joined hands in a unified Workers' Party ballot fell in the 1928 election. The election is called the "Cossack election," as Russian Bolsheviks were used in propaganda from the right and liberals. Dictator Josef Stalin had his hand in the election as the Swedish communists handed Russian money to striking miners right before the election. Having a Russian citizen and Bolshevik in Swedish Communist politburo did not sit well with voters either, as a vote for the reformist social democrats also was a vote for the revolutionary communists in their electoral alliance. Both socialist parties lost 14 seats in parliament as women's and workers' votes went to the right, liberal and agrarian parties. For the social democrats, Marxist rhetoric had been defeated by the masses. A new vision was needed. Folkhemmet. The next chapter will tell the successful implementation of a vague concept.

Reforms 1800 – 1930

1809	Separation of powers of Estates, king, and judiciary
1809	Parliamentary ombudsman[41]
1842	Elementary schooling for all children
1845	Equal right to inheritance for women and men
1846	Abolishment of guilds
1864	Freedom of business
1866	Parliament reformed into two chambers
1868	Freedom of religion
1873	Right to academic grades for women
1891	Government supported funds for sick
1901	Employers' responsibility for work accidents
1909	Suffrage for males over 24 years of age to lower parliamentary chamber
1909	Council on legislation
1913	Pension for all citizens regardless of wealth
1915	Supreme Court granted unions - employers collective agreements
1916	Work accident insurance
1919	8 hour working day (agriculture excluded)
1921	Suffrage to all citizens minimum 23 years of age to both chambers of parliament.
1928	Law on collective agreements for unions - employers
1928	Labour Court established

---

[41] Ombudsman is a term in Swedish which has become global and means an authority with independent supervision of public authorities. Much hailed in Sweden but with little impact as only advisory. Same goes for Council on legislation (Lagrådet).

CHAPTER 3

Hubris 1930 – 1970

By 1930 four out of five Swedish workers were unionized, the highest percentage at the time in the world and never later surpassed. Going neither to the left again, nor to the right, social democratic party leader Per Albin Hansson from 1928 picked up a nationalist term coined by a Swedish right wing professor, Rudolf Kjellén. The conservative term people's home (folkhem) was transformed for other social, more reformist and welfare purposes. Broadly defined, nationalism was a better ground than political ideology for Hansson. Kjellén had also used the term national socialism when referring to his conservative corporatist and nationalist ideology. There are similarities between the folkhem ideology and the national socialism of the German Nazi ideology, but Kjellén never went so far although he was critical to democracy. Swedish folkhem thinking was a mixture of brown and red ideologies. Conservative patriotism was anyway present in most Swedish parties at the time regardless of ideology.

The older Swedish usage of the term folkhem had meant public charity houses where poor people could find some help and contacts or just read newspapers and books. Party leader Hansson wanted to reach beyond the concept of social class to all common men who were being, or felt themselves repressed regardless by whom, including petty farmers, small tradesmen etc. Mythologizing the history of peasant uprisings from the 16th century, social democratic agitation shifted focus from urban workers to also include agrarian classes and lower middle class. But there was a problem. The romantic view held by socialists of hard taxed but proud Swedish farming yeomen in the 1500s fighting local vogts, lord protectors and sheriffs, for freedom from taxation had to end, since the welfare state would tax its citizens even more. Socialists had to keep the rebellious spirit burning in history but not in present time. In medieval history, Swedes were proud and independent farmers opposed to taxes. In mid 20th century, Swedes were told by their socialist masters to be proud to be dependent on welfare services and pay huge taxes according to the new folkhem mythology which most poor people took to their hearts and trusted.

Hansson wanted Sweden to become more like a good home for all folks, with equality and mutual understanding. Traditional class-divided society should then be replaced by the people's home, where there are no privileged or downtrodden inhabitants, no favourites and no step children. In the good home there is equality, care, cooperation and help for everyone. Not quite the communist dream of classless utopia, but just more caring and inclusive homes, under socialist Pater familias.

The less aggressive term folk replaced the earlier class. Prussia's authoritarian welfare systems, German idealist philosophical ideas of social organisms, folk hegemony and corporatism beyond class struggles were ideological influences included in the new concept as well as nationalist and racist elements[42]. Vagueness was useful since many listeners and users could find their own meanings in the term folkhem. The semantic associations within "folkhemmet" to home and people were marks of a genius in political marketing, socialist chairman Per Albin Hansson, and the father of the early modern Swedish welfare state. A replacement of the popular plea for suffrage was found at last.

Ideologically, the Swedish social democracy in early 1930s was quite conservative and the realm of politics did not involve all areas of life. Per Albin Hansson viewed the state as not quite the same thing as society, a distinction which later social democrats did not understand, respect or much care much for. What Hansson wanted in the early 1930s was less of a totalitarian socialist state than a society built around respect, responsibility and reason. He meant that there is "a general feeling that

---

[42]   Swedish Institute for Race Biology was founded in Uppsala University 1921 and supported by socialists, agrarian party and the right. Later social democrats initiated with support from other parties forced sterilizations to avoid undesired citizens. In 2000 the history of sterilizations was documented by a parliamentary report, SOU 2000:20, *Steriliseringsfrågan i Sverige 1935 – 1975*. See also Abelin 2012.

society is good when there is a certain amount of freedom. One is going in the wrong direction when restrictions on large groups of citizens'
[behaviour] are felt as harassment'[43]. This important "certain amount of
freedom" would become less well respected over decades, and demands
for more restrictions would come from all parties. Hansson would never
ride on 1970s the-personal-is-political bandwagon.

WORKERS RULING SOCIETY 1930

Crucial to understanding socialist progress and victory in Sweden is that
the organizational strength of workers in Sweden is a major factor when
shaping public policy[44]. Organized labour was strengthened by the opposite force of organized capital. When employers got together, workers
needed good coordination and organization too. Both parties kept their
disputes out of the courts and worked towards industrial peace. Later
images from fervent agitating union and social democratic ideologists
of tough class-warfare Swedish workers' united opposition against the
harsh bourgeoisie-are simply overstated. Tolerance and neutrality from
the establishment dominated by liberals until 1930s were more important
for success of workers' interests than antagonism. Liberals and the middle classes welcomed representatives of the workers and introduced them
to regular political life. Class war surfaced briefly in 1917 but was quickly

---

[43] Hansson in Ljunggren 1994, p. 28. The right party chided him in his speech on the
folkhem when he claimed for instance that things that politicians should disregard
for example could be people dancing at restaurants alone without a partner. Drunk
yet not hurting anyone. Other guests could take over if the dancing and especially
drinking went out of hand. No need to legislate he claimed against conservative stiff
upper lips and tight liberal prigs denouncing what they viewed immoral behaviour.
Ljunggren 1992, p. 77. argues that the Swedish vision of folkhemmet is similar to
the German radical conservatism of 1920s. Both ideologies argued for a strong state
that could combine modernity with tradition. In Germany the result was national
socialism, in Sweden the welfare state. For diplomatic connections in a similar but
fascist vein, between socialist Stockholm and fascist Rome, see Cantera Carlomango
1995.

[44] Nycander 2007, p. 36

replaced by welfare schemes and reformism. Slow and steady wins the game, Swedes would say.

By 1930 the workers' representatives had led several cabinets, unions were well respected in labour disputes and a new popular culture and consumption for common people emerged outside the urban liberal bourgeoisie and stiff conservative elite. The workers represented the new modern nation. Other countries may have had their cultures and histories. Sweden had modernity and rationalism[45]. The brutal wars of the 17th and 18th centuries, which have brought the end of the Swedish Empire, were forgotten along with victims of Swedish colonies in Finland, Poland, northern Germany, Russia and the Baltic states. The pride of being modern became the pride of being Swedish. Conservative national pride in its history was replaced by socialist national pride for modernity and peace. The bourgeois nationalism of old had changed into the social democratic stateism of new. Nothing displayed this modernist attitude more than the functionalist architecture and minimalist design at Stockholm Exhibition of 1930. The slogan accept! (acceptera, with a small letter) of the exhibition said it all: the future is lean and rational, cool and unstoppable. A surprise to convince exhibition visitors of the benefits of a modernized lifestyle was serving them mass- produced food.

The new attitude of national reconciliation from former socialist radicals was immediately visible when the losing social democratic leader Hansson congratulated the victorious center - right dominated cabinet in 1928. National consensus was the message instead of class divisions. This unity was to be important during the fatal year 1929 when after a world war, a decade of prosperity, Charleston dances and American optimism,

---

[45]   Berggren and Trägårdh 2006, p. 224. "Swedes would come to appreciate themselves as utterly modern human beings that had overcome the past and did not need tales and legends from 19th century to enhance their self-esteem". The term "ultra – modernity" for blind Swedish devotion to modernity is proposed by historian Kazimierz Musal (in Andersson and Hilson 2009, p. 220). Chapter 7, called "The Swedish Exception" in Berman 2006, summarizes the nationalist yet modern Swedish socialism in the first decades of 20th century.

financial depression spread its doom over Western economies. Later a domestic financial crash in March 1932 created by the suicide of Swedish industrialist Ivar Kreuger affected most Swedes, as they lost savings, stocks, jobs and faith in business and free market oriented politicians[46].

Further events built sympathy for social democrats. When in 1931 five demonstrating workers were gunned down in Ådalen in northern Sweden by military partly on purpose, partly by accident, people were outraged. These events were discouraging for the liberal party in power. The social democrats utilized the propaganda, although initially they were as confused as anyone else about what had really happened when striking anarcho-syndicalist workers, enemies of the reformist social democrats, went berserk on the military. Confidence in capitalism was enjoyed neither on Wall Street nor in Stockholm[47]. By fall of 1932 the victorious social democrats had entered their long uninterrupted governance for 44 years, the world's longest-serving democratically elected government, from 1932 to 1976.

Welfare reforms and economic regulations followed soon after a quick devaluation of the Swedish Crown, which helped exports. The minority social democratic led cabinet under Per Albin Hansson had to make compromises with the agrarian party in 1933. Protectionism and unemployment programs were created together with a New Deal-inspired fiscal policy of loaning money to help the economy to recover, which became the farmers - workers united program. Arguments in favour of public spending of borrowed money came not only from the famous John M. Keynes but also from domestic political economists of both socialist and liberal origins, the

---

[46]   The liberal prime minister C G Ekman had to resign six weeks before elections in 1932 due to taking cash from Ivar Kreuger both to his party and to his own bank account.

[47]   The liberal government broke away from free market ideology and regulated milk prices in 1931/32 to defend farmers' trusts. The left criticized the regulation that led to higher prices as all monopolies do against the consumers. But after the 1932 victory the social democrats lay down the populist protests and used market regulations even more in other sectors.

Stockholm school of economic thought (Knut Wicksell, Gunnar Myrdal, Erik Lindahl and Bertil Ohlin). The threat of violent ideologies from Hitler, Stalin and Mussolini abroad made protectionism, consensus and national pride even more important. Nevertheless and contrary to common knowledge even today, the government regulations cannot be credited with restarting the business cycle in 1933. Instead, the economy had recovered by itself just before the regulations came into use, but of course all participating parties have granted themselves the honour of having saved Sweden[48]. Especially the socialists.

MIDDLE WAY SWEDEN 1936 AND 1938

The American journalist Marquis Childs' book *Sweden. The middle way* became popular after its publication when President FD Roosevelt presented the inspiring ideas at a book launch in 1936. What impressed the Democratic Party president, himself an author, was the discovery of a middle way between communism and raw capitalism that Sweden seemed to manage so well. A royal country with a socialist government in a capitalist system. Mixed economy was the term. What further impressed the US audience were family planning and constructive relations within the labour market. Childs' thesis was that Sweden had found a uniquely effective way to deal with social and economic problems, a way that put Sweden between the United States' concentration of economic power in the hands of a few men and the trials and hardships in Soviet Russia. A middle way.

Childs described Sweden's methodology as a modification of the capitalist economy through a strong co-operative movement and government involvement in the economy. At a time when United States was struggling with consequences of the great depression and debating Roosevelt's New Deal, Childs pointed to Sweden as an example of pragmatism and progress. Unemployment in Sweden had never reached such epidemic proportions as in the United States, so there could be things to learn. Reviews of Childs' book were enthusiastic.

---

[48]   Edwardsson 2010, p. 225

"'[It] reads like the best political news in years,' wrote one reviewer in the *New York Herald Tribune*, and continued that 'It sounds gloriously like what we used to think of as American: a method of sane compromise and steady progress, each step tested by the sole criterion: Does it work?'"[49].

President Roosevelt sent a delegation two years later to Sweden to get an impartial account of labour - employer relations. The American phenomena of the closed shop, whereby a union could monopolize a work place, allowing only its own members to get work there, did not exist in Sweden. Non-interference from the courts and government was different in comparison to America's unregulated, sometimes violent and unorganized labour market relations, which made the US interest so keen[50]. Childs' writings were an enormous success for Sweden and links between US democrats and progressive politicians flourished over the coming decades especially through the Myrdal couple and Olof Palme, all three staying in the US for long periods of time and all later becoming social democratic ministers[51].

1938 is seen by many Swedes as the year when workers and managers agreed to work together, although cooperation had been going on for decades and with initial support from liberals. At the fashionable hotel Saltsjöbaden outside Stockholm, employers and unions stated foundational rules in the famous Saltsjöbaden Agreement in unity and spirit. These mutually agreed rules of industrial action have come to be regarded almost as legal principles for conflict resolution, though they are outside of the courts. The agreement cemented the official Swedish social consensus, the norm that opposing parties shall conclude agreements without interference by government. The agreement is still in effect, with the most recent changes having been made in 1976.

---

[49]   Ohlsson 2006.

[50]   Nycander 2007, p. 35

[51]   In 1960 union leader Arne Geijer toured the United States together with Bertil Kugelberg from the employers. JK Galbriath and JFK's advisors listened, see Ohlsson 2006.

The advantages of compromise between capital and labour were many. Government could concentrate on welfare construction and fine tuning of the growing economy with macro- economic Keynesian tools, while export oriented business could focus on innovation and production. Swedish business, economic research and government policy paid little if any attention to the micro economy. Enterprises, small firms and entrepreneurs were not supported. People were to be employees (or if unable, become welfare recipients), not self-standing entrepreneurs with their own minds. White collar engineers were organized into their professional unions, and blue collar workers into theirs. Both unions and employers were interested in uniform working conditions in all geographical districts and trades, leading to standardization. Union and employers gained a better understanding of one another, leading to calm rational negotiations. Informal, yet keeping their distance. The right people at the right place and time. Preferably as many as possible in as large companies as possible.

With high percentage of workers in unions, many became active politically through the social democratic party, as they had almost all been enlisted as members through their union. The absence of large ethnic, religious, linguistic or cultural differences in the population made Sweden homogenous and easy for growing export companies with growing well organized union branches. Volvo, IKEA, Electrolux and Ericsson are some of the companies now well-known abroad that all started during the early welfare state[52]. The homogeneous workforce consisting of men coming from similar backgrounds, some rising to the middle class and some staying on the shop floor, contributed to the smooth running of business. Later this informal management became known as the modern informal Scandinavian style of managing companies and government[53].

---

[52]   Swedish enterprises growing during 20th century booming years are Alfa-Laval, Separator, Swedish Match, Sandvik, Stora Enso, MoDo/Holmen, ASSA Abloy, Boliden, Kopparberg, SCA, Vattenfall, SKF, SAAB, ABB, LKAB, SSAB, Tetrapak, Götaverken and Kockum shipyards.

[53]   *Futureorientation* 2006. In government services, informal management styles dominate too, see Lövgren 1988.

Large companies, a few later becoming multinationals, were crucial in organizing labour and getting employees to understand agreements at all levels. A feature of the Swedish welfare state period in mid 20th century is its dependence on a homogenous and trained work force at large manufacturing companies exporting abroad. The tradition of rural mill towns exporting abroad excluded small business. Unions favoured large companies as each workplace then could be stronger against the employers' organisations, sometimes even stronger than the employers. Small entrepreneurs were not well-liked by the Swedish Employers Association (Svenska Arbetsgivareföreningen) either. Representatives of big industries and employers did not care much about how agreements with large trade unions affected small businessmen who did not have time, expertise and money to follow all rules, negotiated over their heads by their own representatives. Big firms had lawyers and human resources divisions to work with labour union officials. Generally, Sweden has low numbers of small businesses compared to other nations. The Netherlands and Denmark, which have similar welfare structures, have almost double Sweden's number of small business[54]. The reasons for dearth of small business are obvious considering the labour market structure.

FAMILY AND URBAN PLANNING

Legendary social democratic pioneers and Ministers Gunnar and Alva Myrdal wrote in 1934 a classic piece of social engineering on new social and population programs[55]. A lively debate followed over the details and visions of planned parenthood and family life. Since earlier attempts on nationalization of private property had not been favoured by voters or unions, new ideas on planning had to emerge how to organize lives for citizens in a modern welfare state. Instead of relying on old and mostly unsuccessful socialist expropriation of production, this attempt was to socialize consumption. The Myrdal couple, Gunnar the economist and Alva the child psychologist, wrote together:

---

[54]   Ekonomifakta 2012.

[55]   Myrdal 1997 [original 1934]. American expanded edition 1941, *Nation and family* (Harper, New York)

"The tendency will anyway go towards an organization and control of social policies concerning not just income distribution in society but also the direction of consumption within families"[56].

School lunches, child allowances from the government, free health care, and support for better housing and rent control were all means directed towards uplifting the working class into a new kind of radical middle class values. All families, including the middle class, would get same benefits. Children should be reared by expert pedagogues in government child care units where they would get away from the conservative patterns at home and clinging maternal intimacy. Alva Myrdal proselytized, as head of early childhood education teachers' training institute (Socialpedagogiska Institutet) which she founded in 1936, for a new kind of child care that went beyond the child care necessary for working women and kindergarten for middle class house wives. Behind the drive to raise more and better socialized children was the national need to make more Swedes stay in their people's home, folkhem, and not leave for North America.

Instead of loyalty to God, king and nation, children should be raised to honour science, folkhem and welfare state policy, the Myrdals argued. The traditional ideal of the harmonious middle class life of house wives was to be replaced with collective and social order according to the latest findings in social and child psychology, often stemming from American progressive education and social affairs. The power of discourses on children and child rearing had to be in the hands of the experts rather than parents and older family members. Ideas for new child care structures were discussed in detail and proposed in a parliamentary investigation 1936 on population

---

[56]   Myrdals in Edwardsson 2010, p. 233. A strong idea of control of consumption was the goal: "The most important task for social welfare policy, its immediate aim, is to organize and manage the national consumption after other directions that those in the so called free consumer choice in the technologically often too small household units and under mass suggestion and advertising" (in Svensson 2011, p. 60- 61). Gunnar Myrdal meant that people should not be trusted to spend their money as they liked, see ibid.

and sexuality[57]. Explicit Swedish sex on film was a decade away, but the texts on how to manage the sexual lives of Swedish citizens were already in governmental proposals, including mentioning of female orgasms.

Social and family reforms were not yet in place as World War II broke out, but the ideas were all printed in reports about how to transform families into happy population units in new suburban pigeon holes. The Swedish style of a planned economy and society use soft power to educate citizens that in their turn would control market forces through demands as concerned consumers. Clear division: Consumers good, market forces evil. Welfare state good, capitalism bad. Like Trojan horses the reforms in family life, housing and consumption would break up and transform capitalism from within.[58]

Further cleansing of undesired citizens was established in 1934 in a national program for forced sterilizations of vagrant gypsies, single mothers, imbecile mothers, and people with Down's syndrome, proposed by Myrdals and other social reformers. The better half of citizens, those that were not subject to sterilizations, on the other hand did not reproduce enough. A remedy must be found and Myrdals stated that sexual life was not only a private matter for desiring men and women, but of national concern. By sterilizing the undesired and enhancing sex among the desired, eugenics became a government concern.[59]

Housing, in addition to child care, sexuality and population control be-

---

[57]　*Betänkande i Sexualfrågor* in Hirdman 1988, p. 131- 153. Parents and family life were characterized as less fit to raise children in the modern world. The Myrdals lived in USA from 1938 and mostly during WWII, where Alva Myrdal wrote *Nation and family* 1941 to spread the gospel of modern social policy which attracted many progressive democratic Americans. She states the exceptional features of Swedish freedom from feudalism as fertile ground for socialist progress.

[58]　Hirdman 1988, p. 96.

[59]　The Nazist German Third Reich applauded the Swedish racial perfectionism as did all parties and people in the establishment, such as Protestant bishop Arvid Runestam. Forced sterilizations continued until 1976.

came another national arena for futurist socialist experiments in 1930s Sweden. Apartment blocks were built in the suburbs outside Stockholm and other major cities with two rooms and a very small kitchen. The idea was to use more rooms for each family, since houses in villages usually had large kitchens but one nicely decorated room for show and to use only on holidays. To break the rural culture of sitting and sometimes sleeping together in a large farm kitchen, it was crucial to get away from old conservative family patterns and make kitchens unbearably small.

A difference in the Swedish social policies in 20th century compared to efforts in similar countries is the importance of universal welfare policies and benefits. The need based welfare benefits coming from charity funds to the poor in the preceding century continued in many Western nations. In the US food stamps and social project housing were introduced for the poor while market solutions were the responsibility for the working population. Sweden and other Scandinavians nations went a different direction: include all citizens in benefits, rich, poor, middle class. By letting the higher classes get value for their high taxes in receiving levels of sick leave benefits based on their incomes, they did not feel bearing the brunt of all poor on their backs.

Redistribution of incomes rather than alleviating poverty through growth was and still is the defining Swedish social and economic policy for all political parties and much supported by the citizens. Sharing a small cake equally is better than getting a larger cake shared unequally. To avoid stigmatization and support self-reliance this policy was thought to be better if it involved all citizens, not just the poor. Within the social democratic camp there were divisions between the Myrdals, favouring solutions leading each beneficiary to prove his need, and Social Minister Gustaf Möller who would rather have given people a substantive amount of cash and left them alone[60]. The latter system is called universal welfare

---

[60]   This solution was established already in 1913 when pensions were given universally to all, albeit at a low level - and at a time, age 67, when the average life expectancy was age 60. For comparisons with mid 20th century UK social policy and Sweden, see Heclo 2010.

policy, which now dominates in Scandinavia and to some extent in UK. Selective policies dominated by market forces and charity exist in USA, and similar selective policies but dominated by family and corporate insurances are established in southern and central Europe.

WORLD WAR II 1939 - 1945

During World War II, the neutral Swedish nation collaborated with England, Nazi Germany and the Soviet Union trying to keep everyone at peace. "Miss Sweden wants to be alone", an English paper wrote alluding to the secretive Swedish film star Greta Garbo in Hollywood at the time, and to her national origins. Some not so graceful samples of national compromises:

- Censoring the press and entertainment to prevent anti-Nazi agitation
- Registering anti-Nazi activists and harassing them
- Letting Nazi soldiers travel by trains through Sweden to occupied Norway
- Not giving the Norwegian king refuge in Sweden nor acknowledging the Norwegian government in exile in London
- Not helping Finland when as promised they were attacked by the Soviet Union
- Refusing admittance to German Jews at Swedish borders by returning them
- Acknowledging the Soviet occupation of the Baltic states
- Creating a governmental Information Institute that told Swedes only to write well about the country in letters to relatives abroad
- Continuing sending machinery and goods to Germany until a US threat in fall 1944 stopped the support for the enemy
- Having pro-German ministers before and during the war (Arthur Engberg, Christian Günter, KG Westman and sometimes also King Gustav V),
- Thanking Hitler for invading the Soviet Union 1941
- sending German deserters back to a sure death 1940-1941

- Establishing Swedish internment and labour camps for communists, foreigners, supporters for the Allied forces, anti-Nazi
  activists and radical union activists that could make trouble.
  When Hitler's troops started to lose, Sweden used the same internment camps for pro-Nazi Scandinavians and collaborators
  that a year before had been used to keep anti-Nazi activists away
  from the press and public meetings and not disturb Germany.

Sweden was neutral but kept turning to the winning side. By 1945, the
Soviet Union wanted 150 Baltic families and soldiers extradited. These
citizens of the former independent Baltic States had by then wound up in
Sweden after fighting on the German side. The Soviets considered them
traitors as Estonia, Lithuania and Latvia were Soviet republics after 1945
and by their resistance to occupation these soldiers were at fault. Sweden
bowed down and sent them to certain deaths.

The war period was endured by a coalition left-center- right government
(apart from the Soviet-allied communists SKP) and a planned war economy in many areas that would stay on after 1945. Social democratic and
nationalist institutions used the war as an excuse to make Sweden a more
planned economy. The social democrats aspired in their 1944 party program for socialization of insurance companies and petrol trade, government regulations of foreign trade and investments and a billion Swedish
crown credit to Soviet Union[61]. Taxes had been raised before the war but

---

[61]   *Socialdemokratins partiprogram*, 2001. p. 39-50. The program had 27 points which also
        included higher pensions, governmental unemployment- and sick leave insurances,
        general child allowance, shorter working day, higher housing standards, continu-
        ing war time regulations (rent control and food rationing for instance), more public
        sector, extended price control, radical agricultural reforms (expropriation) and gov-
        ernment support to construction. The communists did not make their own program
        but adopted the socialists'. The proposed billion credit to Soviet irritated relations to
        USA but trade minister Gunnar Myrdal tried to keep both sides happy. He had lived
        happily in USA and written *An American Dilemma: The Negro Problem and Modern De-
        mocracy* in 1944 and was well acquainted with US diplomacy, but said that "Sweden's
        overall political interest is to reach intimate and good relations with Soviet Union ",

with these proposed reforms much more money was needed. Inspiration for socialist and welfare state reforms did not come from Karl Marx, but from the mild British social liberal Lord Beveridge, who appealed to both social democrats and welfare state supporting liberals and conservatives, especially the liberal party chairman, Bertil Ohlin. Ohlin was a true social liberal, professor of economics, eloquent speaker and later Nobel laureate.

The political wind did not blow to the left after the war, with a promise of loans to dictator Stalin and a program for taking over private property, but even more travails were to come for the post war left-politicians. A blow to the communists, which had their strongest electoral support of 10 % in 1944, was a fatal strike in 1945 by the metal workers' union. Influenced by hard line communists, workers led a strike for better wages but lost. In the 1946 election, communists got 6 % and their support in parliament for the social democratic minority cabinet was diminished. The influence of organized Swedish communists and radical social democracy was stalled by this defeat for exactly three decades. In 1976, the radical socialist proposal of wage earners funds would finally break the four decade rule of socialist rule.

POST WORLD WAR II 1945

Prime minister Per Albin Hansson died suddenly in 1946 and was succeeded by the mild yet staunch leader Tage Erlander, who would reign as Prime minster for the next 23 years. Swedish politics from end of World War II was going in the direction of a planned welfare state, regardless of party adherence. A debate started between liberals and socialists between 1945 and 1948 on the socialist proposed program for a planned economy. The debate was actually about how much planning the Swedish economy should have, not whether planning was good to begin with, which most true Western liberals would like to discuss. Yet some few liberal politicians and independent minded individuals managed to stand

see Edwardsson 2010, p. 277. He had to leave office in 1947 but by then the damage was done and the voters were scared of communist domination and his party almost lost power.

up for liberty after a long period of ideological neglect and submission
to leftist thinking and the wartime consensus under coalition cabinet led
by socialists. The liberal economist Fredrick von Hayek's book *Road to
serfdom* became useful in fighting totalitarian tendencies when the employers' federation translated and issued Hayek's argumentation against
planned economy in 1944. Help from the left came too. The social democrat and cooperative leader Anders Örne was first and foremost a co-op-
eration pioneer and defender of consumer rights. He tried also to steer
away from planned economy in his writing *Ekonomisk demokrati* in 1946
by proving that consumers would be better off with private property and
sound capitalist competition on open markets. The freethinking social
democrat Örne warned for the consequences of a socialist victory for
planned economy:

> "Democracy is not to be unified with a state power that dis-
> poses of and can command all the means of production in
> society./.../ such a state will by its nature become totalitar-
> ian, that is, ruler of all human beings and the regime will
> practically be dictatorship"[62].

Theories of freedom are not often used in political debate, but with the
Soviet Union close by and socialist government rulers at home wanting
more power, alternatives became obvious for some clear headed Swedish
politicians. The debate over a planned economy in late 1940s made the alternatives clear even though the social democrats tried to muddle the arguments with a debate over the negative and positive concepts of liberty.
Businessman and Right party politician Harald Nordensson was firm in
defending the negative concept of liberty[63]. Ernst Wigforss, finance minister and scholar argued that the negative concept was too limited and
true liberty could only be realized with a positive concept. The positive

---

[62]   In Edwardsson 2010, p. 271.

[63]   Norberg 1999a, p. 34. Ernst Wigforss insisted on equality and found the base for
it when saying that "Poverty is tolerated with equanimity if shared with others. It
becomes unbearable when daily compared to others' wealth", in Svensson 2000, p.
29.

contribution would be material goods, security and social welfare. The coercion and lack of freedom that such a positive arrangement would entail was the price people would have to pay. The Soviet Union would argue with the same strategy in discussions of the UN universal declaration of human rights and vote blank in 1948, thus seeing full employment and decent housing as important as rights to life and freedom, i.e. negative freedoms not to be killed or enslaved. Swedish socialists offered little defence of human rights and went along the same road of argumentation and some policies as the Soviet Union did.

But not everybody was fooled. Many Swedes did not want to pay a higher price for lesser freedom. In 1948 the social democrats lost the initiative when the fiercest antagonist to socialist planning, the liberal party led by Bertil Ohlin, doubled its electoral share. Contributing to the losing left parties' arguments for a planned economy was the fact that the business cycle after the war rose unexpectedly leaving plans to direct the economy in the dustbin. Full employment came with an unfettered market economy, a devaluation of the Swedish crown, and by 1950 Swedish firms had to go abroad to find enough workers[64].

In 1947 two governmental reforms were introduced that made welfare policies easy to fund. One was the mandatory personal identification number consisting of a person's date of birth augmented by four random digits. The second was the retention or withholding tax which obliged all employers to pay taxes for their employees direct to the tax office. Before this tax reform, people had to pay their taxes themselves and then count in their own wallets on how much was given over to government. Now this was concealed and no one could flee from the control imposed by the unique ID number, which is used by all government agencies as well as private enterprises, making Sweden an excellent country for targeted marketing actions.

---

[64]   Immigrants came mostly from Italy, Greece, Yugoslavia, Turkey and Austria and quickly integrated in work force and Swedish society.

LABOUR AND FOREIGN POLICIES 1950

After the war, Swedes were tired of rationing, regulations and nationalism. The USA became even stronger in its dominance of culture, opportunities and business contacts. Working life was well-ordered enough, with regulated labour market mechanisms, whereby government institutions provided council, transport, housing and training to cities for jobless rural peasants and workers. Structural and geographical transformations were led by industry, unions and government - all in same direction for prosperity and peace. Union leaders understood early that if they were to get better wages, industries had to expand and rationalize production. Smaller industries and sometimes whole trades had to close down and workers be taken care of by Labour Market Directorate (Arbetsmarknadsstyrelsen, founded 1948) for training, unemployment benefits and new jobs[65]. This differs from similar governmental labour initiatives abroad in that the Swedish unions fully accept these rationalizations.

A unique feature in labour relations was fair wage policy, an idea that had roots in British political thought (Bentham, Ricardo, and Mill) but became real in post war Sweden. The idea is simple. Wages could only rise if production rose. To spread a fair wage policy for all workers, less productive firms had to close down under the pressure of central agreements between unions and employers. These agreements were made with the exporting industries in mind, where higher wages could be paid from good profits,

---

[65]   The Labour Market Directorate was led by social democratic director - generals from 1948 until 2008 when the first non- social democratic leader were hired by center-right cabinet. This fact cannot be over emphasized when discussing Swedish labour policy and control over national statistics of unemployment, research and legislation. Research done to support social democratic labour policies that were done at Institute for working life (Arbetslivcentrum/ Arbetslivsinstitutet) was finally closed down 2007 by center-right government. From 1976 to 2007 it was illegal for employers not register open positions at the governmental labour agencies of the Labour Market Directorate. Businessmen not registering available jobs could get fines in court for not showing their available positions to everyone. In all these areas, socialist ideologies dominated entirely no matter what reality showed to be true of labour market functioning.

but were instead held down in favour of higher wages in the less productive sectors and public sector, leading to higher taxes and public sector expansions. Two trade union economists, Gösta Rehn and Rudolf Meidner, designed in 1951 a model for full employment, high growth, low inflation and fair wage distribution. The employers gave the model their support from 1955 to 1980 since unions in exporting industries could hold back wages. Profits for investments and efficiency were encouraged by government regulations. Private investment funds could be exempt from taxation if put under government control during good years and spent in bad times. Government spending in bad times and saving in good times was the official Keynesian social democratic policy, but also supported by most parties to the political right. However, the spending was actually higher than the savings. The Swedish working population became used to yearly increased wages and higher welfare state benefits[66]. Sections of society came under government control without open total socialization, a step which would become even more unpopular later. The model was named functional socialism. Control of vital functions, rather than ownership of business, became the strategy of Swedish welfare state economy.

The 1950s, in Sweden as in many other Western countries was a time of rising prosperity and calm on the international front with the violent exceptions of Korea and Indo-China. Sweden became recognized for its success in sports (ice hockey World Cup gold 1953, football WC silver 1958, and boxer Ingmar Johansson WC gold 1959), avant-garde film maker Ingmar Bergman and international diplomacy (negotiator Folke Bernadotte in Israel, Dag Hammarsköld UN secretary general, Swedish disarmament initiative in UN and vocal support to liberated colonies in Africa and Asia). A balance in its international relations played off rather well. Sweden stayed officially neutral from NATO and the Soviet Bloc but had secret links to NATO in case of a Soviet invasion. This fact did not become publicly known until many decades later.

---

[66] Magnusson 2010, p.401–426. Labour policy reforms were a success, Rothstein (1996) claims comparing labour reforms to education reforms. Social democratic school policy got caught in bureaucracy as Max Weber would have predicted, unlike union led negotiations outside government.

Even more astonishing than public ignorance of military secrets was the fact that the social democratic foreign minister Östen Undén (in office 1945-1962) was not informed about any NATO loyalties. The secrecy was a verbal agreement among the prime minister, high military officers and some opposition party leaders. Undén was thought to be too closely linked to the Soviet Union to be trusted, a loyalty than would continue later with Olof Palme. When Soviet cannons shot down two Swedish airplanes 1952 as they spied over their waters in the Baltic Sea, foreign minister Undén protested. But he did not know that Swedish planes had been collecting information over Soviet waters that were given over to USA as an informal top secret agreement in return for Swedish air force using advanced US intelligence technology.

Officially Sweden was neutral but the Soviet Union knew well that the airports were designed so that US bombers could land, and the same with sea ports. A secret Stay Behind network of civil and military leaders that would coordinate opposition in Sweden if Soviet occupied was created after World War II modelled on the successful strategy during German occupation of Norway[67]. Military wise, neutrality did not play any significant role as it was a domestic issue for ruling social democrats to prove their worth in the Cold War. Thus the government was well trusted by citizens to keep Sweden out of any war by not being bound to either side, neither West nor East. The secret NATO deal would have been pulverized the moment it became public, so anyone

---

[67]   NATO used its Allied Clandestine Committee/Special Operations Planning Staff (ACC/SOPS) where Sweden was secretly represented by industry manager Arvid Lindencrona. None of this was known officially until the fall of Soviet Bloc in 1989 and onwards. Soviet did not get fooled by Swedish neutrality, as the Swedish parliament, citizens and world community including UN did, but kept itself well informed through air force officer Stig Wennerström, a spy that had told the Soviet Union everything they needed until getting caught in 1963. Regular talks were held with CIA by Swedish secret services, see Rauscher and Mattsson 2004, p. 127. The Stay behind network is acknowledged in a 2002 parliamentary report but no details are given (SOU 2002: 108). See Jallai 2011 for fictional arguments for the assassination of Prime Minister Olof Palme and NATO/CIA.

that knew anything lied openly to the public and parliament for decades. The consensus for rejecting Swedish nuclear weapon became strong in late 1950s and was supported by social democrats, communists and popular movements. Soviet claimed later that if Sweden had gotten atomic bombs, it would surely be a target in a heated militarized North Atlantic war. Of this, common Swedes would know nothing if nuclear bombs would start to fall.

There were more secrets than military in the calm 1950s Sweden. Pastor Karl-Erik Kejne at Stockholm mission found out that young men were being abused sexually by another pastor. Kejne himself became the victim of police harassment and a minister, Nils Quensel, tried to cover up the story with little success. Soon the press wrote about a homosexual mafia in Stockholm. The writer Wilhelm Moberg managed to smuggle documents out from a court room that showed how the minister had used his force to secretly have some other homosexuals imprisoned in mental asylums. These men were sane but most had committed homosexual acts with the minister. The accused pastor was sentenced to 40 days but died of mercury poisoning while jailed. The body was cremated before anyone could verify the cause of death. But by then other more embarrassing links within the Swedish establishment became known. Another homosexual, Kurt Hajby, revealed that he had had sexual relations with the Swedish king Gustav V in 1930s. He was then first sent to USA with royal cash, but was deported and again sent abroad, now off to Nazi Germany. The story was covered up by the court, politicians, media and police officers, but the social democratic cabinet in charge was discredited by the cover up and what little leaked to the press[68]. More socialist scandals would follow of more importance and in many of them would sexuality, hetero and homo, paid and unpaid sex, play significant but sad roles.

---

[68]   Half a century later Prime Minister Tage Erlander published his dairy from 1952 where he acknowledged that king Gustav V had most likely been intimate with Hajby.

PROSPERITY 1950

Television became popular during the decade but as was the case with radio after 1925, there was a government media monopoly: one TV channel and two radio channels, one for serious talk and one for classical music. Swedish youth had very little space for the emerging pop and rock and roll music scene. No commercials were allowed. The state used every possibility to broadcast its propaganda regarding life style matters and political consensus building. In 1961 the government radio faced competition from a private run station, Radio Nord. It was a private broadcasting service from a boat outside Swedish waters. Pop music and entertainment were broadcast to many young listeners until law enforcement in 1962 shut down the initiative[69]. It would take until 1987 when free commercial television was allowed and free radio 1993.

Literature flourished though in this prosperous calm decade. Children's book character *Pippi Longstocking* was the crazy anti-authoritarian heroine for young and old, created by the popular author Astrid Lindgren, a true genius. She would rock the socialist establishment decades later, even as her creation Pippi fit well into welfare state campaigns against repressive families, conservative traditions and tough teachers in favour of children's rights. Without prosperity, such a self-expressive character would not have been accepted. Refer to the position of Sweden in the World Values Survey, rich and tolerant, untraditional and rational.

---

[69]   Another radio station, Radio Syd continued to broadcast from international waters beyond Swedish law. But in 1966 government banned Swedish ownership of private radio stations settled abroad but broadcasting to Sweden. Radio activist Britt Wadner was sentenced and fined. She had to leave Sweden when law enforcement tried to take over her property rights to her house. UN declaration no 18 of right to free speech was violated with no attention. Instead union representative Gunnel Granlid at the national public radio, which had absolute monopoly declared: "Freedom of choice is confusing. Freedom of choice will lead to people not choosing informative programs. People will become less conscious. It is wrong to give people what they want ", in Johansson 1998, p. 31. Private radio activists Britt Wadner and Jack S. Kotschack were ahead of their time.

Gross Domestic Product (GDP) rose by almost 4% each year 1950
– 1960. With the Swedish economy linked to the monetary Bret-
ton-Woods system and to trade organisation GATT, the neutral high
powered country could sell mechanical products and natural resources
to all war torn countries and less developed nations. A large devaluation of the Swedish currency in 1949 helped boost the exports. This
method would be used many times by failing Swedish governments
when the economy did not rise, but would prove disastrous in the long
run. Income taxes rose from 20 % to 30% but were still lower than in
USA at the time. The winners included workers and the lower middle
class, losers were the traditional middle class and upper class. Sweden
had reached the highest equal living standard in the world by the mid
1950s. Living standards were higher in the USA and Switzerland, but
these countries had less equal distribution. Everyone seemed content
and had few disturbing demands. The concept of service democracy
was coined in 1956 by political scientist Jörgen Westerståhl to picture
the calm country's dedication to prosperity, pragmatic politics and
smooth administration with little public dissonance. Similar non-ideo-
logical trends were prevalent all over Western scholarship and debates.
Gunnar Myrdal and liberal editor Herbert Tingsten proclaimed the
death of ideologies along the same lines as sociologists Daniel Bell,
S.M. Lipset and Raymond Aron.

Alongside social democratic democratically led institutions of local, regional and central government, socialist movements and corporations
had by 1950s organized a well-functioning corporatist network of organizations, networks and structures. They all were a part of the working
class movement, or just the Movement (Arbetarrörelsen, or just Rörelsen),
a term still much in use by socialists. Communists were included and
tolerated as some eager little brothers and sisters, not quite grown up
and too wild but on the true left ideological track. From cradle and preschools to graves and funerals homes, housing, insurance, groceries, savings, adult education, kiosks, restaurants, lotteries, petrol pumps, dance
halls, youth clubs, charter trips, and pensioners' councils - all areas had
their socialist dominated corporatist structures. Foreign observers will
not easily appreciate the political stand in buying milk at the socialist and

cooperatively owned Konsum (Coop) rather than the private franchise ICA, a stand true even today.

Swedish society was and still is divided into two camps, center-right vs. center-left, with farmers and peasants in middle, especially in smaller towns and industrial cities. But few dared in the 1950s to speak about party politics as it was and still is often considered a private matter, impolite and embarrassing to bring up. Growing up absurd in docile socialist Sweden was as maddening as in socially conservative and materialistic American 1950s[70]. Workers went to the co-operative stores and used social democratic run insurances, the middle class to private stores and private insurance companies. The compromises between labour and capital together with a political consensus and homogeneity lead to corporatism where social democratic and labour organizations settled deals outside democratic influence. Mussolini's 1920s dream of harmonious relationships between workers and managers was rather realized in small Swedish mill towns than in Italian fascist corporations[71]. Sweden was

---

[70]   As in the maddening accounts of American hysteric conformity by Paul Goodman, *Growing up absurd* 1960 and Allen Ginsberg's *Howl* 956.. Poet and later Swedish Academy member and Nobel laureate Harry Martinsson told in 1956 of the mental depression living under possible nuclear terror threats and destructive technologies (he foresaw negative effects of television and computers) in his poetic science fiction story *Anira*. The coldblooded space passengers live passive but secure unemotional lives in a spaceship, drowning themselves with entertainment and repressed by a totalitarian master. See Martinsson 1998. Another sign of the nervous and complacent state at the time is *A clean, well-lighted place: a private view of Sweden* by Kathleen Nott from 1961, an account of the Swedish neurotic complacency and conformism. Being silent and rational while watching absurdity was a national trait. "Political controversy does not lie in the nature of the Swede. His interest is in good administration alone", Huntford 1971, p 77.

[71]   Edwardsson 2010, p. 290, 242- 247 and Sejersted 2005, p. 335- 342. Dahlkvist 1974 and Anners 1976 criticized the social democratic corporatism from the left and right, respectively. Nycander 2003 defends the agreement between labour and capital as a sign of democratic corporativism. Huntford viewed Swedish corporativism as a modern system of medieval guilds. For analysis of the Swedish social democratic

never fascist but with the strong labour market agreements and a constitutional right of non-government bodies to be considered in legislation,
corporatist directions in Sweden are very strong yet almost without clear
boundaries between government, enterprise and organized interests[72].

The links between the chairman of workers' trade union LO and the social democratic party executive board are striking examples of corporatism
that is undemocratic yet legal. The union chairman is by default also a
member of the party executive board, a practice which continues even in
2012. If the social democratic party is in power, as was the case for 44
years, the LO union chairman has direct access to cabinet without being elected but through meeting ministers every week informally at board
meetings. The party executive board is often seen as the real power center
in Sweden, rather than cabinet or parliament. Other similar features are
the unemployment funds which are owned by the unions but financed to
90 % by taxpayers. The unions execute a governmental duty to support
jobless people. Through the funds, members are recruited both to unions
and earlier also to the social democratic party through collective enlisted
membership. Corporatism is still alive in Sweden, ingrained in culture and
mores, supported by many political parties and vested interests also outside
the labour movement where corporatism is traditionally strongest.

PENSION REFORM 1960
Bland politics in late 1950s gave way to consumerism and the social
democratic government was in need of a popular issue that could draw

---

nomenclature, see Isaksson 2006.

[72] British economist Andrew Schofield wrote in 1974: "In Sweden there is a society in
which interest groups are so strongly organized, their democratic basis so firm, and
their habit of bargaining with one another independently from the government so
well established, that here, if anywhere, 'indicative planning' in the full sense - that is
planning without any dependence of the state - looks as if it ought to be feasible. /. . .
./The government is meant to keep its distance. It is not only that it is excluded from
the colloquy between the two sides: it does not even, any longer, attempt to exercise
guidance", in Nordfors 2006, p. 8

support as their parliamentary backing was thin, surviving only with support from the agrarian party. Most unions had reasonable pensions for their members through collective agreements with employers, but a few trade unions for workers had prioritized immediate higher wages instead of fees for pensions later. For their members only meagre national pensions existed by the time of retirement. The social democratic government proposed a mandatory system that deducted fees from wages to a new national additional pension system, ATP. Debate followed and an advisory referendum with three alternatives was arranged in 1957. The social democrats wanted a mandatory system and the center-right parties two different voluntary systems. No alternative got majority but the center-right alternatives had together 50 % of the votes and social democratic alternative got 45 %. Since the referendum was only advisory, the left cabinet claimed victory and started negotiations, which then fell through. A snap election was hurriedly organized in which the outcome was a tie, 115 – 115. Social democrats did not back down and put the pension bill to parliament.

With one liberal swing vote the daring social democratic strategy worked. The system was a mistake from the beginning since pensioners-to-be did not pay for their pensions, but for the older generations before them. By passing the buck, the new pension system became a great chain letter pyramid built on the promise of high growth, low unemployment and equal population growth. If any of these parameters were unbalanced, government had to raise taxes to fulfil the promise of pensions. This would happen later when there was not enough payroll taxes paid into the system from wages when unemployment rose or during recessions.

A payroll tax of 3,5 % was introduced in 1960 to finance the pension reform, but there was little discussion as the tax was not seen on pay stubs the way direct income taxes were. The pension reform shifted the whole political field more to the left. Liberals and conservatives that had been opposed to socialist and forced welfare systems became partners in the coming decades in welfare state building, even if trying to keep expansion at to a slower pace. A few critical voices were marginalized and considered reactionary, as arguments for individual responsibility and free market economy that were at least heard of before the pension reform were silenced after the pension reform in 1960[73]. The debate steered away from social welfare for bringing a basic standard for the needy to social welfare as a civil right and guaranteed income by government social policy. Social democrats would use indirect and excise taxes to provide more welfare services for free, while pretending that someone else paid, not the wage earning citizens. With no links between benefits and contributions the system was doomed from the start[74].

The 1960s was the last decade in which the Swedish welfare state lived up to its promise. The liberal and conservative leaders criticized each other rather than the ruling social democratic governments and lost elections. Taxes rose higher in Sweden than in USA and Europe. Leading American economist, admirer of Sweden and advisor to democratic presidents, John K. Galbraith was hailed in Sweden as a theorist of the new industrial state beyond capitalism and communism, built on technology and rationality. His emphasis on the importance of government planning for successful capitalism suited the social democrats well, especially Olof Palme and his generation of young progressive politicians. But the Swedish socialists thought that US was also a threat to world peace, and they were not alone in this view in turbulent 1960s worldwide.

---

[73]   Book publisher Johan Hansson, head of Labour History & Archives Tage Lindbom, writer Vilhelm Moberg and economist Sven Rydenfeldt were lone defenders of liberty and free markets in 1950s. See *Revolt mot välfärdsstaten* 1958 and Sandberg 2009. A small group of liberal workers under Dalecarlica county miner Arne Montan was formed but was too weak against the social democratic rule over labour organisations, and with little support from the liberal establishment, see Norberg 1999b, p. 286- 89. For the complacency of the center- right parties towards welfare state expansion in mid century Sweden, see Uddhammar 1993, Garme 2001 and Findlay, Jonung and Lundahl (eds.) 2002, ch. 6. Authors critical of welfare state paternalism and conformism during 1950s were Folke Fridell and Kurt Salomonsson, both with firm working class background. But most authors were loyal to socialist thought and rule (even to Stalin), especially some of the members in the Swedish Academy giving out Nobel prizes of literature, notably Artur Lundkvist.

[74]   Burenstam Linder 1983.

ANTI- AMERICAN 1960s

Abroad Sweden rose and became a kind of self-proclaimed international moral authority with its foreign aid program SIDA (Swedish International Development Agency), UN secretary general Dag Hammarskjöld and the wealthy, left leaning country's neutral stand in the Cold War. Leading social democrats but also other respected government officials and intellectuals adhered to the view that super powers, the Soviet Union and US, were equal in respect of freedom, civil rights, rule of law and economy. Much criticism had been lashed against US' treatment of its black population already by the 1950s but this anti-racist theme became a sign for Swedish moral correctness globally and anti- Americanism for decades. Socialist Swedish authors had in 1947 hailed Josef Stalin and commemorated the 30 year memory of violent Soviet takeover of Russia in 1917. These authors refused next year to critique the Communist coup in Czechoslovakia 1948, as they thought criticism of only the Soviet Union could be viewed as one sided and pro USA. These influential cultural socialist elite, some writers who later became members of Swedish Academy selecting Nobel Prize winning authors, had formed an influential so called non-aligned and governmentally supported group of writers that advocated criticism only of USA. Artur Lundqvist was among the most vocal author loyal to the Soviet Union, vice chairman of communist World Peace Council, member of the Swedish-East German friendship committee, received the Lenin Prize in Moscow 1958 and yet a Nobel committee member at the Swedish Academy. When the 31 authors congratulated Stalin, evidences were available to read of the Russian dictatorship, similar to five years earlier when anti- Nazi Swedish intellectuals were silenced as the evidences from death camps and pogroms surfaced from Germany. A few writers had the integrity to stay out of the glorification of communism hailed by the majority of writers at the time; Karin Boye[75], Bertil Malmberg, Margit Abenius, Eyvind Johnsson and Wilhelm Moberg.

---

[75] Karin Boye portrayed the terror regimes of Hitler and Stalin in her dystopian novel *Kallocain* in 1940 with similar usage of technological and medical means as Orwell and Huxley. Her visit to Soviet Union and earlier membership in communist group Clarté led to strong skepticism of left wing utopias and repressive welfare state mechanism. See Boye 2002.

In Sweden and in other such naïve international quarters, neutrality meant that both super powers were at fault. The CIA understood the Swedish attitude as a "plague on both your houses" [76.] The Soviet Union with its occupation of the East Europe, Gulag labour camps, surveillance and the invasion of Hungary in 1956 was viewed as being equally as good as USA with its free elections, free enterprise and unforced union membership, freedom of speech and press, not to mention differences in standards of living in the two countries. Another target for socialist critique was the apartheid regimes in southern Africa that often were aligned with attacks on the US for supporting racism. Swedish criticism of segregated schools attacked American policies as if the civil right movement and the anti-segregated school verdict of Brown vs. Board of Education in Topeka 1954 did not exist. Only Swedes were tolerant towards other races, citizens were told by establishment and media, while they were proud of blond and blue eyed men in blue berets serving under UN flags. Sweden was heaven, the outside was hell.

By 1965, the US' policy in the Vietnam War came in focus in far off and uninvolved Sweden, as young minister Olof Palme spoke against US involvement. He held his speech without informing other cabinet ministers including the foreign minister. Palme was not alone, as the son of Alva and Gunnar Myrdal, rabidly radical writer Jan Myrdal, was arrested the same year for demonstrating against US Vietnam policy in central Stockholm[77]. From apartheid to anti-colonial struggles, strong socialist and left liberal opinion was brewing in Sweden. Decolonization in the

---

[76]   "Kålsuparteorin" in Swedish. P. 226 in SOU 2002: 108 (from the now public CIA memorandum entitled "Sweden Guidelines Paper., 6 June 1962).

[77]   Jan Myrdal is a Maoist publicist and independent scholar of the new left in post war Sweden. His book *Confessions of a Disloyal European* was hailed by NYT 1968 of that year's 'ten books of particular significance and excellence'. His breakthrough was an uncritical and panegyric report from Maoist China in 1963. His hatred of his parents Alva and Gunnar and the Swedish social democratic party have been topics of his many books. He has supported socialist and communist dictatorships in Albania, Cambodia, Vietnam, China, North Korea, Soviet (under Stalin, but not under Khrushchev) and armed Maoist rebellions in India and Latin America.

third world was excused at the price of democracy. The social democratic student club in Uppsala *Laboremus* claimed openly that one-party socialist states were welcome and must be excused for not living up to democratic standards. The non-aligned movement lead by Tito in Yugoslavia was cherished by young radical students who wished that their own less utopian social democrats in Sweden would become as radical as some heroes and leaders in developing and some socialist countries.

Helping emerging countries to modernize without going through a market economy, as Marx thought was mandatory on the road to communism, the Swedish government used a foreign aid program to fund transition in developing countries from agriculture to industrial communism with no intermediate period of liberal democracy or market economy. The foreign aid program rose by 20 – 25% every year in the 1960s. Swedish private corporations working abroad were supported by government contracts. All political parties supported using aid to finance exports of national products. Swedish money made many new nations dependent on more aid and offered few market economic incentives. Repressive, socialist Tanzania is the worst example and biggest recipient of Swedish aid, though hailed as a success in Sweden and supported by the close friendship between Julius Nyerere and Olof Palme dating from the 1950s. Other socialist and authoritarian recipients of large amounts of Swedish aid have been Angola, Cuba, Nicaragua, Ethiopia, Vietnam and Mozambique.

Just as the admiring Americans hailed the exceptional Swedish welfare state in the 1930s, Swedish foreign policy was hailed by progressives around the world in 1960s. That Swedish history had become more peaceful than histories of other nations was the national proud message to the world. No one remembered the fierce, ruthless Swedish wars in Northern Europe during the Swedish Empire in 17th and 18th centuries, except people in Poland and the Baltic nations, but their voices and victims were never heard then or later[78]. Swedes themselves did

---

[78]   Zaremba 2003 told about a public meeting in southeast Poland in 2002 for the 200th year commemoration of lost lives in battles against the Swedes in 1702. Swedish diplomats were not present.

not remember their war torn bloody history as future and modernity replaced memories of the ugly compromises made during World War II. The nation was truly an exception and had a mission to tell the world what was right and wrong, the Swedish establishment believed. A new moral superpower was born, but the world was not always impressed. *The Times* commented by 1970 that "Sweden is known for 'the export of unsolicited advice' "[79]. But director general of foreign aid agency SIDA and loyal social democrat Ernst Michanek stated without modesty that "the most successful social democracy in the world", i.e. Sweden, had a duty to spread knowledge of modern society building to the world and that the interests of the international under class was the responsibility of Swedish trade unions and social democratic party[80].

YOUTH PROTESTS 1960
Sex for friendship's sake, contraceptives in grocery stores, nudity on film, vocal feminism, communist activism, anti-imperialism and counterculture were mixed in 1960s Sweden with advisory centers for sex debuting teenagers, anti-commercial happenings, the cool Stockholm Museum of Modern Art (where visitors could enter an exhibition through a gigantic vagina 1966), politically radical scruffy singer-song writers and support for radical filmmakers documenting the cultural changes.

The Center-right parties were less satisfied with the emerging liberating social movements but that would change. Liberal party youth league members were sometimes more radical than the young socialists. Young liberals organized trips from Poland for abortion-seeking women in 1965, demanded that society "must take the children from their parents" to balance parental daily governance[81], supported socialist dictatorships and violent revolutions abroad and viewed economic growth as exploitative capitalism. These counter cultural attitudes were mostly tolerated and sometimes supported by the establishment. Especially Olof Palme

---

[79]   Huntford 1971, p. 74

[80]   In Edwardsson 2010, p. 310

[81]   Liberal Youth League leader Per Garthon 1968, in Svanborg- Sjövall 2011, p. 106.

used his intellectual curiosity and international travel experiences in 1950s from anti –colonial and progressive efforts in Africa, Asia and USA to relate to the rebelling youngsters. Government funded Swedish Travelling Exhibitions toured the country offering an anti-imperialist critique in 1968–70 blaming Swedish corporations and government policies for supporting capitalist repression abroad. The exhibition was criticized but tolerated, a situation which would be a routine later when the times were a-changin´. . .

In 1967 Olof Palme was interviewed briefly in the avant-garde leftist film *I Am Curious (Yellow)* (Jag är nyfiken (gul)), a film rated X in USA due to its obscene content with a kissed penis and other nudity. One cannot imagine other European ministers being in same movie with actors showing their genitals. Swedish sex was nothing to be ashamed of but properly supported through government campaigns for contraception and sexual education. Swedish filmmakers including Ingmar Bergman had shown naked breasts since 1951, so what was the fuss about, many Swedes thought. Next year in February 1968, education minister Olof Palme took another revolutionary message to the streets and walked the Stockholm streets alongside with communist North Vietnam's ambassador to Russia in a manifestation against the USA' s involvement in Vietnam. In May 1968 during worldwide global protests, he went to a Stockholm university student union building and spoke to the young protesters who were occupying their own premises, just like in Paris' student quarters weeks before.

In the next decades these radical baby boomers born in the 1940s would become Palme's greatest supporters and his most loyal employees in the bulging Swedish public sector. Especially radical women loved him. Swedish 1960s were never as divisive and radical as in other Western nations around 1968 as there was little to protest against a soft state with tolerant civil servants and political leaders sympathetic to radical reforms. Palme was also a hard working central bureaucrat that had been involved in, among other tasks, a government housing project 1965-1975 to build one million flats in functionalist modern style for common people. In 1967 as communication minister he successfully had led the change of traffic from left-hand side driving to the right-hand side. His organizational talents in common areas were useful assets when his radicalism and international experiences scared off regular voters and sympathizers.

WOMEN'S LIBERATION

Modern Sweden was by 1960s still built on its history of farmers, rural manners and popular trust in equality that gave the grand futuristic projects coming from radical reformers and social democratic government an informal and popular touch. Little distinguished workers from public employees and managers by the end of the turbulent decade. Hats and ties were taken off by young men who let their hair grow. Women took off their brassieres under the blouses. These young women would not become housewives, but remain independent. All were not in accord with the changed sex roles, however. Socialist campaigns for women's right to work were out in front of the male dominated trade unions and some dissenting social democratic female leaders, such as the fiery Nancy Eriksson. Still the mood was in favour of women's emancipation, or of the need to bring more numbers into the workforce as some more pragmatic advocates analyzed the feminist calls.

Women were to be liberated from home through work, from undesirable men by divorce, from unwanted children by abortion and from unexciting abstinence or monogamy through free sex. The small feminist Group 222 of liberal and socialist men and women working as newspaper editors, radio and television producers, politicians and journalists, became influential using the government monopoly on broadcasting channels in radio and television, government contacts and high rhetoric against common family life and what they viewed as obsolete family traditions. Their agenda was open and clear. Since people were so conservative, they needed to be informed and disciplined to make the right choices[82].

---

[82] Johansson 1998, p. 26-27. The influential group 222 members were Krister Wickman, Marianne Höök, Gunnar Fredriksson, Monica Boëtius, Eva Moberg, Gertrud Sigurdsen, Gabriel Romanus, Anita Gradin and Olle Alsén and about 20 more. Even today the left leaning journalists with condescending attitudes dominate, for instance at the national radio program Studio Ett every weekday afternoon. The

Social projects for juvenile delinquents, addicts, mentally unstable people and other marginalized groups were established outside regular municipal social services and in opposition to the capitalist system, which was blamed for all social ills from which these victims suffered. Social workers mixed informally with clients and took a stand against hospitalization and medication. The establishment left and right wavered in their support for the liberating social tendencies and new movements, as many radical experts and politicians also wanted to fight the medical authority, one which they also viewed as often dominated by bureaucracy and inhumane treatment. In 1965 the prison system was reformed and punishment was replaced with treatment of criminals. Individual responsibility for actions was replaced by emphasis on social structures which could be monitored so the criminals would change their behaviour. Initially the prison reformers proposed to abolish the idea of punishment in law but that did not happen, even if in practice the result was the same: focus on treatment, not punishment[83].

WELFARE STATE FINISHED

The political feeling by end of 1960s was that the Swedish welfare state was almost complete. Social democrats were looking for good campaign slogans but settled for Increased Equality (Ökad jämlikhet), thus rivalling communist calls for Equality in 1968 election[84]. With this meek slogan, social democrats had their best election result ever during times of peace, over 50 %. Author Göran Hägg, born 1947, wrote:

> journalists, who have been found to mostly vote in favour of socialist politics, always seem to know best and any problem can usually be solved with more state regulations, politically correct values and tax money. This paternalist and maternalist tradition is strong especially in gender equality discussions and policies in Sweden in all political quarters, although a majority of Swedes support freedom of choice of child care, including the option to choose which parent should stay home on government funded parental leave 1-2 years.

[83]   The socialist treatment system of criminals of 1960s has not worked as hoped and is recently analysed in the parliamentary report *Nya påföljder* SOU 2012:34.

[84]   Equality was mentioned 513 times in social democratic party congress papers in 1960 and 4 682 times in 1969, see Östberg 2002, p. 71.

"It is a supreme favour to have experienced the year 1967 in Sweden. Such unfettered optimism and collective irresponsibility is hard to imagine. I have tried often to find similarities together with contemporary friends. To be an enlightened French aristocrat in mid 17th century might have felt the same. But here it was actually the whole population that encompassed the illusion"[85].

What is paradoxical is the verve and fervour with which the left activists tried to paint Sweden as an imperialistic and capitalistic hell to live in for all when in fact never had so many had it so good, at least materially.

On 14 October 1969 at age 42 Olof Palme came to power as social democratic party leader and Prime minister. Under his reign, Sweden turns another chapter, from hubris to humiliation. "Sweden: Hot Soup from Olof", *Time Magazine* chronicled his victory[86]. Little did they know how hot Swedish soup could get under the red aristocrat Palme. The next chapter will describe the most extreme period in the land of extremes.

---

[85] Hägg 2005, p. 231. "Hyper rationalism" has been coined for Swedish mid 20th century efficiency and social engineering, see Elmrud and Glans 1998, p. 153.

[86] *Time magazine.* 10 Oct, 1969. *The New Yorker* wrote same year on Palme that he probably was the only acting prime minister who had read student rebellion theorist Herbert Marcuse.

Reforms 1930 – 1970

1934 Unemployment insurance by unions funded by government
1938 Ban to fire pregnant or married women
1942 Rent control
1943 Expansion of government child care
1947 Retention (withholding) tax
1947 Identification number for whole population
1948 Child allowance for all families
1948 National labour market agency
1949 Regulation and expropriation of land legislation
1949 Experiments with comprehensive 9 year education
1951 Three weeks paid vacation
1952 Foreign aid program
1952 Right to leave the Swedish Church
1955 Legislation for sick insurance for employees
1955 Abolishment of alcohol regulation
1955 Mandatory sex education in schools
1957 Social welfare legislation
1958 School corporal punishment abolished
1959 Pension system reformed
1960 Labour – employers agreement to abolish women's lower
       wages
1962 9 year comprehensive primary schooling for all
1965 One million apartments' construction program
1965 Beer with alcohol sold in grocery stores
1967 Change of driving to right-hand side of traffic

CHAPTER 4:

Humiliation 1970 - 2000

The 1970s mark a watershed in Swedish policy as Olof Palme with his energy and international outlook redirected Sweden into a socialist experiment state headed downwards into humiliation. His posture as a radical aristocrat angered many center-right politicians, common workers and voters. Sweden was transformed by Palme; his legacy is still felt, for better or worse. Secretly some Swedes were proud of his initiatives, but there was open hatred of him until his yet unsolved murder on 28 Feb, 1986. To openly criticize Olof Palme today is still often viewed as disrespectful.

His manic political activism and sudden death has made him into an international icon, with streets named after him in India, Hungary and Italy. Prizes are handed out to his honour, such as the Olof Palme Memorial Lecture at Oxford University[87] and Der Olof Palme Freiden Preis by Germany's Social Democrats. What made him so successful was his embodiment of the combination of an effective high ranking civil servant of high class heritage who effectively could serve in any regime and his linkages to the emerging radical generation of 1968. He was 20 years younger than the young rebels of 1960s, of noble and wealthy origin, a reserve officer with a law degree, yet open to women's liberation, ecology, workers' rights, international solidarity and equality for all citizens. Being an aggressive politician playing the majority card rather than seeking consensus through cooperating with opposing parties, Palme was similar with the fierce turn of the 19th century liberal party leader Karl Staaff, neither being well-liked by his contemporaries but admired posthumously. Like Staaff, Palme was also called a renegade by his fellow upper class members, and he did not always sit comfortably within the traditional tranquillity of Swedish politics[88].

---

[87] Funded by the Swedish Olof Palme Memorial Fund and with lecturers like Noam Chomsky, Martha Nussbaum, and Wole Soyinka etc.

[88] Lewin 2002, p. 43. The distinction between politicians leaning on cooperation or

In the late 1960s, the character of social democratic party gatherings transformed from brass bands traditionally playing the socialist anthem "L'Internationale", while some mild but boring spokesperson speaking into a malfunctioning microphone, to one of a well-lit stage with pretty film star Monica Nielsen swaying and singing the latest radical pop tunes, interacting with the handsome Palme in his early 40s, delivering cool one liners to a stunned congregation. A political rock star was born. Progressive, intellectual, noble-a European John F. Kennedy or Jawaharlal Nehru. Palme is a forerunner of young smart progressives Bill Clinton (less cool) and Tony Blair (very cool) but with the experience of a FD Roosevelt or a Clement Attlee. Charismatic, quick, energetic, but yet in the end, destructive[89].

The new left movement presented both a support and a challenge for Olof Palme and his social democratic party in the 1970s. Palme was ahead of the party and unions in most policies but navigated well the tide of reforms in labour legislation, expansion of the public sector and international engagements. It is probable that his left-leaning version of traditional Scandinavian social democracy prevented the non-communist leftist fractions from splitting off, as they had done in Denmark (Socialistisk Folkeparti 1959) and Norway (Sosialistisk Venstreparti 1961). His star quality as the wonder boy of modern politics became known to the world as he became friends with Fidel Castro being the first Western leader to visit Cuba since the revolution, sometime lover to American film star Shirley Maclaine, and managed to divide a nation forever before and after his death at age 57.

The combination of his energy, his descent from a wealthy educated and conservative family, and his radical views transformed the radical 1970s into a political work and play field for radical teachers, social workers and government employees. The public sector expanded and Palme became

---

on majority is useful. Lewin argues that the majority consensus building politics was reestablished in 1990s crisis when left, center and right parties united in battling financial problems and collaborated for the EU membership in 1994.

[89]   See Derfler 2011 for Olof Palme's legacy in English.

the red extremist CEO of the capitalist Swedish kingdom. In no other democratic country did the state rule over such a large and growing public sector. During 1970s the highly taxed citizens' money was mostly spent in adding almost a million employees to the government payroll, whereas the private sector rationalized and let workers off. In fact, the private sector did not hire any net new employees at all after 1970. The new public employees were mostly women, who took jobs in the social sector caring for children and parents other than their own; the socialization of family life that was viewed in as a liberating action. Whatever name one gives it, it was a losing game as there was little economic growth to pay for the expanding public services.

STRIKES AND PROTESTS 1970

Palme had his hands full the first months of his administration as miners in the state-owned LKAB mine fields went on wildcat strikes in 1969-70. The strike was Sweden's first televised labour conflict, and the new left leaning monopoly channel TV2 covered the workers' opposition in detail. What surprised the Palme cabinet ministers was that these government employed miners went on strike against a socialist government that the large majority of miners themselves had elected. Palme blamed the uprising on Finnish communists and media, though he was humble enough to tell the party leadership that it did not know enough about the hardships among miners. Radical intellectuals and academics provided support and money to the strikers, who were shut out by their socialist union representatives and had no access to strike funds. In the end the workers were successful in their demands and some of them had learnt a new term, alienation, which was repeated by all serious social scientists who had been analyzing workers since the May 1968 Paris uprisings. The workers carried placards expressing the same message in their slogans; "We are not machines", "Now or never!" The miners' strike was followed by more wildcat strikes in other industries and services, and by next year a conflict within government sectors including railways and the military. By 1970 Prime Minister Palme had enacted legislation to enjoin the public employees from striking, as their demands could become a threat to law and order. Some strikes he supported, some he fought when threatened.

In Stockholm, inner city protests at a projected subway station adjoining a park led to a similar rebellion in 1971. Hippies, urban environmental activists and conservative ladies joined hands against inner city modernization. The city of Stockholm had gone through a large architectural makeover which had turned most of old downtown into rubble and replaced it with high skyscrapers and grand, modernistic plazas. Soviet Bloc countries had never succeeded so well with their Stalinist programs for urban planning, but Sweden was able due to more affluence and even less respect for tradition[90]. The social democratic mayor of Stockholm Hjalmar Mehr had to back down, giving the alliance between young greens and old conservatives a victory. A romantic and anti-modern feeling united people of all political stripes and ages. A few years later this environmental and anti-bureaucratic tendency would bring down the long reign of social democratic regimes after 44 years. The welfare state was increasingly heavily criticized by both left and right for its anonymity, bureaucracy and reliance on industrialization.

The centralizing tendencies of the Swedish welfare state did not go unnoticed by international observers. In 1971 the conservative UK broadsheet *Observer's* correspondent Roland Huntford published his thoughts in a sour but accurate commentary on Sweden, *The New Totalitarians*[91]. By linking Swedish socialist planning and social engineering to George Orwell's *1984* and Aldous Huxley's *Brave New World*, he raised many eyebrows. Some Swedish commentators agreed with his analysis, though

---

[90]   Landin 2002, p. 11-12. Swedish new social movements and radicals are analysed in Johansson 1998 and Östberg 2002, from right and left respectively. Arvidsson 2008 tells the autobiographical story of the leftists who knew everything. The 1968 left wing movement in Sweden was not very intellectual and actually resisted a scientific discussions in favour of emotions and activism. See Segerstedt 1979 , Almqvist ed. 2008 and Ljunggren 2009.

[91]   *Det blinda Sverige* 1972. An updated analysis of the book and comparison of Sweden after 2000 is Ljungberg, et al. 2007. Foreign readers may still find Huntford's views worthwhile reading. Swedes will choke. Still.

they were equally stunned by his harshness. Many high placed officials and politicians had been interviewed, but only anonymously. Thus a broad and open debate had been avoided, a pattern that would be repeated later in interviews with angry policemen and nurses who dared not give their names to media.

Sweden is not truly part of the West, Huntford stated, having not been occupied by the Romans, never having experienced feudalism, nor ever taking part in the Renaissance. He then quoted the current parliamentary ombudsman who stated that Swedes regarded the source of security of life as social welfare, rather than the rule of law as in other Western nations. Swedes are still medieval in their rural trust in the welfare society and would rather be taken care collectively than be individually responsible. Corporatism together with technology had made Sweden into a control state.

The relation to control fascinated Huntford, who noted that life would have been better if Swedes had done like smart Russians did when they were to obey a stupid communist order. The Russians said to the communist rulers -Yes, whatever you say, Comrade! - But they did not carry out silly orders. Instead Swedes executed all orders well, whether silly or not. Result: compliant citizens and an unopposed bureaucracy. The same adherence to questionable rules would later make Sweden the best pupil in the EU class, implementing everything Brussels said.

The Social democratic administration, social democratic cabinet and social democratic party (and executive board) created a monolith that left little room for new non-socialist rulers even if they were to gain power, Huntford claimed. He would be proven right later in the same decade. Politics aside, his analysis went to heart of Swedish conformism and rational attitudes in everyday life. Huntford was not alone in viewing Swedes as being so obedient that no external force was necessary, since the citizens controlled themselves so well. French historian Michel Foucault, who spent two years in my hometown of Uppsala in late 1950s, writing about disciplinary thought patterns in mental maladies and institutions, seems to have been influenced by similar thinking, as were other foreign commentators on Swedish welfare services and culture, such as American writer Susan Sontag and Finnish film maker Jörn Donner[92].

SOCIALIST TROUBLES

Palme himself stirred up more trouble in 1972 by using the UN conference on the environment in Stockholm as an opportunity to criticize American Vietnam policy. His talk drew a strong reaction from Washington. At Christmas the same year he gave a radio speech comparing the fierce US bombings of Hanoi in North Vietnam to the Holocaust massacres of World War II and other international crimes against humanity. Washington froze diplomatic relations with Sweden for two years, as Nixon called him again "that Swedish asshole"[93]. But Palme secretly maintained good relations with the US establishment to ensure help against the Soviet Union. Officially he was still neutral, but from 1970 on he was strongly anti- American.

The parliamentary elections of 1973 were indecisive, as the two opposing party Blocs, socialists with communists on one hand, and center- right parties on the other, received same numbers of parliament members, 175 each. Palme stayed on as prime minister of a minority cabinet, but had to use a lottery at times to resolve tie votes. What was more disturbing for him and his party, that year there was a public disclosure of a secret intelligence bureau. IB (Informationsbyrån) had, without permission from parliament and in opposition to the routines of secret services, registered and persecuted left wing activists and others that the ruling socialist party disliked or feared. The two journalists who revealed the IB affair, Jan Guillou and Peter Bratt, were sentenced to prison under espionage legislation, exactly at the time of Watergate scandals, for which no American journalists had been jailed for doing similar investigate journalism. The

---

[92]   Sontag 1969, Donner 1973 and Berggren and Trägårdh 2006, p. 369- 37. Dissatisfaction of the 1960s - 1970s labour movement from a worker's point of view is well captured in Bengtsson 1972. Later journalistic and more pessimistic writings in same vein on Sweden are Nilsson 2005 and Jalving 2009.

[93]   Hägg 2005, p. 266.

bureau did not exist officially within the intelligence services, so there was no applicable law on military or civil intelligence procedures.

The astonishing part of the shady secret activities was the powerful and illegal links between the social democratic establishment and a network of spies who worked neither for military intelligence nor for the secret police, but only and clandestinely to serve the socialist government. They worked under highly placed socialist politicians with experience of secret intelligence networks, such as Prime Minister Olof Palme himself. Decades earlier, he had worked with student politics supported by CIA spying on European and Asian communists, and as a Swedish military intelligence officer in 1951. Palme did not acknowledge any awareness of the unconstitutional secret bureau IB in 1973, but there is no question that he knew of its existence and routines. Center-right politicians did not like this strange use of state power and money by a political party, but conceded that the growing leftist movement had to be surveilled in some fashion, which was a defeat of open society, constitutional rights of freedom of speech and thought and basic liberal values[94].

The Swedish parliament was made up of two chambers until 1974 despite decades of constitutional dithering. Since the social democrats had taken power 1932 they had withheld their earlier critique of the existing two chamber bicameral system, which was supported by conservatives. Socialists soon realized that a system that made electoral changes slowly and with few cabinet shifts could be of benefit to them as it had been to the conservative governments earlier. The liberal party was mostly alone in its fight for constitutional reforms[95]. Social democrats knew that if they lost a lower house election they could still maintain power for another eight years through the first chamber, making the temptation to

---

[94]   Unlike in the earlier decade when liberal–conservative scholar Sven Rydenfeldt and journalist Janerik Larsson revealed similar secret registrations of leftwing activists. Tolerance and freedom of speech for all views was Rydenfeldt's and Larsson's motives, even when they defended their communist opponents. See Norberg 1999b, p. 300.

[95]   Ahlmark 2011, p. 89 – 102.

keep the old system strong. There was little resistance to maintaining the inherited system of representation through two chambers, was sure as constitutional changes were a hard sell to the many voters not interested in such details.

Still, the 1974 constitutional change did not meet the requirements to ensure civil rights, rights to property, sound electoral support for minority cabinets and an independent judiciary. A minority cabinet could stay on if there was no opposition majority n parliament, which is an unknown procedure in many Western democracies. Social democrats made peace with the liberal party by 1974 as they had done before with the agrarian party to secure support as minority government. Demands for a catalogue of civil rights were brushed away by minister of justice Carl Lidbom and legal experts schooled in legal positivism. He and his predecessor Lennart Geijer viewed natural law as old fashioned, as an obstacle to the administrative powers of elected governments. Laws are tools the ruling party needs to reach its political goals. Might is right. With no separate spheres of legislative, executive and judicial powers as in many other normal Western constitutions, there are no limits to what the ruling government can do. In 1976 government officers were exempted from personal responsibility for their actions performed as a civic duty, which made questioning of their decisions impossible within Sweden. The only way to question Swedish constitutional law and ruthless government decisions was appeal to the European Court of Human Rights, to which Sweden was brought many times from 1970s onwards. Olof Palme did not mince his words, expressing fear and contempt when he called the European Court a playground[96].

---

[96]   Medborgarrättsrörelsen 2008. In 1982 the European Court of Human Rights decided that the Swedish constitution did not give enough protection to individual property in the Sporrong-Lönnroth case. Later in 1987 Sweden was again sentenced the second time in the European Court of Human rights when bus service owner Bengt Pudas was neglected by all legal courts in his attempt to oppose a juridical decision in favour of another bus company. He came all the way from the rural cold north to Stockholm inner city and settled himself in a wooden box on the main square outside parliament. For three months bus entrepreneur Bengt Pudas became

Trade unions became the next battleground for Palme. Should the successful collective bargaining between the unions and employers continue, or should workers' demands be converted into legislatively conferred rights? Trade union LO leader Arne Geijer had by 1965 already become suspicious of Olof Palme and his radical ideas for a union reinforced by legislation. Such mechanisms would make the employers less powerful and aggressive and rock the delicate balance between the two, he claimed in a secret discussion at the American Embassy[97]. But the tide was turning. Even center-right parties were openly discussing new ideas of corporate democracy and the social democrats felt sidelined. Palme launched a formidable labour legislation program, one which has beleaguered labour relations since the fervent 1970s. Over ten reforms were enacted into laws through which the right to employment protection and employees' right to co-determination in the workplace have become mostly impotent, ineffective and controversial.

Employers felt threatened when they were not allowed to fire employees as needed , either for performance or due to market changes, and by having to cooperate with unions in serious decision making. Some unions had young radical members and wildcat strikers who welcomed the changes, but the central union leadership at LO tried to back down. What followed was exactly what the union leader Arne Geijer had predicted. Employers campaigned against the changes and their organization, the SAF, later withdrew from all national central collective bargaining. The national union LO then had no national and central counterpart.

center of attention, hailed as hero against government and a popular campaigner for his sake. Sweden had to change legislation to make it possible to question an administrative decision. If a constitutional court had existed, the Pudas affair would not have happened, nor the Alvgard tax affair later. Swedish constitutional law was under attack from the strident jurists Gustaf Petrén and Jacob W F. Sundberg who did what they could to fight socialist executive legislation and uphold ideas of rule of law. Still the juridical system favour municipalities and government against civilians, see Zaremba 1992, Warnling – Nerep 1995, Sandberg 1997 p. 25, Thelin 2000 and *Sydsvenska Dagbladet* 20 Oct, 2010.

[97] Nycander 2010a and Nycander 2010b.

All negotiations had to be made trade by trade, not by centralized talks from confederations of employees and employers. The fundamental social contract that had lasted since the first industrial relations agreements in 1906 was broken. But during the maddening industrial relations in 1970s even more eccentric ideas of industrial relations were proposed.

WAGE EARNERS FUNDS

What tipped the balance of labour and capital was not only bureaucratic and one-sided employment legislation in favour of employees, but another unwanted demand from radical union activists and leftwing campaigners; funds to socialize the economy, dubbed wage earners funds (löntagarfonder). The neologism containing "wage earners" was coined to gather support from both workers and the middle class. The term also avoided associations with Yugoslavian workers' councils or their Russian counterparts, "soviets" as workers' councils are called in the Russian language. Yugoslavia, as a communist country outside the Soviet Bloc, attracted many leftists and even liberals at the time, and the Yugoslavian workers' councils were admired and studied. Strangely no one seemed to ask young immigrating Yugoslavians why they left their good socialist country for jobs in bad capitalist Sweden. How to gain influence and ownership of business became a fiery issue, first and foremost for social democrats, but also for center-right parties who campaigned to give more power to employees. With radical reforms such as forced union representatives in banks and government regulated investments in private companies together with a new social democratic party program proposing that - "the right to decide over production and its distribution [should be] placed in the hands of the whole people", i.e. socialization of private property - unions and social democrats were ready by 1975 to take over capitalism itself.

Wage earners funds were proposed with the objective of successively allocating profits that were saved in exporting industries due to the fair wage, to be administered by union representatives. The higher a company's profits became, the quicker it would be taken over by workers, which of course would discourage recognizing high profits, though no one seemed to notice the contradiction. Another result would be that no businessman would allow his company grow beyond 19 employees, since with 20, it would become common property. Within 20 years socialism would become the dominant form of economy[98]. The liberal idea from 19th century, of employee shares in companies, was transformed into an instrument of social democratic corporatism, as unions would serve as both the voice of management and the workers' voice against management, not unlike in Soviet Bloc economies. Employers and center-right parties presented good arguments against the social democrats and their union-supported wage earners funds. The socialist party was taken by surprise at the LO union congress at summer 1976 when the fund initiative gained support, two months before elections. No initial talks were held with the employers or anyone else at the social democratic party establishment, so it was easy for the center-right opposition to portray the ruling cabinet as having been taken over by a radicalized union leadership.

Prime minister Olof Palme and union leader Gunnar Nilsson, who did not get along well, recognized the potential to curb the radicals through reformist versions of the proposed funds, but it was too late to manoeuvre. Voters did not like the funds, which smacked of the Soviet Union and its soviet councils. In 1976 the social democrats lost, partly due to the funds, partly a united right of centre coalition, but also because many spectacular affairs had made the socialist government appear power hungry, immoral and ruthless. Here is a selection of unsavoury events.

---

[98]   "All companies operating at a profit were to transfer annually to union funds newly issued shares equalling 20 per cent of their profits. If the proposal was carried, union funds would soon acquire a controlling interest in most profit-making Swedish enterprises. Sweden had acquired a unique economic system: private property would be confiscated by funds combining the functions of trade unions, employers/company managers and owners. The result would be an extreme combination of power and ownership, in that, before long, all profit-making concerns in the country would be owned by one single organisation", Sandberg 1997, p. 17. On Olof Palme's position on the union funds, see Arvidsson 2006, p. 198- 219, Östberg 2009, p. 247 – 59 and Berggren 2010 p. 529- 533.

SOCIALIST SCANDALS – PART I

1. Fall 1972. Croatian terrorists hijacked a plane at Malmö airport, asking money and for the release of Yugoslavian terrorists who had killed an ambassador and occupied a consulate in Sweden. Minister of Justice Lennart Geijer could not prevail against the terrorists and gave in to their demands.

2. Spring 1973. The labour unions own faltering construction company BPA was rescued unconstitutionally by Olof Palme through the award of a foreign aid project for Algeria, a corruption pattern that would unfold later[99].

3. Summer 1973. A bank robbery in central Stockholm led to robbers holding hostages for five days. Sympathy developed between robbers and hostages leading to the expression "Stockholm syndrome". Olof Palme emerged as soft on crime, granting the robbers for a 45 minute conversation which was taped by the police. However 20 minutes of the dialog. remain conveniently lost. Palme used the tense occasion, once tear gas had disarmed the robbers, to speak as a politician rather than a statesman and thereby exploiting the crisis for an electoral advantage.

4. Spring 1975. The West German embassy was occupied by an extreme left wing terrorist group, the Baader Meinhof gang, leaving four people dead and some severely injured terrorists. The injured were immediately sent to West Germany in spite of doctors' recommendations and without negotiations with German officials. The minister in charge, Anna-Greta Leijon was one year later hunted down by the same terrorists, who wanted to take revenge by kidnapping her; the plot failed due to clumsy planning by the terrorists. Swedish left wing activist Pia Laskar was sentenced for planning the kidnapping of the minister, but was later nonetheless brought into leftwing, social dem-

---

[99] Arvidsson 2006, p. 118-19. For the corrupt dealings by Olof Palme with Swedish weapons to Rajiv Gandhi in India 1986, see p.131-32.

ocratic and union circles as leftist icon on queer and leftist activism[100].

5. October 1975. A spy working for the social democratic party was revealed at Gothenburg municipal hospital where he surveilled left wing activists. Two leading social democrats, police officer Hans Holmér and journalist Ebbe Carlsson, were involved but not charged. They were however charged later in 1980s for other illegal actions doing police work without legal authority.

6. October 1975. Pentti Ketola, a Finnish social democrat, was stopped at the Stockholm airport with cash coming from Germany to help finance a Finnish union campaign against communists[101].

7. January 1976. Hans Eriksson, leader of Transport workers' union, vacationed in fascist Spain at the employers' expense, in spite of the union Blockade of Spanish general Franco's dictatorship. Eriksson would later resign due to mismanagement of union funds.

8. January 1976. Ingmar Bergman, world famous film maker, was questioned by tax authorities in front of actors during a rehearsal at National Theatre Dramaten, after which he left Sweden for Germany for six years.

9. March 1976. Astrid Lindgren, the world famous children's author, paid a double tax amounting to a total of 102 % of income, and wrote a satire in Sweden's largest tabloid, *Expressen,* about the greedy witch Pomperipossa in the land of money.

10. May 1976. Brothels with politicians, royals, judges, military officers and heads of government agencies as customers were linked to the social

---

[100]   Pia Laskar was also charged with bank robbery and burning down a Spanish travel agency. Other left wing and social democrats sympathetic to German terrorism might have been involved. Persson 2012 tells a fiction that probably is true.

[101]   The money to Finland may be traced back to CIA through Germany and Sweden, see Arvidsson 2006, p. 111.

democratic party. Polish prostitutes associated with the communist country's Stockholm embassy courted military officers and ministers. Underage girls were involved. Police investigation was hampered by leading socialist leaning police officers and government officials. Documents are still in 2013 partly restricted from release as classified.

11. August 1976. A female clerk at parliament who took notes for ministers including Palme was cohabiting with a major drug dealer, who was given pardon by Minister of Justice Lennart Geijer. The woman was given a new job in the labour movement[102].

12. November 1977. Lennart Geijer, by then a former social democrat minister of justice, was named in the press, among other politicians including Olof Palme, for visiting prostitutes. Palme lied about Geijer and the whole affair in parliament and to media.

By far the most important affair was probably the earlier mentioned 1973 affair about the social democratic party supported secret service bureau, IB that worked outside of all legal restrictions. But the public criticism from children's fiction writer Astrid Lindgren, who just as Ingmar Bergman declared herself a social democrat, led voters to swing against Olof Palme. With a gain of eleven parliament members, the government shifted to the right of center[103]. The agrarian Centerpartiet became the largest party in cabinet with a new prime minister, farmer- turned-politician Torbjörn Fälldin. His honest rural personality won debates against the more witty but arrogant Olof Palme. The pipe-smoking Fälldin vs. Palme with cigarettes, countryside vs. urbanity.

CENTER- RIGHT GOVERNMENT VICTORY 1976

The three party coalition of the liberal Folkpartiet, agrarian Centerpartiet and conservative Moderaterna was unprepared for the transfer of power.

---

[102]   The affair "Kanslihusflickan", see Rauscher and Mattson 2004, p.50-59.

[103]   By 1976 the parliament had 349 MPs to avoid the embarrassing stalemate of 175 – 175 of 1973 election.

The Palme government had hidden figures of the failing economy. Business leaders had tried in vain to inform the minister about the crisis but
were told to come back after the elections. The economy was heading for
disaster[104]. Sweden was the fourth richest country in the world in 1970,
a never reached position before or later, but from then the economy was
going down fast. Average annual growth in 1960s was 4.5 %, but only
1.9 % in 1970s. This humiliating downfall of the Swedish welfare state
was felt by citizens with oil crises 1971-1973 and a deep recession leading to stagflation. This new phenomena combined stagnated growth and
high inflation for which no Keynesian cure could help. Private citizens
with big loans benefited as they were allowed to make tax deductions for
interest rates of the loans that withered away during high inflation, 7 %
1970 and 13.8 % in 1980. Middle class families with loans on houses and
condominiums were at advantage, workers in rented housing not.

During the dire decade more money for public spending was needed and
the only way was to raise taxes by all means. The tax share of GDP had
risen to 40 % 1970 and would rise to 53 % by 1990. Payroll tax was 12 %
1970, 36 % 1979 and by 1990, the astonishing level of 39 %. Value Add-
ed Tax (VAT) had risen from 3 % 1960 to 25 % by 1970s. Inflation was
60% between 1970-1976. Four devaluations in 1976-1981 by center-right
governments helped some, but Swedish exports faced competition from
other less expensive nations both in Europe and Asia. Due to the agreed
fair wage policy in union–employer relations, higher oil prices could not
be compensated with lower wages for the workers. Together with rising
payroll tax, labour costs rose 40% in just two years, from 1974 to 1976
during socialist regime. Later analysis by economist Assar Lindbeck revealed that the budget processes were more lax in Swedish 1970s-1980s
than in other countries.[105]

Important changes were made in labour legislation in mid 1970s that
went against the current trends of deindustrialization. Since staff in industry was easier to replace by other unskilled or quickly skilled workers,

---

[104]   Garme 2011 and Ahlmark 2011, p.197- 230.

[105]   Lindbeck 1997, p. 1280

labour laws were created that protected workers with seniority when cutbacks had to be made. This system could be defended when most workers did similar routine jobs. But with higher levels of training needed for
workers and jobs being lost in crises and market competition, defending old, untrained workers unfamiliar with high technology became less
relevant. Industry lost jobs to the service and professional sectors too.
Sweden enacted labour laws that did not keep the skilled and educated in
the workforce, if they had been later hired than the less skilled. In an age
of transformation to lean production, these protectionist laws did much
harm, as did higher taxes on people than on machinery. Valuable brain
power in the heads of trained workers and educated professionals can
walk out any day, draining business of efficiency, innovation and talent,
but the Swedish taxes and labour legislation were still founded on a vision
of routine industrial jobs in which individual efforts and minds weighed
little against collective forces.

The center-right government did not handle of economic crises well, as
it supported failing unproductive industries (textiles, shipyards, mines)
and went through its own internal coalition quarrels. Four short-lived
cabinets ruled 1976 – 1982 with center party leader Fälldin heading three
and liberal leader Ola Ullsten one. Nuclear power and taxation disagree-
ments split the coalition, even though voters re-elected them in 1979
with only one parliament member in favour. A referendum on nuclear
power with three alternatives was held in 1980 to solve governing center-
right coalition troubles (two pro-nuclear power parties and one against
in the coalition):

> **Alternative 1.**   The moderate party was pro- nuclear.
> **Alternative 2.**   The Liberal party and social democrats were
>   pro-nuclear but for   dismantling later.
> **Alternative 3**   The Center party and communists were for im-
>   mediate dismantling of the 12 Swedish nuclear
>   power stations.

Alternatives 1 and 2 won together and nuclear power has since then produced a fourth of Swedish power supply. A formal ban of research on

nuclear power at Swedish universities excluded all subsequent serious decisions.

Swedish welfare state policies did not change much during the non-socialist years. In fact, two of the ruling coalition parties made peace with Olof Palme on taxation reforms in 1981. Mutual interests in finding solutions in the political center still worked as it had previously, isolating left and right wings. Moderate party leader Gösta Bohman left the center-right government 1981, angry for having been deserted by his coalition partners, the liberals and center. On the controversial wage earners funds, the ruling majority was weak and did not even dare to give new rules to the parliamentary committee looking into the various fund proposals. Instead directions from socialist Olof Palme continued to guide the committee after Palme himself had left office. Total public sector employment continued to rise, reaching its peak in 1982, the last year of non- socialist government. Political scientist Emil Uddhammar writes:

> "The hitherto predominant view of Swedish politics has unduly exaggerated both the role of the Social Democrats, as the presumed sole primus motor behind the growth of the big state, and also the extent of the non-socialist parties' opposition against state expansion/ . . . /In order to find real opposition against state expansion during this period [20th century], one would have to search among farmers and people without university background"[106].

TWO HARD MEN 1980
Two men stand out in the late 1970s and 1980s Sweden as defenders of the market economy and individual freedom, ASEA industrialist and employers' confederation leader Curt Nicolin and moderate party leader Gösta Bohman. Parrying calls from social democrats and other welfare state advocates in the non-socialist camp, they pitted their knowledge, wealth and strategy from business life to campaign against wage earners

---

[106]   Uddhammar 1993, p. 483-84.

funds and in favor or free enterprise. The non-social democratic government had continued after 1976 with the same anti-market policies, thereby ruining companies by keeping them afloat with state subsidies when
they did not produce enough. Nicolin argued against his weaker business
colleagues who could not see clearly what was going on. Subsidies to
industries are like drugs Nicolin said, making employers feel good at first
but get them hooked and wanting more. By getting subsidies through negotiations with government, companies pay less attention to innovation
and keeping market shares[107]. Nicolin was firm in his opposition to wage
earners funds, unlike some other business leaders who tampered with
their own corporate/employees/share fund experiments while preparing
for the worst, nationalization of private property. He stated that employers should not have any alternative concerning funds. To plan for wage
earners funds or any kind of anti-business funds would be a step in the
wrong direction and lead to failure. Pehr Gyllenhammar, who was CEO
of car manufacturer Volvo and an old friend of Olof Palme's, aspiring
for liberal party leadership, disliked the new aggressive tone against the
social democrats and unions. But Palme had started a fight from which
business leaders could not back away, Curt Nicolin thought.

Many business leaders were used to calm negotiations, corporatism and
intimate talks with union leaders and government ministers in retreats at
the state run Harpsund mansion or royal Haga castle outside Stockholm.
With Nicolin the Swedish consensus on industrial relations changed, as
he broke with tacit understandings and actual fear among many Swedish industrialists in relation to the powerful social democratic leadership.
Nicolin understood the need to get support from small and middle size
business men, since few large Swedish multinational companies wanted to
fight the establishment at home. It was better just to shift the head office
to abroad, the leaders of IKEA, Ericsson and Tetrapak said openly. Small
entrepreneurs were therefore much better spokesmen against ruling socializing tendencies, as they were hard working people with huge tax and bureaucratic burdens stemming from Palme and his supporters. Fortunately
Nicolin was not only former CEO of multinational ASEA (later ASEA

---

[107]   Larsson 2011, p. 38.

Brown Boweri, ABB) but, he also owned some small business in small towns. He knew how to talk to businessmen of all sorts and used his links when the media needed reliable spokesmen for small business.

Curt Nicolin was convinced that the question of wage earners funds was the most challenging issue for his generation of entrepreneurs and businessmen. If they did not oppose the initiative, the next generation would find themselves being perhaps managers of their former companies, but no longer owners. The wage earners funds were called small steps of tyranny by liberal party leader Bengt Westerberg, and Nicolin could not have agreed more. Reformism was in this sense all the more dangerous, as there were no obvious communist coups as had happened in Eastern Europe[108]. Palme won the 1982 election by steering attention away from the funds, and faced little opposition from the center- right coalition by then in shambles.

In 1983, two weeks after the traditional Midsummer celebrations in June when all Swedes went on vacation, Palme had a wage earners fund program ready to take to parliament, one financed by higher payroll taxes and taxes on corporate profits. From the hard working Småland County, under the leadership of local businessman Gunnar Randholm, came a roar that was heard all the way to Stockholm. Randholm had protested locally earlier but was called by industry leaders to stage a national manifestation, taking protests to the streets just like the left did when protesting. On 4 October 1983 employers' leader Curt Nicolin was king with over 75 000 subjects marching the Stockholm streets shouting with

---

[108]   From 1970 to 1976 a total number of 281 laws were created that made business life problematic, as well as for individual lives. See Arvidsson 2006, p. 310. Sugar cubes could be sold in kiosks but not granulated sugar. Panty hoses but not socks for men, see Svanborg-Sjövall 2011, p. 22-23. Socialists and the center party joined the unions in defending the rules. Telephones were not to be bought from any other supplier than the governmental telecommunications authority until 1980s. In 2012 there are more than 11 000 business laws, orders and rules to follow which costs $13 billion to process for employers and managers. To get a permit from local environmental boards for business may take four years, see Fölster 2012c.

flags. The employers' confederation and trade organizations, business-men and supporters united in demonstrating against wage earners funds in the largest street manifestation ever in Sweden. Over 500,000 signatures were collected and handed over to Olof Palme, who refused to accept them. Instead, the center-right leaders got media attention when they gladly welcomed the signatures. But they had played a dangerous game in not acting against the funds themselves, with the exception of Bohman. The same goes for the employers that rather cooperated with socialization proponents, apart from Nicolin. Without these two hard men, Sweden would have socialized its industry in the 1980s, a few years before the Soviet Bloc disintegrated. Courage and foresight saved Sweden, though few today praise or understand their important role or how close Sweden was to a real existing socialism. Palme had a majority behind him in December 1983 for approval of a vague fund proposal that was never implemented.

The second hard man, moderate party chairman Gösta Bohman, was as important as Curt Nicolin. He was a self-made entrepreneur who with wit and tough rhetoric fought against the ideologies behind high taxation, conformism and expanding welfare services. As finance minister in the first non- social democratic cabinet in more than two generations, he knew the bad state of Swedish economy. Bohman had sought support against the wage earners funds from the employers' confederation before the 1976 elections but had been refused[109]. Not until Curt Nicolin headed the employers could these two tough men make a united front against socialist dreams of taking over Swedish private property. Bohman launched two ideological terms that defined his liberal-conservative legacy; new insecurity and new individualism. He stated that a new insecurity has risen due to too much power being concentrated in the hands of government. Individualism was a reaction to this disempowerment. Freedom was superior to equality he claimed, contrary to social democrats like social minister Alva Myrdal, who had viewed freedom as a means to collective ends, to equality, but not as a goal in itself. She had also questioned in a report the rights of parents to keep their children outside government

---

[109]   Ehrencrona 1991, p. 293.

day care centers. The heads of the Labour Market Directorate called housewives "enemies of society" who should not "count on the privilege to stay home"[110]. Bohman wanted families to be free to choose their own ways to care for their children. His desire that this right become a constitutional civil right went against the development of Swedish pre-schools and child care centers, which had begun in the 1970s. Today such a right is again being viewed as backwards and anti-feminist by the media and government but not by Swedish families according to polls[111]. Bohman did not care.

Anti- socialist Bohman and Nicolin were not afraid of the neo-totalitarian social democratic propaganda, though they changed their strategy without backing down. Moderate party ideology sounded better than conservative, but moderate party leader Bohman took the change further and changed the party ideology from conservatism to liberal-conservatism. He wanted his traditionally conservative party to become more liberal and individualistic. The new individualism he wanted was in the tradition of classic liberalism, confusing media and voters at first. Bohman made the traditional liberal party Folkpartiet so angry that it needed to add Liberalerna to its name later, to distinguish it from the rising neo-liberalism of 1980s and from Bohman and the former Right party in particular. The need to distinguish liberals from moderates was important as any ideas viewed as right leaning or conservative were extremely touchy, a view that still exists in media, education and government due to decades of socialist loyalty and welfare state liberalism.

But Bohman meant that liberalism was shared by many parties, his own right leaning party among others. Sweden needed a liberal revolution and this liberalization is aligned with conservative traditions of slow changes. His conservatism dealt with how this liberal change would take place,

---

[110]   Edwardsson 2010, p. 318. Government child care centers should inform children about the Vietnam war and how to change capitalist views argued socialist minister Birgitta Dahl and union leader Gunnar Nilsson respectively in their proposals for new child care centers in 1974, see Arvidsson 2006, p. 289.

[111]   Lifvendahl 2000, p. 28- 29.

not the content. Bohman disliked the military, royalty and churches as much as anyone else in Sweden. Conservatism was an attitude of caution and responsibility for others and oneself as individuals, not only as taxpayers. Swedish liberal conservatism has its logic[112]. Bohman differed from traditional enlightment liberalism in his distance from its optimism and belief in reason and science. The future is much more undecided than we think so plans must be made carefully.

Bohman had read Hayek's *Road to serfdom* with great interest. Hayek had received the Swedish Nobel Memorial Prize in Economic Sciences in 1974. Milton Friedman, of a similar school of economics, had received the prize two years later under heavy police protection during his Stockholm visit, as left wing protesters tried and succeeded in disrupting the ceremony. But it was not until Margret Thatcher and Ronald Reagan were elected that a neo liberal ideology made an impact. Under the wings of Gösta Bohman rose younger, liberal minded but moderate politicians, such as his son-in-law Carl Bildt. Bohman's fight for freedom was rewarded in the 1979 election, when his moderate party became the biggest of the three center-right parties, overtaking the more rural center party. Since then the moderates have remained the largest of the center–right parties.

Gösta Bohman was the first party leader for the moderates, the former Right party (Högerpartiet), as it changed name and leader 1971. To be politically right leaning, or just plain a political middle class during Swedish 1970s, was like being a communist under McCarthy in the 1950s US. Children's television, a state monopoly, showed either sad Czech fuzzy cartoons or left wing clowns singing about environmental threats, capitalist profits or hailing liberation struggles in poor countries. Not even the victory in 1974 Eurovision song contest by super pop group ABBA cheered up the left wing media and establishment. Instead Sweden boycotted the contest in 1976 as left wing groups threatened to sabotage

---

[112]   "Conservatism wants to keep what has worked earlier. Liberalism has shown itself to work well. Thus it is conservative to be liberal" stated Stig-Björn Ljunggren 1992, p. 331. Ljunggren's dissertation *Folkhemskapitalismen* on the history of the Swedish right proves that even the right was behind the welfare state expansion.

the event for being too commercial[113]. ABBA was especially hated as they had become rich, which was an even worse sin than being right of center politically. One ABBA member, Anni-Frid Lyngstad, even dared to speak for the employers' causes while earning her riches, for which she became especially hated by the leftist dominated state media and leading press.

Unquestionable national heroes of that era included tennis player Björn Borg and alpine skier Ingmar Stenmark. Sport was still somewhat beyond politics but not culture. Parliament had set new goals for cultural affairs by 1974, directing that culture should contribute to a better social environment and quality and opposing the negative effects of commercialism on culture. The social environment meant government, not culture by civil society organizations or creativity from independent artists. Culture, which had been the mental backbone of middle class life and a glimpse of creativity and dignity for the rising working class authors from 1930 such as the great Ivar - Lo Johansson, Harry and Moa Martinsson and Eyvind Johnsson, had become means to social ends, not simply valued as art. Similar to the degrading of independent culture and the eradication of small business was the transformation of education and schooling. Deemed conservative, bourgeois and authoritarian, primary and secondary education was "reformed," to ensure that the young were schooled to be servile subjects, as the next digression on education will show.

SCHOOLING SOCIALISTS

Social democratic policy had earlier viewed educational reforms as a means to open the gates to higher learning for all. To raise the best and brightest from the working class by giving them entry to the former closed schools for middle and upper classes was the goal. But after 1945, according to socialist education planners, schools themselves needed to change. The learning of the higher social classes had to be brought down to conform to new less knowledgeable students, the socialists thought, thereby downgrading their own class. Criticism was first directed towards what was viewed as bourgeois and traditional values and knowledge. The new society needed

---

[113]   http://sv.wikipedia.org/wiki/Melodifestivalen_1976

new knowledge that was relevant to society, not to simple perpetuate the old education system. Earlier knowledge had been thought to be objective and eternal, but now this attitude had to make way for a more pragmatic, relative and social view of knowledge. Later socialists would also abandon the very idea of knowledge itself, as postmodern critique would become influential in the dominant left leaning educational policy.

Alva Myrdal, who was eager to make her mark in education as well as in family planning, supported both modern progressive pedagogical methods and time management methodologies from industry to ensure students' efficiency. American progressive educator John Dewey inspired the Swedish system throughout the 20th century. Schooling as a social enterprise with every public institution and student participating together in social relations fitted well with the folkhem welfare state vision based on scientific knowledge used for utility, everyday life and democracy[114]. Education and knowledge for its own sake were viewed as useless, boring and bourgeois.

Socialists had early plans to reform a school system which was both hierarchical and complicated. In 1948 a model for grade progression was proposed by a parliamentary school commission: In grades 1-6 all pupils would be together, in grades 7-8 some differentiation by ability, and by grade 9 separate classes. A trial period of ten years with various patterns followed, but by 1957 the rules had changed. Now, a mere 6 years together in same class was viewed as unequal and unfair. Instead 8 years together, plus a final differentiated year was proposed and tested. Educationists Torsten Husén and Kjell Härnqvist, who led school experiments with differentiated streams for various students according to talents and attitudes, wrongly assessed the outcome of the experiment, in favour of non-differentiation, a handy result for the social democrats[115]. The misin-

---

[114]   Larsson 2011, p. 65, 67. Dewey's educational thinking and methodology was translated already by 1912 into Swedish.

[115]   Hadenius 1990, p. 170-171. Karl- Georg Ahlström, professor in Uppsala university and opponent of a dissertation in 1962 that tried to prove what any layman with minimal statistical sense could see was not right use of data, did a remarkable job

terpretation stated that keeping classes together up to 8-9 grades was not detrimental to high achieving students. But the facts were more nuanced. Differentiated streams were better for high achievers, while non-differentiated streams were not better for low achievers. Summing up the effects, a non-differentiated class would result in lower expectations for actual learning, but higher expectations for social bonding. This suited the socialist dream of schooling well.

The blunder of misinterpreting the results of the experiment with differentiated and non-differentiated streams was not revealed in time to affect parliament decisions in 1962. Swedish primary education changed into a system with grades 1 to 8 + 1, where the last year was optional for more academic or vocational streams. Social democratic education leaders Stellan Arvidsson and Alva Myrdal were educational radicals and viewed traditional schools as hostile and reactionary. Differentiation according to achievements, attitudes and talents would be only possible within the main class, they argued, thus having one teacher for all but making all students individually appreciated as John Dewey had wanted. The theory went that students who were tired of books and learning would become interested by being in the same class as more motivated students, and those who lagged behind were merely lacking intellectual stimulus. Thus, providing more bookish knowledge to those who rejected it was the answer. They could not explain in detail how teachers would teach whole classes at various levels and neither Arvidsson's party comrades nor the parliamentary allies in the agrarian party were persuaded. Nonetheless, Arvidsson argued for an even more non-differentiated system, 9 + 0, meaning that the last differentiated year would be omitted too. In 1962 this was not possible but Olof Palme would later succeed.

1962 represents the start of the Swedish primary school (grundskola),

---

but in vain. Internationally reclaimed professor Torsten Husén later regretted the mistakes. His colleague Urban Dahlöf had concluded by 1967 that the results from experiments with 9 year primary school differentiated and undifferentiated was written in sand, i.e. inconclusive. Same conclusions are drawn today by psychologist Laurence Steinberg in *Adolescence* (2011, New York: McGraw-Hill), p.192- 195.

which has been hailed internationally. The achievement level at grade 8 was lowered to at best what had formerly been expected in grade 7, meaning that at least one year was lost for all. Further changes were a reduction of time devoted to theoretical subjects, reducing vocational subjects, introducing a norm-referenced system relative to student population, and giving more time to crafts and sports. The goal for primary education as stated in the 1962 curriculum was to support the varied developmental levels of the pupils and thus bring them knowledge and train their skills. Note here that the order of the notions; development comes first, knowledge and skills second and as an effect from pupils' development. This order remained in all subsequent curriculum reforms, even today. Knowledge is not the overall general aim for schools, but development in social context.

Fear of meritocracy led to a streamlined curriculum so that more advanced students would not be supported in their quest for higher education, but given less time for academic subjects than before and left on their own. All students were being promoted to the next grade despite their record of achievements, and grade retention became an exception. British sociologist Michael Young who 1960 wrote *The Rise of the Meritocracy* was translated into Swedish same year and made an impact on Swedish school reformers. What would happen to equality if the brighter students were to enter higher education irrespective of their social backgrounds and make up a new aristocracy of intelligence? Sports were viewed as an exception in which a good runner might succeed, but same student would be held back in other subjects, especially mathematics and science. This is still the case in Swedish schools. Excellence of bodies is permitted, brains not.

Olof Palme was named minister of education 1967. He initiated two reforms. The first was to abolish the last differentiated year, 9th grade and make all students attend all 9 years together. Separate classes according to ability and aspiration were by then only allowed in mathematics and English, but this too would be abolished later. His second reform was to introduce a special period of free electives from any field, including leisure studies.[116]. These electives were not, repeat, NOT, to be used for remedial studies, teaching or homework. The process towards conformism accelerated, when the former 9th year with its vocational and academic streams was abolished and replaced with more general subjects, thus making primary education geared towards a middling level at which all students were supposed to be satisfied. Vocationally and academically motivated students got less time for their respective interests. What is astonishing is that the vocationally interested students, often from working class backgrounds, got less time for vocational subjects in the new system. Their time was filled with free electives, consumer studies, crafts, sports etc. As if the socialist process of degrading education could not go fast enough, teachers, with Stellan Arvidsson, the leading social democratic school reformer at the fore, were sent to the communist dictatorship of East Germany to be inspired.[117].

Olof Palme stated in late 1960s in an address to school children that one does not go to school to achieve anything personally, but to learn how to function as a member of a group. His successor as education minister and later also Prime minister, Ingvar Carlsson, maintained similar views on the purpose of schooling as being the production of well adjusted, good members of society. Schools would teach people to respect consensus, and not to sabotage it through dissenting views. Deputy education minister Sven Moberg expanded on the topic saying that the purpose of education

---

[116] Fritt valt arbete, also called Palmes strimma, see Hadenius 1990, p.218. The idea of a mandatory elective choice of six hours/ week originated from Palme himself. I recall having photography and music but others were repairing their mopeds (guys) or baking cakes (girls). Homework strictly forbidden. Palme said in parliament that the electives were directed towards making schools more student friendly, enhance communal feelings and fun for less motivated and rebellious students.

[117] Swedish parliamentary education committees, School Agency, deans of teacher training, ministers etc. went to communist East Germany to find inspiration from 1960s, see Skolvärlden 10 Dec, 2010. Leading social democratic school organizer and dean of Stockholm School of Education (Lärarhögskolan i Stockholm), Stellan Arvidsson, headed the Swedish-East German Friendship Association, at the time.

"is to turn out the correct kind of person for the new society. The new school rejects individuality and teaches children to collaborate with others /.../ we want to produce individuals who are integrated in society "[118].

In comparison to the start in 1962 of primary schooling in Sweden, Palme reformed in the system 1968 to dedicate less time to preparatory studies for secondary education. The results were 10 hours per week less time for academic studies in comparison with the pre 1962 school system. Languages including Swedish and science were levelled down. All optional subjects, not only foreign languages but also art, home economics and technology would count when applying to secondary schools. Thus the threat of the rise of any meritocracy was greatly reduced. Palme said to parliament that education had four aims;

1. a profitable investment
2. self-realization
3. independence of views and values
4. higher equality in society

In none of these aims for education was bringing knowledge to learners mentioned[119]. Two decades earlier the minister of education, also a social democrat, had stated that knowledge of foreign languages; mathematics and practical skills were the aims of Swedish primary education. In the 1960s socialization had become all, and knowledge acquisition forgotten. The words education and teaching would later be replaced with school work for all, teachers and students.

But all did not work out as planned; in the early 1970s students rebelled

---

[118]   In Huntford 1971, p. 204, 210- 211.

[119]   Hadenius 1990, p. 227. This emphasis on social values rather than knowledge was true for all welfare nations in Northern Europe and openly defended as being natural. "In the *golden age* [the most expansive and extreme period, my italics] of Nordic social democracy, social virtues such as equal opportunity, cooperation, adaptation and solidarity were considered to be the main goals of compulsory schooling", Oftedal Tellhaug et al 2006, p. 253.

and disrupted classes. From accommodating around 2-3 % of the student population, special education surged to an unimaginable 40 % of students found in need of special treatment. Only a few of these students had physical handicaps. The majority had disciplinary problems. Special clinics for disruptive and unmotivated students were established, though they could seldom cope with all the problems. For welfare state propagandists it was an ideological failure to have disruptive students taken from their class. The phenomenon of rebellious and less motivated students was investigated by a parliamentary committee in 1976, resulting in that pointed in the wrong direction, i.e. towards special education in separate groups from which at least some of these students could benefit. As had been done before in the Swedish welfare state, politics and ideological motives triumphed over empirical evidence and the committee recommended reintegration of students with special needs and showing disruptive behaviour back into the regular classroom[120].

Another remedy was to keep all students in school for longer duration and to tolerate some level of disruption. To keep students in schools for longer hours, free but mandatory classes were organized in arts, crafts, cooperation with organizations outside schools, sports etc. One extra hour per day with mandatory yet free activities for all students whether they wanted or needed such care, and no matter what their parents thought. All parties agreed with this reduction of family responsibility except the moderates. Free yet mandatory activities would come back later by late 1990s, supported by socialist minister Wärnersson in the non-subject life skills (livskunskap). An optional subject with no curriculum, no marks and no syllabus yet mandatory. Socialist schooling, schooling socialists.

In spite of evidence that few of the least interested students could benefit from more studies, more study-oriented activities were proposed. A new curriculum, LGr80, was assigned as a remedy for the problem of unruly students. The solution now under center-right government, was to bring subjects together in thematic studies, student oriented ac-

---

[120]   Ibid., p. 252- 253.

tivities emanating from student questioning, project methodology and homegrown versions of progressive education. Along with broadening subject studies and lowering entry to secondary studies by not requiring advanced studies in English and mathematics, report cards were only given from grade 8. From grade 1 to grade 7, parents and students were informed about school progress by talks each semester with class teacher in charge. Neither documents nor grades were given to parents about the progression of their children for seven years. This non grading school system continued until 2011[121].

Giving report cards each year had been a matter of great discussion in the 1970s in Swedish education policy debates. The national School Agency, social democrats, communists and most liberals wanted to abolish all marks and report cards, believing that grades did not enhance real knowledge but only fictional knowledge relating to tests and appropriate behaviour. Ingvar Carlsson claimed in a parliamentary report that "the role of report cards so far as the principal ground for selection to higher education and work entails that school work is at risk of being directed towards giving knowledge and skills "[122]. The overall social aim for schools could be dimmed by too much emphasis on marks and academic progress Carlsson explained. The risk of learning something was still threatening.

Since industry production relies on science and technology, these subjects were ruled as reactionary, implicit capitalistic and too hard to study for the new soft schooling of young socialists. These tough subjects lead to exploitation of workers and mindless jobs in dirty industrial working conditions in ugly factories that produced industrial waste. Science was bad, so-

---

[121]   Not until 2006 did the sad state of Swedish education start to change in a better direction, as international comparisons showed to the Swedes their expensive, inefficient and violent schools. Vouchers were introduced in 1992 and have helped aspiring students to leave bad schools for better, but more must be done as primary schooling started on shaky foundations in 1960s. See McKinsey 2010 and Sahlgren 2010.

[122]   In Ohrlander 2009, p. 95.

cial science good. Humanities forgotten. Industries and technology were
at fault for decades for all ills of society, so students knew what subjects
not to choose. Since the radical 1970s, not enough students have chosen
math or science to guarantee an adequate supply of scientists, engineers,
doctors and technicians. The few students that start higher education in
these areas often need remedial classes. Social sciences are almost ten times
more popular than the hard sciences. Swedish students do not prepare for
careers that are in demand; they start later and finish higher studies later
than students in other countries[123]. There a dearth not only of engineers
and technicians in Sweden. Vocational careers such as welding, plumbing
and other traditionally male manual labouring jobs, cannot find enough
young apprentices. Skilled workers from Poland and the Baltic states find
jobs in Sweden, but there are not enough of them. These working class
jobs were also looked down upon by the progressive post-war school policy makers and socialist education reformers who dismantled trainee programs, theorized about vocational studies and resisted vocational careers
by not valuing manual work. Socialists have not only shown disregard for
skilled work, but also for unskilled work (see statements from party chairmen Sahlin and Juholt in Socialist scandals II below).

The focus in education policies since the post-war period has been to
replace studies of real subjects with activities in new, vague subjects or
plain leisure. It should come as no surprise then that few students choose
difficult subjects, and that they do not study enough.

LEFTIST DOMINATION

It is hard to understand how during the 1970s so few people in the entire
nation protested against the Swedish media with its host of extreme programs and events; increasing dominance by left wing journalists, TV and
film producers, psycho babbling theatre performances and self-indulgent
female authors spreading tales of their repressive family life and their

---

[123]   Fölster et al. 2011, p. 21. Only strong immigration of well-educated people will make
up this need, but Sweden welcomes instead immigrants with no education at all
which makes the situation worse.

need to do household chores now when they, the radicals, had children themselves. What emerged as extreme in this decade would become normal later. In 2012, the early art experiments and radical politics of the 1970s are viewed with nostalgia by the old radicals and their younger successors.

A propaganda strategy combined with laid back socialist-leaning teachers at schools, a teenage sexual revolution at home and sex education in government policy made sex life exciting but also dangerously balanced on the edge of extremes even in Sweden. Swedish sin on film exploded and a government commission proposed lax legislation on incest, paedophilia and sex between adults in charge of youth[124]. State television could show yelling divorcing couples (director Bergman), copulating drug addicts (Jarl) and serious state news anchors telling about the terrible hardships people suffered living outside safe socialist Sweden. Working class people and the marginalized underclass were idealized by red middle class vanguards in media, government and education, who tried to dress down and use slang from outcasts and deliberately rude people. Junkies and criminals were romanticized as victims of cruel capitalism, bourgeois class repression and harsh families. Social democratic leaders could even

---

[124]   In 1976 a parliamentary committee (Sexualbrottsutredningen, SOU 1976:9) proposed lower penalties for rape equal to parking ticket, incest permitted, legal age for sex with older person to which one can be dependent to 14 (a male teacher could have sex with 14 year old girls), lower age for sexual harassment to 10 years (touching children age 10 sexually would be ok), lower penalties for rape if the victim was inviting to sex by dress and attitude. A pedophile group from Swedish Federation for Lesbian, Gay, Bisexual and Transgender Rights (RFSL) was represented and referred by the committee which took to their views and proposed lower penalties for pedophiles and lower age restrictions. The proposals did not reach parliament and were replaced 1977. The committee was directed by Lennart Geijer, socialist minister of justice, who had been to prostitutes and under aged girls since 1960s. Palme was warned in 1970 that Geijer could become a threat to national security with his sexual affairs but left it to be. Seven years later the sex affairs exploded in the largest daily, denounced by all ministers but the reality of some socialist ministers going to prostitutes was proved to be right, see Mattson and Rauscher 2004.

openly defend car theft as Leila Freivalds did before she became minister of justice and foreign affairs[125].

The middle class was the target, never the upper class which was easy to control and co-opt. Since the 1938 Saltsjöbaden agreement on industrial relations, the two top establishments in business and politics had worked well together and would continue discussions even on wage earners funds. The middle class was a completely different game and a real threat to socialist dominance. It was much harder with people with strong middle class traditions and professionals who could speak up against domination, wrongdoings and faults in government. The ability for independent thought was wrested by the socialists from the hearts of middle class values, culture and education, in much the same way as the Soviet Union and other communist countries had tried to do. High taxes were used to curb opposition. With money in savings, people could stand up against authority, decide their own parental leave, rise with self-confidence, ambition and merit and not be as servile as if they had nothing. Swedes have unusually small amounts of savings compared to other similar countries due to high taxation and low incentives for savings. In Italy where people earn less than Swedes do generally, savings are six times as high[126]. Yet Sweden has an unequal distribution of wealth caused by a tax system which does not let more people become wealthy by work, just a few through speculation and inheritance. During the 1970s taxation was extreme but some radicals wanted even higher taxes for the few rich and many middle class citizens.

---

[125]   Edwardsson 2010, p. 329. Freivalds was 28 years old and had a law degree at the time in 1970. But she told television reporters that she agreed with working class youth who needed cars on their way home at night. Public transport had stopped by then so others' private property had to be used. Lennart Geijer, the incumbent minister of justice, agreed saying that those who did not have cars could basically take from those who had, see Rauscher and Mattsson 2004, p. 34. Freivalds is the only minister that has left office in midterm due to scandals twice, once as minister of justice 2000 and as foreign minister 2006. In total four scandals.

[126]   Munkhammar 2011. See also Mitchell 2007 and Laakso and Lerulf 2011.

Waves of inbred theories from splinter Marxist groups and Swedish sin on films were replaced by mid 1970s with ecology and feminist morals but the message was the same: social structures define human beings. When socialism as a term was not useful anymore, equality was the term of the decade. Who could be against equality? Resentment and envy grew towards those fortunate in talent, wealth or personal integrity and style. The enemies of equality were always the same, repressive bourgeois traditions and capitalism. The two hard men representing the causes of all misery were obvious to all; the cruel old Right party that now called themselves moderates under the forceful Gösta Bohman and the greedy businessmen lead by stone faced Curt Nicolin. A simple political view for an infantile nation, but one which was broadcast every day from state television and radio to all citizens from toddlers to pensioners. Give us your tax money, your integrity and we will protect you from Bohman and Nicolin was the message in state media and in the privately owned press.

In television studios a balance was established with the opposing left on one corner bashing the social democrats for letting down the working class. In this way opposition between two leftist alternatives was all there was. Socialists seemed normal compared to the wild extra parliamentary leftist groups and the parliamentary communist party VPK (Vänster-partiet kommunisterna). The extreme was normal. Palme often called himself a democratic socialist, his successor Carlsson, rarely, and his successor Persson, never. Calling oneself socialist was safer than communist and more daring than being a social democrat, which was viewed as too square and rigid after 1970. Socialists could relate to freedom struggles in the third world while working in and for the expansion of the public sector at home. Being a socialist meant that one thought better of oneself and others, especially the downtrodden and other socialists. Having high hopes for mankind, socialists always knew better, at least until early 1990s when the Soviet Bloc fell and Sweden had to pick up the welfare bills. By then the leftist do-gooders had softened their tone a little but remained true to their optimistic ideals about the goodness of all mankind and a society free from domination and history. It was reality that had failed them.

PALME BACK 1982

Olof Palme was busy and content dealing with international relations during his absence from Swedish domestic politics 1976 - 1982, something he preferred. Secretly some Swedes, even his enemies, hoped he would become the second Swede after Dag Hammarskjöld to lead the UN as Secretary General. Instead he became the UN peace envoy 1980 for the Iran – Iraq war, lead the Commission on disarmament at the Socialist International which was received by the UN in 1982, and was a driving force in the Five Continent Peace Initiative for disarmament in 1984. He had good relations with the non- aligned movement and used his socialist European friends Willy Brandt and Bruno Kreisky to build relationships for peace and international development in his own smooth yet anti-imperialist way[127].

Back in power 1982 after his largest victory ever, 45.6 % votes and without the need of communist support to form a cabinet, Palme used the last four years of his life to move his party and Sweden reluctantly towards more openness. But there was a lot more to do to revive the staggering economy, and Palme acted quickly. In the morning before he declared his new cabinet to the king and parliament, he decided to devalue the Swedish currency by 16 %, something that surprised everyone but helped to boost exports. Palme promised it would be the last devaluation. Sweden had cheapened its currency six times in the years 1976–1982 and inter-

---

[127]   Palme can be viewed as pro Soviet Union in his calls for a nuclear weapon free zone in Scandinavian peace initiatives in 1980s, former KGB spy Oleg Gordievsky has argued in revealing the Soviet infiltration in these peace movements. See Arvidsson 2006, p. 396-397 and Östberg 2009, p. 324 for two opposing views on Palme's relationships to Soviet interests. See Ahlmark 2003, p. 220-221 for details of further Soviet submission by Prime Minister Carlsson and foreign minister Sten Andersson that both claimed as late as 1989 that the Baltic States were not occupied by Soviet. Same year, the Baltic States sung themselves without violence free from communist repression. Sweden watched and ministers Andersson and Carlsson never apologized. Civil society and religion helped to liberate the repressed countries against a brutal government. But these non-state communal features are little valued and understood in the land of extremes and state individualism.

national trade and finance were not impressed by this instability. More important was the 1985 decision to dismantle regulations for banks and citizens, to allow people to borrow as much money and in whatever currency they wanted. Sweden was among the last Western countries so have such capital controls and banking procedures. The 1985 deregulation has been called the most important financial decision since 1945 in Sweden; it brought dire consequences later. Palme seemed not to understand the seriousness of this decision, but neither did many others, including the governor of the National Bank of Sweden, Bengt Dennis and Finance Minister Kjell Olof Feldt. Olof Palme himself by this time had other things to ponder over, Russian submarines for instance.

In October 1981, a Soviet submarine had run aground in Sweden's south eastern coast. The submarine had nuclear weapons and the Russian captain seemed drunk. Immediately the event was called Whiskey on the Rocks, as the submarine code in NATO terminology actually was Whiskey 137 and the submarine was sitting steady on Swedish granite rock[128]. Soviet officials stated that the submarine had taken a wrong turn which no one believed. The government under the center-right party coalition protested, while keeping the military alert around the intruder and informing Olof Palme who had good relations with the Soviet Union. Next year under Palme's returned social democratic government, new submarines were supposedly detected outside Stockholm waters, but not caught. What followed was a series of exchanges between Palme and his ministers, a raucous exchange among a joint parliamentary commission on the submarines assaults, moderate foreign policy expert Carl Bildt, and Soviet ministers and diplomats. Everyone blamed and misunderstood each other, at times on purpose. Some leading ministers questioned whether the undetected submarines actually existed and if so, were they from the Soviet Union? Other ministers went to the media telling that the Soviet Union surely was to blame. A moderate member of the parliamentary commission, Carl Bildt, went to Washington telling them that Palme was soft on Russia. Not being a minister or spokesman for Swedish foreign policy that was not well liked by all

---

[128]   Brown 2010 coined actually the slogan, p. 86, for British *The Spectator* which became an instant media hit.

involved. Palme was of course furious at Bildt talking to Washington without authorization. Carl Bildt would later replace Palme as Sweden's voice in the international community[129]. But he was not alone in his thoughts about Swedish defiance against the Soviet Union.

Twelve naval officers did not believe the assurances from their commander in chief, Prime minister Palme and protested openly in the press stating that the prime minister of Sweden did had not stood up against the Soviet Union's intrusion into Swedish waters. The search for Russian submarines continued, with more comical than tragic episodes, after around 10,000 coastal Swedes later said they had seen submarines or traces thereof, which might have been from animals (minks and fish have been seriously suggested). Deeply ingrained in the Swedish historical psyche is fear of neighbouring Russia. The media got a good story with a foolish Russian captain spying from a submarine, but the suspicions of the Soviet Union actually trying to inspect and invade Swedish coastlines would not later be questioned.

PALME ASSASSINATION 1986

The remaining years under Olof Palme were tough. His son Joakim Palme was awarded tuition at Harvard University in exchange for a lecture, but Palme himself did not admit to the exchange nor bring attention to it in his private income tax return. Very petty but embarrassing for a socialist minister defending high taxes. Wage earners funds finally won approval in parliament but were watered down and not favoured by many union members and social democrats. Liberal ideas had started to influence the social democrats, although unions defended the old corporatist ways. A defence of government totalitarianism came from LO union economist Anna Hedborg who questioned whether people should have the right to work part time. Such a small contribution did not yield enough taxes and these people with some self-chosen leisure could use their time to bake their own bread, paint their windows and in that way avoid spending money on goods and services, she said but did not gain

---

[129]   Incidentally they had grown up together in the same upper class building on Östermalm, Stockholm and knew each other. See Berggren 2010, p. 12

any support. She had been quite influential though in creating the first proposals for wage earners funds.

New public management methods on public private partnership, client oriented welfare services and privately run pre-schools became heated topics. Socialist finance minister Feldt was interviewed in 1985 saying that privately run nursery schools and kindergartens were not much to fret about. A furious Palme telephoned afterwards and spoke to the media comparing private child care with Kentucky Fried Children, a slogan which was printed on children's t-shirts to scare off voters. The multinational home appliances corporation Electrolux had started a small pre-school, Pysslingen. The social democratic government responded in 1985 with a law that banned all child care organizations run by corporations for profit. But by then the genie was out of the bottle and campaigning for child care cooperatives run by parents or employees started to gain headway. Palme tried to make apply a social democratic twist to the liberalization in mid 1980s in order to humanize and democratize the public sector, but failed to pay interest, even though he stated many times after the loss 1976 that the party had become too bureaucratic[130].

After some more affairs leading to criticism in the parliamentary constitutional council or change of ministers not being up to marks - in their private finances (minister of justice Ove Rainer), being too open to media (foreign minister Lennart Bodström), playing down Swedish criticism of Soviet submarines in front of Soviet ministers (Sweden's ambassador to UN Anders Ferm), constitutionally dubious meddling in the government corporation NCB (industry minister Roine Carlsson) – Olof Palme was

---

[130]   Palme fell asleep repeatedly when listening to what his socialist friends Ingvar Carlsson and Bo Holmberg thought about liberalizing public sector. See Östberg 2009, p. 297-98. Some reformers were liberal minded socialist economists at finance ministry and prime ministers offices. In 1983 several books were published that openly criticized the Swedish welfare state foundations and its rationalistic tendencies, see Segerstedt 1983, Alapoeus 1983 and Burenstam –Linder 1983. The year before Hans-Magnus Enzensberger had visited Sweden and gave his depressing account on lack of personal freedom and socialist hegemony in Sweden, see Enzensberger 1987.

tired. By the time he met his assassin in 28 February 1986 he had made his political contribution. The assassination was never solved, as Swedish authorities were quite unused to political violence; it was the first assassination since 1792, when King Gustaf III was shot by a nobleman. To cover the criminal investigations would take several volumes at least, not to mention the conspiracy theories. Strangely, fiction is closer to the truth. A novel on the Palme murder by Swedish crime fiction writer and professor of criminology Leif GW Persson, *Between summer's longing and winter's end*, is best guess yet with a probable story idea of a planned murder by right wing individuals in the Swedish secret police and intelligence services [131].

Replacing Olof Palme was hard, but his close friend Ingvar Carlsson did what he could at 2 AM 1 March, 1986. A humble social democrat from a working class background, brought up single handily by his working mother, Carlsson appealed immediately to the shocked Swedes, from left to right. Carlsson was calm, kind and sincere. Others around Palme were not. Palme's allies and fellow social democrats, police commander Hans Holmér and former government information officer Ebbe Carlsson went immediately to hunt for the murderer in their own way. They had both engaged in extra-legal espionage against the communists and regulations at Gothenburg hospital a decade earlier, and had done damage control during the prostitution affair which had badly affected the failed election 1976.

Head police officer Holmér took charge of the police investigation personally without actually being designated as such, an action which would

---

131   Persson 2010. See also Jallai 2011. Former head of Swedish intelligence police SÄPO, Olle Frånstedt, has spoken openly of the murder coming from Swedish assassination plot by military or police. These right wing officers did not trust Palme who turned towards Soviet KBG, see Focus 2011. A close friend of Palme, an American professor who had worked for CIA at the same time as Palme had in 1950s, had shifted his loyalty to Soviet and KGB. Palme tried to stop Swedish intelligence exchange with CIA, an order that never was obeyed. Sweden continued cooperation with British M16 and CIA which both were suspicious of Olof Palme's radical socialist views and loyalties to the Soviet Bloc.

lead to later accusations of a breach in operative routines. He disregarded all leads that did not suit his hypothesis, which was that the Kurdish terrorist organization PKK was to blame. After one year the police investigation fell apart and he had to resign. But his friend Ebbe Carlsson continued his extra-legal investigations beyond all established police investigations through his contacts with minister of Justice Sten Wickbom. When the state attorneys refused to follow order from Ebbe Carlsson, Wickbom stepped in and sidestepped the police investigation. In other countries the law and the police would be organised into separate domains, but in Sweden there are no such distinctions. Amateur detective Ebbe Carlsson managed to import spy equipment in 1988 with the help of the new Minister of Justice Anna–Greta Leijon[132]. She had written on a Swedish government ministry letterhead that Ebbe Carlsson, at the time working for a private publishing house, represented the Swedish government in the Palme murder investigation.

But Ebbe Carlsson was a free-lance amateur detective with no official relation to the police or secret service, but with high connections in the social democratic establishment. The spying equipment import was detected and minister Leijon, head of police Nils Erik Åhmansson and head of secret police Sune Sandström all had to leave their posts. Knowingly or unknowingly they all had let Ebbe Carlsson run his own show, at the expense of and with tacit permission from powerful socialist connections in the government, without any official designation to investigate Palme's assassination. Prime Minister Ingvar Carlsson denied all information about Ebbe Carlsson's scandalous ways, but many believe he knew more than what little he said when called to constitutional court in parliament[133]. The separate secret service directed by socialist party au-

---

[132] Justice minister Sten Wickbom had to leave office due to a scandalous escape of Stig Bergling, a Swedish military intelligence officer that spied for Russia in 1970s. Bergling managed to escape in 1987 while on leave from the correctional institution and under lax surveillance from secret police.

[133] Ebbe Carlsson's homosexuality may have given him extra free reign with the social democratic establishment rumours say when questioning why so many powerful people stood up for him as he might have private power over ministers involved in

thorities which had been revealed in 1973 IB affair was still in operation.

By the late 1980s, the Swedish economy started to look like a casino with heavy private loans, an accelerating real estate market and with thriving but risk-taking entrepreneurs. Business was good but government could not quite keep up with the pace, and the speeding economy lead to bust. Wall Street crashed on the Black Monday in 19 October 1987 and currencies became a safe haven. Speculation against the Swedish currency started because the crown was correlated to a fixed currency mechanism. New reforms of liberalization and lower taxes lead to an overheated economy. But many people, politicians from left to right, even the National Bank of Sweden officials and finance investors, failed to see what was coming.

By 1990 the economy was boiling over. Prime Minister Carlsson tried to back up the failing financial system with government bans on strikes, increases of wages, rent and taxes, forced savings and no dividends to shareholders. Sweden was in bad shape and needed help. The Soviet Union was about to fall like its East European satellites close to Sweden had done. The possibility of applying for EU membership was mentioned. During the crisis, the Carlsson cabinet had to resign and parliament had to elect a new social democratic cabinet supported by the liberal party. EU membership was favoured by center- right parties but only by the upper levels of the social democratic establishment. Most Swedes, especially union activists, were sceptical of the EU. But the rules had changed and so did voters.

CENTER- RIGHT BACK 1991

The minority social democratic government under Carlsson was defeated in the 1991 election, as it had been marked by hard crises. Voters wanted more liberal policies than the social democrats could accept. A center-right government lead by moderate party leader Carl Bildt was elect-

---

sexual dealings. In parliament hearings these matters were mentioned but rejected as evidence was lacking.

ed. His intention was to make a clean cut with earlier social democratic policies, abolish wage earners funds and to make a decisive shift in the welfare state system. But his government inherited a financial crisis that had been building for the last 50 years. The deregulation of the Swedish currency and loans in 1985 had turned loose an enormous overheated financial crisis that foreign investors used for speculation, but which harmed savings and wages[134].

After months of defending the crown by raising National Bank of Sweden interest rates, eventually to an unimaginable 500 %, making two futile joint crisis packages with social democrat leader Ingvar Carlsson, moderate Prime Minister Carl Bildt had to let the Swedish crown float in relation to other currencies. At 14.28 pm, 19 November, 1992 the Swedish crown fell by 10 %. Banks went almost bankrupt and the government had to keep them afloat with public money and to socialize them like the center-right government had had to do in 1976 with failing industries and trades. The resolution of Sweden's financial crisis imposed a fiscal burden-that is, required a taxpayer-financed bailout — equal to 6 percent of GDP or around $70 billion in 1992. But a pattern of high taxation and humiliation was broken:

Sveriges skattetryck förr och nu

Skatteintäkter som andel av BNP

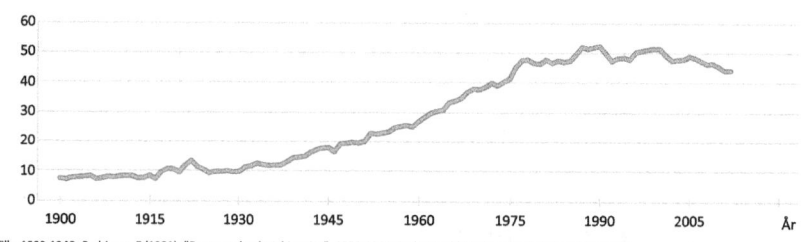

Källa: 1900-1949: Rodriguez, E (1981); "Den svenska skattehistorien". 1950-1964: Rodriguez (data skatteintäkter), SCB (data BNP). 1965-1992: OECD (data skatteintäkter), SCB (data BNP). 1993- : SCB.

The diagram shows tax revenues in proportion to GDP 1900- 2011 peaking in 1990 and a decisive shift in 1991 with the center-right government going towards 46 % in 2011 (UK 35 %, OECD average 34 % and US 25 %)[135].

---

134   Lars Jonung 2002

135   Statistics generated by www.ekonomifakta.se from Swedish and OECD sources.

The financial crisis in early 1990s pushed the Swedish economy into a depression in which unemployment rose to levels not seen since the 1930s, around 10 %. Fewer cars were sold in 1993 than in 1953. GDP showed negative growth. The public sector let go of employees, since taxes did not keep coming in as people in the private sector were laid off. The social democrats used the depressing times as an opportunity to demand more social responsibility and were re-elected 1994. The number of people working in the Swedish population had by 1993 shrunk to 71 % from earlier high rates by 1990 at 86 %. With mass education and unemployment programs the social democratic government had kept people occupied, but rarely with meaningful activities. Many adult education projects for the unemployed were organized to keep laid off people somewhat pleased. The management theorist C. Northcote Parkinson rephrased his law on always expanding organizations by adding a Swedish law, stating: "Policies designed to increase production increase employment; policies designed to increase employment do everything but".

When the economy started to grow again in the late 1990s, many of the laid off workers were not rehired. Production had become lean and in need of a computer skilled workforce. Some of the unemployed had during the long absence from work become unhealthier and less attractive to hire. In early 2000s, 12 % of the workforce were either on long term sick leave or had gotten early retirement. Some of them were satisfied with being on benefits, some (former) socialist economists found out, enraging the party leadership[136]. The re-elected social democratic government used these welfare state mechanisms to hide unemployment, not unlike the Soviet style of communist full employment. Single mothers, young people and immigrants were more marginalized in the economic revival. Child care and schools were crammed with more children.

A referendum on EU membership was held in 1994 with a marginal victory of 52 % votes in favour of joining. A reluctant member of EU on the periphery of Europe, Swedish EU interest manifested even less support in a referendum on entering the monetary Euro zone in 2003 with 56

---

[136]   Lindbeck 1997, Lindbeck et al 2004 and Lindbeck 2008.

% against. Euro scepticism runs openly in three parties, the Left party, the Green party and the Sweden democrats, and less visibly in the Social democrats and the Center party. The remaining liberal – conservative parties are more positive towards the EU and Europe, but they are in minority. With Sweden's turn towards USA after World War II and its striving for modernity, anything old and historical like Europe was and still is seen as conservative and backwards. The aforementioned Polish-Swedish writer Maciej Zaremba noted in a speech 2003 that Sweden has since long time rejected the four C's of Europe: Capitalism, Colonization, Conservatism and Catholicism[137] . Not quite European to begin with, during the 19th and especially the 20th century Sweden wanted to break away from any old continental ties. European languages apart from English were of less interest. The Euro scepticism of Sweden runs deeper than elsewhere in Europe and Zaremba asked again in a series of articles what Sweden is doing in Europe, when there seems to be no interest at all, not even if a new constitution would make EU into a federal union[138]. The Swedes simply do not care, but pay EU fees and want to be left alone. It is state individualism on an international level.

LIBERALISATIONS 2000

Social democrats had started to decentralize the education system in 1990, but the center- right coalition went further in liberalizing school management in 1992. A school voucher system was introduced which became such a success that no party would dare to abolish it, not even the returning victorious social democrats in 1994. Vouchers give government money to public and private schools according to a set rate if schools meet education requirements and legislation demands, just as Milton Friedman had proposed already in 1962. During social democratic and continuing center-right governments, the Swedish education sector was deregulated from 1990 in curriculum, grade system and governance, independent schools (non-profit and for- profit) made legal and new pedagogies based on information technology and student centred learning environments.

---

[137]   Zaremba 2003, p. 22

[138]   Zaremba and Malmström 2003.

Sweden was going through a liberalization phase that affected all areas. The Bildt and Carlsson governments agreed together on an individualized pension system where citizens could invest their shares in private pension funds themselves. For Swedes to get an option to plan pensions as individuals rather than as tax payers were such new phenomena that an anthropologist studied their minds and actions[139]. The 1960 pension reform ATP that had been the crown jewel in the social democratic social policy had failed, just as some had predicted. Systems similar to the losing liberal alternatives in the referendum in 1957 replaced the then winning but in 2000 losing ATP pension system.

It is due to the hard decisions made by socialist and center-right governments from 1990 that Sweden survived the tough years before the millennium shift. The center–right government under Carl Bildt was not re-elected in 1994 as crisis and talk about neo-liberalism had scared off voters, but similar liberal reforms continued, as they were in great demand. A new social democratic leader and former finance minister, Göran Persson, did what the center-right government never could do, and with some support from the working class and lower middle class majority. He went to rebellious union assemblies with hard messages but did not receive much support. Instead the trade union LO discussed to lower the funding to the social democratic party, something of which it had been the backbone since 1898, but without a resolution[140]. Workshop clubs and districts could rebel, but most of the LO establishment supported Göran Persson and his tough measures.

In parliament Persson said that he would condemn any Swede who spoke negatively about his country abroad. He had all reasons to be firm. The Swedish economy in mid 1990s was almost where Greece was in 2012. Persson had been to Wall Street, Frankfurt and the City of London where smiling young finance brokers and investors asked him why they should buy more Swedish government bonds. The media called them finance puppies (finansvalpar) and Persson hated them, but did what he had to do as quickly

---

[139]   Nyqvist 2007.

[140]   Ström Melin 2010, p.40.

he could with as little attention as possible. Little talk and much action, the opposite of what Greek ministers under similar pressures have done.

Persson's socialist ministers cut down some bloated welfare services reformed the public sector and lay off employees. Considerable cuts in government spending together with a high production growth in exporting industries helped to boost the failing economy. Government made low inflation instead of low unemployment as the overriding goal for economic policy and made the National Bank of Sweden independent from parliament and cabinet interferences. The earlier high inflation had not lead to real wage increases since 1980, so people understood the need for change. Employees had been fooled for decades in a spiral of higher wager and higher prices with no real values behind, just higher numbers. Lower taxes, privatization in tele-communications, railways and electricity, strict budget ceilings, EU membership in 1996 and more efficient administrative reforms made Sweden into a success story in early 2000, similar to Finland which pursued similar crisis management at the same time. Leading ministers at the Bank Support Authority taking over bad loans paying with public money were invited to the American congress in 2008 to give advice concerning the by then failing US financial system[141]. Cutbacks in state administration did harm to the tradition of parliamentary commissions which had been given wide responsibilities and enough time earlier, but now were done single-handedly in shorter time, of lesser quality and often with a clear result in mind given from ministers[142].

---

[141]   Welfare state reforms and financial crises in Finland and Sweden are compared in parliamentary committee report *Two of a kind*, SOU 2000: 83. For USA and Sweden comparisons, see *New York Times* Sept 22, 2008.

[142]   Professor of economics and former social democrat Assar Lindbeck who headed the parliamentary commission on economy and financial crisis strategies, called Lindbeckkommissionen SOU: 16 1993, is the exception when one man albeit with good help in very short time did a bipartisan in depth study of Swedish economy that the center-right government ordered and subsequent socialist government used to some extent if not fully. Being an independent researcher Lindbeck has given talk at classical liberal Mont Pelerin Society in 2009 on the Swedish model, see his web site at Stockholm University http://people.su.se/~alind/ and his memoir Lindbeck 2012.

Over half a million jobs in industry and the public sector were lost during the crisis in a population of nine million citizens. The Swedish auto industry became American; SAAB went to GM 1998, Volvo to Ford 1999. Traditional mill towns with strong socialist support were mostly hit. In Pajala, a working class small town above the Arctic Circle, over 35 % of the adult population was on early retirement, unemployment benefits or work re-training programs in 2000. But there were winners during the liberalized economy, such as towns with high degree of small entrepreneurs like in the southern Gnosjö district for example, which saw over 90 % of its adults employed in same year. In 1997, after three years with austere budget cuts under a social democratic government, Sweden started to get out from the financial chaos as a more mainstream north European and globalized modern welfare state. Almost a normal nation economically. The center-right parties applauded the pro-business changes and the ruling left government executed free market policies with great force[143]. But did the model survive?

REDEFINING THE SWEDISH MODEL

A globalised high-tech economy suited a reformed and lean Sweden well by the new millennium. The Swedish model seemed to survive by adaption and reforms. Some of the old institutions survived during the hard 1990s but the social contract between rulers and ruled had been re-negotiated. Citizens had to take more responsibility. But was there abandonment or just an adjustment of the Swedish model? Analyses diverge depending on political views. Social democrats usually say change but no abandonment. The left believes abandonment with hard consequences has taken place. Right of center parties diverge as some voters and leaders wanted a fully blown neo-liberal government policy in the 1980-1990s, but had to settle for a social democratic watered down version.

Lindbeck was a member and chair of the Committee for the Prize in Economic Sciences in Memory of Alfred Nobel 1969 – 1990.

[143] Josefsson 2005, Bergh and Erlingsson 2008, Bergh 2009 and Magnusson 2010, p. 227- 452.

This version was still working quite well at the end of the 20th century by the actions, hard work and foresight of four men who saved Sweden during the turbulent financial crisis and government cutbacks in 1990-2000; prime minister Carl Bildt from the right, prime minister Göran Persson from the left, former social democrat and economist Assar Lindbeck as expert and Urban Bäckström executor as governor of Reserve Bank of Sweden. The continuity of ten years (1993- 2003) and trust from two different cabinets of Bäckström was essential. Even if he was a moderate economist appointed by moderate Prime Minister Bildt, socialist Prime Minister Persson did not change horses in midstream. Bildt had shown similar respect for Lindbeck who was a social democratic economist when Bildt needed his advice. Tradition, pragmatism, expertise and consensus had worked again.

The Swedish welfare state has still high taxation and strong traditions of big government but has gone through some transformations. Economist Andreas Bergh noted:

> "The one-size fits all, and homogenous, Swedish welfare model is arguably dead. But in many respects, the model lives on. The most important welfare services during life cycle are still publicly funded to an extent that separates Sweden from most other countries"[144].

In the third millennium, Sweden managed to get out of the traditional social democratic welfare state policies successfully after a hard, mostly home-grown financial crisis. Taxes remain high, even increased with an extra tax of 5 % for the upper middle class. Olof Palme's vision in 1985 of Sweden as "a society with full employment, welfare and democracy /.../ the highest level of civilization any society has reached historically" was replaced with a goal of not being indebted, as his more modest succes-

---

[144]   Bergh 2010, p. 117. Same message but in other words: "The Swedish economic model is perhaps the most ambitious and publicized effort by a capitalist market economy to develop a large and active welfare state", Freeman et al 2010, p. 1

sor Göran Persson proudly said a decade later[145]. From being among the richest countries in 1970, Sweden fell to around 20th place by year 2000 in OECD rankings. Other countries have caught up with the long exceptional growth that neutral Sweden experienced from 1870- 1970, starting with liberalization by finance minister JA Gripenstedt in the mid 1800s and accelerated after the wars which excluded Sweden. The period of humiliation that started and partly was caused by the Swedish experiment of Olof Palme in 1970s would end by 2000 and Sweden could experience hope again. The next chapter will discuss these necessary approaches.

---

[145]   In Ehnmark 2000.

Reforms 1970 – 2000

1971	Five day working week of 40 hrs.
1971	Separate taxation of spouses
1974	New constitution, one chamber in parliament
1974	Legislation on employment protection
1974	Legislation on union representative in corporations
1974	Legislation on employees' right to education
1975	Municipalities obliged to organize day care centers
1975	Legislation on employers' duty to report vacancies to government agency
1975	Public employees exempted from personal responsibility of public services
1977	Legislation on cooperative corporate decision
1977	Legislation on five weeks' paid vacation
1977	Legislation on working environment conditions
1977	Higher education reforms giving non-academic members majority in university governance
1979	Ban on domestic corporal punishment of children
1979	Legislation against gender discrimination in employment
1982	Legislation on working hour schedules
1985	Deregulation of currency flows and credits
1988	Lower marginal taxation
1988	Deregulation of railway system
1989	Mandatory savings (cancelled 1990)
1990	Taxi services deregulation
1992	Abolition of wage earners funds.
1992	Radio and television monopoly ends
1992	School voucher system introduced
1992	Domestic flight monopoly deregulated
1993	Private employment agencies allowed
1993	Swedish Telephone Agency transformed to company
1993	Lower benefits in government unemployment insurance

1994   Swedish Postal Agency transformed to company
1994   Subsidies to house construction and real estate lowered
1995   Legislation on extended paid parental leave
1995   Sweden joins EU
1995   Four year government election periods introduced
1995   Spending ceiling on national budget
1995   Time limit for municipalities to organize day care (3 months)
1996   Electricity and power transformed into market areas
1997   Budget framework transformed making all increases financed
1997   Early retirement due to unemployment abolished
1997   National Building Society sold
1997   Personal computers subsidised to all citizens by government
1998   Personal candidates within parties allowed in election
1999   New pension system with private shares introduced
1999   Securities Register Centre sold
2000   National Audit Office independent from parliament
2000   National Bank of Sweden independent from parliament

CHAPTER 5

Hope 2000 -

Prime Minister Göran Persson had stated in 2000 that his social democratic government must be absolutely loyal to the objectives of social equality but fickle regarding the means. The tough reforms since 1990s led to good economic freedom rankings, as Sweden rose from number 43 in 1970 to 19 by 2000. Marginal tax rates shrunk to 50 % from world record 80 % earlier, foreign trade almost doubled as share of GDP and public debt dropped[146]. Sweden could feel hope again.

In 2001 Göran Persson chaired successfully the European Union for six months, but the end at the EU summit in June focusing on EU enlargement, sustainable development, economic growth and structural reform issues became a disaster. The summit was visited by US President George W. Bush, a fact that enraged many anti-American demonstrators inspired by thrashings in Seattle before. Swedish police was prepared for similar protests with non-violent looking, so-called dialogue police officers working with the many peaceful demonstrators and well- organized ecological, socialist and anti-imperialist groups. However, information about possible terrorist bombs and violent foreign activists led to a police charge that resulted in 150 people being injured, one stone throwing young man shot and over 500 demonstrators taken into police stations. The anarchist group reclaimed the Street thrashed shops, cafés and McDonalds, but the material damages were mild compared to other similar events. Some left leaning parents supported their children in their protests against capitalism and global warming, but there was no general popular support for the protests among the Swedish public. The anti-globalist group Attac, which had lots of peaceful supporters earlier, lost most of their members after the violent events. For the first time since 1931 demonstrators had been shot down by the authorities and it rocked Sweden out of its peace again. But the next event was worse.

---

[146]   Munkhammar 2007, p. 168 – 174.

Anna Lindh was a social democratic wonder girl almost of same class as Olof Palme. She was foreign minister in her mid 40s and was according to most observers the next party leader after incumbent Göran Persson. During shopping 10 September, 2003 in Stockholm city, she was knifed down and died the same evening. Similarly to the time of Palme's murder, she did not have body guards when a mentally unstable and criminal man of Balkan origins stabbed her without any reason. Later he claimed that his immigrant identity lead to confusion and hatred of Swedish politicians. He was sentenced to closed psychiatric care due to momentarily mental illness, but has recently claimed that he fooled the court and doctors to avoid imprisonment. Anna Lindh and Olof Palme were charismatic and energetic leaders that attracted much attention but also hatred, quite rare in calm Sweden. Swedish politicians have since gotten much better security[147]. Unfortunately she was succeeded by Laila Freivalds who not only had excused car theft as a young jurist 1970, but had to resign as minister of justice in 2000 due to a real estate scandal and would later resign again for mishandling of an emergency situation for Swedes in Thailand and censoring websites.

LABOUR TROUBLES FOR SOCIALISTS

Sweden had more troubles the following year 2004, but now from the new European Union. Swedish constitution forbids ministers, parliament and government agencies to decide in court cases. In spite of this legislation, social democratic ministers Hans Karlsson and Göran Persson claimed that the Swedish construction workers' union that was keeping Latvian workers off a work site in a conflict had the legal right to do so. The background was that a Latvian construction company had won a contract in Sweden and kept their workers on Latvian union–employer's agreement, not Swedish. The Latvian workers had not asked for help from Swedish

---

[147]   Olof Palme met his predecessor Tage Erlander 1953 when they both rode a regular train, something Erlander always did when not using the cars of the postal service to get around. Olof Palme had his telephone number in the public directory until 1970 when he had been prime minster for a year. He liked to take the subway train from socialist utopia Vällingby suburb to parliament just like any Stockholm commuter.

unions, which did not have any members at the work site. The Latvian company was willing to sign a contract, but not pay higher wages than what regular Swedish workers had. The Swedish unions demanded that the Latvian workers must get at least 10 % higher wages more than average Swedish construction workers. Union activists stood outside the Latvian closed site shouting "Go home, go home!" The Swedish Labour Court took a temporary decision in December 2004 to grant the unions the right to protest. Labour minister Hans Karlsson said that the case was thereby closed. Swedish workers had the right to protest. The Latvian company went bankrupt after not having been able to complete any work. Fellow EU member nation Latvia protested loudly. The Labour Court brought the case to the Court of Justice of the European Union in 2005 since the Swedish decision was only temporary, although neither the minister Hans Carlsson nor the unions believed so and told the press to forget the case. In 2007 the European Court decided in favour of the Latvian company. Swedish unions had to pay the company owners and Swedish labour legislation had to be adjusted to EU laws.

Another old union rule was also later ruled illegal by same European Court. Construction workers union had an agreement with building employers since 1976 that gave union officials the right to inspect and monitor how wages were paid and on what basis. These monitoring fees were deducted directly from salaries and paid by the employer to the union. The agreement covered all employees, regardless if they were members or not. A worker had to pay 1.5 % every month to the union whether or not the union official actually inspected work sites and did any wage control. The union dealt with the collected fees as they liked and spent on all kinds of expenses, not only control visits. As all blue-collar workers' trade unions support the social democratic party with money, non-organized and politically neutral or center-right voting workers had to support the socialist party with their own salaries. These party contributions could become very large, around $8 per Swedish inhabitant, which is six times more per head than US former president George W. Bush used in his campaign 2000[148].

---

[148]   Segerfeldt 2006, p.17.

In 2001 a case was filed by five workers (Tommy Evaldsson and four others) in the Swedish Labour Court and later to the Court of Justice of the European Union. The union monitoring fees were criticized and the negative right to not be organized or forced to pay to an organization when not a member was brought to the European Court. The unorganized workers won the case against the unions in 2007 as the right to property, i.e. the wages being deducted 1, 5 %, was violated[149]. Social democrats and unions did not have much public support in their criticism of the verdict. Sweden has a long unfortunate tradition of letting unions harass employers who have unorganized employees and even single businessmen without employees to make them sign collective agreements with unions. Unions have the right to use disproportionate industrial actions and use other unions to block off workers and isolate employers from transport, electricity etc. Other countries have laws against unions participating in other industrial actions than their own, but not Sweden[150].

Social democratic minority cabinets had to use parliamentary support from the ex-communist Left party and the Green environmental party in elections since 1998. The Swedish constitution gives the ruling prime minister all power to make a cabinet unless there is a majority against that minister. Nevertheless after an election there is considerable freedom to make a cabinet with confidence from parliament to vote for a new cabinet. After 1998 and 2002 elections incumbent Prime Minister Göran Persson never dissolved his cabinets and ruled supreme even with a 9 % loss in 1998. His government came under many attacks in its human

---

[149]   "Every natural or legal person is entitled to the peaceful enjoyment of his possessions. No one shall be deprived of his possessions except in the public interest and subject to the conditions provided for by law and by the general principles of international law", Article 1: Protocol no 1 in European Convention on Human Rights.

[150]   Rankka and Segerfeldt (eds.) 2007, p. 191- 213. A union harassment case was brought to European Court of Justice in 1996 but the employer Torgny Gustafsson on Gotland island lost due to the Swedish social democratic government's intervention with unsubstantiated evidence. In 2007 the salad bar Wild and Fresh in Gothenburg had to close down due to union interference unwanted by employees, see Appelgren 2008.

resources politics, where high administrative posts in regional and central government were given out to people loyal to any of the involved parties[151].

By Christmas 2004 an enormous water wave from an earth quake at sea, a tsunami, hit beaches in Thailand killing over 500 vacationing Swedes and injuring 1500, apart from killing 230 000 Asians. Foreign minister Laila Freivalds and her staff did not respond well and the affected Swedes did not get enough help in time. An independent commission investigated the dealings of ministers and government officials afterwards. Lack of coordination, responsiveness and capacity resulted in severe criticism of responsible ministers and officials but no minister had to leave office even if they were named in the commission for being at fault. No cabinet had gotten such severe criticism in modern times, but the response was an excuse from prime minister Persson to parliament and as he said, "To take responsibility, that is, stay in power" and not resign. Two years later at the start of center – right government victory in 2006, the secret tapes from the ministries involved were found. These tapes had not been used in the earlier parliamentary investigation as they had been hidden by officials at the foreign ministry loyal to the former social democratic party[152].

---

[151]   Rankka and Segerfeldt 2006, p. 19- 62. Socialist Prime minister Göran Persson "is meddling in practically every nomination, disregarding how unimportant" socialist journalist Olle Svenning noted, ibid, p. 29. Svenning had in 1960s worked with former social democratic ministers like Tage Erlander and Olof Palme and knew well the power games. See also Beckman 2006 and Sundström 2009.

[152]   Two parliamentary investigations, SOU 2005:104 and SOU 2007:44, were needed to sort out who did what, responsibilities, communication and preparations for catastrophes abroad. Inga-Britt Ahlenius, formerly head of Swedish Audit Agency and at the time head of UN Audit Agency, said that after such a negative report a government should resign, see *Aftonbladet* 1 December, 2005. In any other European country resignation should be the result. She claimed that even with the highest tax rates in the world, Sweden does not have the highest functioning state when handling crises like murders of Olof Palme and Anna Lindh, the sea catastrophe with over 500 dead outside Estonia 1994 and 2004 tsunami. The minimal conception of

Persson had more problems. The Social democratic Youth league SSU was reported in 2005 to the police for using fake memberships to obtain government financial support. By reporting older family members and people like Kjell Olof Feldt, ex- finance minister and certainly not a young man at age 74, and not letting members leave the organization registers, around half of 30 000 socialist youth league members were revealed as ghosts. High membership looked good when applying for public grants paid by taxpayers. Police investigation was dropped but members fled and some grants were paid back. But it was not over yet for young socialist outlaws. The socialist youth league president Anna Sjödin could not keep calm. At Crazy Horse bar in Stockholm on a late Friday night in January 2006, she hit guards, yelled racist remarks to them, committed theft and behaved badly being drunk. During the election campaign her case was in court and by Christmas same year she was sentenced and fined.

SOCIALIST SCANDALS -PART II

Swedes view social democratic politicians and union leaders as having to be more moral than other politicians since socialism is an ideal, a higher moral ground. What social democratic politicians and union leaders do with public and private money, members' contributions and government funds are a matter of harsh criticism and sometimes also popular ridicule. The following list shows party and union representatives being no better than average people.

Scandals in social democratic party and union establishment 1994-2011 (a selection):

---

what a state should be capable of includes since discussions by 17th century state theorist Thomas Hobbes a strong preparation for such crises. But in a welfare state trying to do everything and spread itself thin, the core tasks for any state, to protect its citizens, goes. Swedish police organisation is still not prepared to major crises such as Gothenburg uprisings 2001 and the two political assassinations, see Rönnegård 2008.

1. 1994. Business minister and union leader Björn Rosengren went to porn Club Tabu using union money ($8000 for one night), claiming he did not understand what kind of establishment he gotten into so late at night. Evidence of him being with prostitutes at the time is still around but not substantiated.

2. 1995. Finance minister Göran Persson told in parliament that he would curse with force anyone anywhere who talks badly about Sweden abroad.

3. Fall 1995. Mona Sahlin, then labour minister and deputy prime minister, later party leader 2007- 2010, had to leave her posts when parliament discovered that she had used public cash to purchase private services and goods, paid nanny services illegally, not paying childcare fees, taxes, 98 parking tickets and TV/ radio fees in time forcing her to the Swedish Enforcement Agency (Kronofogden). She had just accepted the post as party leader after Ingvar Carlsson in 1995 but left all political positions next year. During her personal crisis she went on a vacation to tropical island Mauritius with three staff members paid by government.

4. 1996. Former public municipal employees' union leader and Örebro county head Sigward Marjasin was charged with mismanaging public and private finances but later freed in court. Leading social democrats denounced him.

5. Winter 1998. Stockholm social democratic leader Mats Hulth had been buying drinks on taxpayers' behalf for many years, media reveals. Municipal rules for alcohol consumption had not been followed. Hulth was supported by the local social democratic club but had to resign.

6. 2000. Family ties within the social democratic party and sphere becomes obvious when the son Thomas of former minister Lennart Bodström and the daughter Brita of former minister Anna-Greta Leijon become ministers too. Families Nuder, Larsson, Toreson, Carlsson, Palme, Holmqvist, Damberg, Marén, Lindh and Holmberg were also

using the social democratic party nepotistic and intimate networks.

7. Fall 2000. Foreign minister Laila Freivalds bought an apartment which had been changed from rental status to private real estate, against the policy of her party. She resigned and was succeeded by Bo Ringholm (note 11) below.

8. Winter 2001. Extraordinary rendition of two refugees after 9/ 11 by CIA at Swedish airport to Egypt without guarantees of the men not facing torture. UN, Human Rights Watch and Swedish parliament objected afterwards to the deportation. Responsible minister was the deceased Anna Lindh whom every involved social democrat conveniently later could blame.

9. Winter 2002. Prime Minister Göran Persson›s wife Anitra Steen headed supposedly the Swedish alcohol monopoly Systembolaget when systematic corruption was revealed between suppliers of wine and liquor and the Swedish government buyers. She claimed unaware of what her subordinate managers where doing.

10. Winter 2002. Minister of migration Jan O. Karlsson received salary also from the EU at the same time which made his earlier cray-fish party at the expense of taxpayers getting much media attention and public outrage.

11. Spring 2004. Party leader Göran Persson bought a mansion with 500 acres for $2 million. Many hard working Swedes did not forget this, even if the purchase was perfectly legal.

12. Summer 2004. Finance minister and deputy prime minister Bo Ringholm was criticized for being lax in illegal wages paid by a sport club Enskede IF where he was president for ten years. Police investigation was started but closed since possible crimes were done too long ago.

13. Fall 2004. Metal union officials went to sex clubs, bought liquor and dildos (to give to loyal women) for union members' money in Troll-

hättan. One evening in Brussels three union officials spent $7000 on liquor and prostitutes.

14. Winter 2004. Prime Minister Göran Persson was made honorary doctor at Örebro University on dubious grounds. The official motivation for his degree in medicine, science and technology (subjects which non-graduate Persson never had studied) could be viewed as a reward for his support of Örebro University College when applying for full university credentials. Earlier attempts had been refused by academic authorities but Persson made way for the new regional university.

15. 2005. Trade union LO fired two officials (Jan Edling and Olle Sahlström) when they wrote about how the union and socialists used false labour statistics (real unemployment 20 % rather than officially 5 %) and corruption in housing foundations meant for poor widows of workers' families going to union officials.

16. Spring 2005. Gunilla Ekberg expert on sexual trafficking and prostitution at a government ministry threatened female journalist Evin Rubar and other women organizations, but minister in charge Mona Sahlin did not react.

17. Spring 2005. Social democratic parliament member Ola Rask was forced to leave his leadership of socialist and union education center due to having two positions, a pension at the same time and using funds for family purposes.

18. Spring 2005. Government Employment Agency in Nyköping threatened to withdraw benefits unless unemployed construction workers went to Stockholm to protest against budget cuts in unemployment benefits together with the union. The government Employment Agency official signed the letter together with union officials and both stated that the march was mandatory.

19. Summer 2005. Center Against Racism, created by ministers Jens Orback and Mona Sahlin, did not use their government grants properly

and had little activity but many expenses on hotels and restaurant. The anti-racist center got new grants each year without control.

20. Fall 2005. Police used union officials when checking on foreign transport companies after a storm in southern Sweden. Unions checked for collective agreements (optional according to Swedish law) while the police looked at safety arrangements. Unions used the uniformed policemen to obtain secret information from foreign chauffeurs that they had no reason to give to union officials.

21. Fall 2005. Zakarias Winberg was fired from his position at a trade union after writing an article declaring his loyalty to Christian Democratic Party, not to the labour movement.

22. Winter 2005. School minister Ibrahim Baylan stopped a report from National Agency for Schools which had found that private schools made better results and that teacher qualifications did not matter. In Sweden agencies are independent from ministers, but Baylan made the agency remove the report from internet immediately. An edited version was uploaded later and Baylan had to explain his actions to constitutional council at parliament.

23. Spring 2006. Göran Persson was sentenced but with no punishment in court for illegal constructions at his mansion under the care of his brother. Neither of them knew that laws taken under socialist parliament made such constructions mandatory to be reported to municipality and a plan for working safety must be prepared.

24. Fall 2006. Göran Persson threatened to withdraw government bonds in telecommunication multinational Ericsson because CEO Carl-Henrik Svanberg said that a shift of political power could be refreshing.

25. Fall 2006. Leading lady of Stockholm municipal social democrats Annika Billström lost her political position but used regulations to fund her private business while being supported by taxpayers after

her lost election. Legal but immoral many thought.

26. Spring 2009. Union leader Vanja Lundby- Wedin did not act or understand when as board member of the union pension fund AMF, she supported its CEO with extra $9 million when he was laid off on top of his $6 million early retirement fund.

27. Fall 2010. Two local socialist politicians went to Stockholm, got drunk and brought prostitutes to the union premises. Buying sex is illegal in Sweden and the legislation is heavily supported by the social democratic, feminist, green and left parties.

28. Summer 2011. Party leader Håkan Juholt had parliament pay for his apartment while his woman stayed there too. He also mismanaged rented cars and travels to Belarus on parliament funds.

29. Fall 2011. Driver Fredrik Lantz was excluded from Transport workers union because of his membership in nationalist Sweden Democratic Party, represented in municipal councils and national parliament.

30. 2008 – 2012. Socialist chairmen Mona Sahlin and Håkan Juholt, finance spokesman Tomas Eneroth, Stockholm municipal delegate Karin Wanngård and socialist youth league head Anna Sjödin spoke degradingly about jobs for manual workers in service sector. They want no one to have such jobs or be forced by workfare schemes to accept them.

CENTER – RIGHT GOVERNMENT BACK 2006

Persson's cabinet did not last after the September 2006 election as may be understood from the above list of small and big scandals in the socialist and union camps. Lax education and immigrant policies came under hard criticism from the liberal party and lax unemployment welfare benefits from the moderates. These parties had formed an Alliance for Sweden together with Christian democrats and Center party that had sorted out their differences enough to make a realistic alternative to the incumbent social democratic government. The Moderate party made the most definitive change in order to win against the social democrats being the largest opposition party. With the slogan " The New Moderates, the new Working class Party " they did what Tony Blair did to Thatcher 1997: taking over the enemy battlefield by asking same questions but give other answers and having a young leader that could appeal to all. Especially young working people were tired of the left rhetoric leading to no jobs but raising taxes even on low incomes. Like David Cameron's red Tories and many Obama democrats, Swedish new right embraces marriage for gays and lesbians, scepticism of royal traditions, cuts on defence, government staying liberal in value disputes. Many traditional conservatives sighed to the changes but the strategy worked. The New moderates got 11 percentages more shares of votes in 2006 than before.

Voters were not sure in 2006 how Persson and his social democratic government would deal with its two coalition parties, the left and greens. The greens insisted to have their own ministers, but the Left party did not support a coalition cabinet without them. The center-right coalition made themselves spokespersons for the working people, while the center-left came to defend lax policies for the unemployed, those on long-term sick leave and early retirees, thus promising to hand out more benefits. Two blocs against one another: Workers against people on benefits with few incentives to work or even to look for work. By 2006, a million Swedes were on unemployment schemes, early retirement, long term sick leave (without being asked to try new occupations or to move to jobs) or on social welfare benefits. That meant one of four adult Swedes were not in the workforce. More than a tenth of the adult population was in early retirement in a country that has good health care and modern safe working conditions. Statistics show that people in rural areas are more often on benefits than urban dwellers since doctors and government officials do not pressure them to either change occupation or move to where work is found.

Since the social democrats had used working life, labour unions and employment programs in their policies since 19th century, their core was attacked when they could not explain how to manage an economy with so many people on benefits. For decades social democrats had used sick

leave, early retirement and often useless unemployment training programs to hide the real unemployment rate which was over 16 % rather
than 5 % according to global audit agency McKinsey and former union
economist Jan Edling[153]. The Swedish government Bureau of statistics
(SCB) did not count unemployed using same methods as recommended
by the EU and global methodology until 2007 after the center-right government made the bureau change the parameters. A working class party
with few working people did not rhyme well with voters. Adding to the
socialist damage as a working class party was also its disregard of vocational secondary education, inability to train enough skilled workers and
contempt for unskilled workers in cleaning, guarding, sales and other
low paid jobs in the services sector. The social democratic labour party
did not attract working people from any classes who pay taxes, but was
supported by the recipients of welfare benefits and welfare state employees who handed out benefits. Simple equation: Vote for us, we give you
money and someone else pays.

Statistics showed that people on benefits supported the social democrats
and left, but they were not enough, just about one million adults. Left
leaning voters seemed defeatist about the future while right leaning voters were more optimistic at the time[154]. The left took the losers, the right
the winners. 20 % of all working voters cast their votes for socialists,
whereas 75 % of people on benefits did. Political scientist Stig- Björn
Ljunggren analyzed:

---

[153]   McKinsey 2006 and 2012. Recommendations from McKinsey: reduce regulations,
reduce labour costs, facilitate competition, reduce restrictions in firing and hiring,
and improve productivity in public sector. Sweden had the worst ability to create new
jobs in OECD 1992- 2003. In 2009 the Swedish government initiative Globalisation
Council presented its final report and recommended same policy changes, see Globaliseringsrådet 2009. See also Edling 2005.

[154]   Holmberg and Weibull (eds.) 2007, p. 34-35. Social democrats acknowledged that the
elections 2006 and 2010 were lost due to leaving the question of creating jobs to the
right and being stuck with giving out benefits to jobless, see *Dagens Arena 2010*. For
less realistic analysis Isaksson 2010 and more realistic, see veteran finance minister
Feldt 2012 and for the more optimist, Hamilton 2012.

> "The aim of the moderates has been to become the domi-
> nant party in urban Growing Sweden while they have given
> over the Losing Sweden to its main opponent, the labour
> movement, which with strange joy and energy has taken
> the task to its heart. Social democrats have left the 'workers
> party' to the moderates while they themselves willingly have
> taken the role of 'welfare recipients' party'"[155].

One main campaign aim for socialists was to keep the unemployed in-
finitely on government benefits, while the center-right declared that one
and a half year was enough. Same with early retirement and long- term
sick leave, which meant to see a doctor and test working abilities in more
working areas than before leaving the workforce.

NEW MODERATE WORKERS' PARTY

The center-right government did well from 2006 and was re-elected in
2010. Central to the victory was to make more people work and liberalize
the labour market. The two earlier center- right governments in 1976 and
1991 inherited failing economies due to social democratic mismanagement. But in 2006, the economy was good for a year until the financial
crisis on Wall Street spread instantly. The social democratic party had
changed its leader to Mona Sahlin, the first female ever to lead the party,
but that did not help win either. Her earlier faults with private money
were always following her. Crucial for social democrats losing both 2006
and 2010 elections was the weak red-green coalition, lax welfare policies
and defence of hard taxation.

Moderate Prime Minister Reinfeldt had chaired the European Union in
fall 2009 with the same efficiency as Persson had earlier, but faced much
tougher issues on climate change, problems with member states on rati-
fication of the Lisbon treaty, the financial crisis coming from US banks

---

[155]   *Svenska Dagbladet* 7 Oct, 2011. Svallfors 2010 agrees but is more loyal to their party.
British labour historian Tony Judt 2009 said "If social democracy has a future, it will
be as a social democracy of fear", but skipped the pessimistic line in Judt 2010.

and armed conflicts in Gaza and Georgia. The Stockholm Programme on justice and homeland security in the EU was an accomplishment that drowned in the financial crisis and constitutional dealings with stubborn Irish and Czech presidents[156].

Some gain was given to the social democrats due to center-right government mishandling policies for benefits and rules for sick leave which was utilized to a maximum by the center-left populist opposition, portraying the ruling center-right coalition driving dying cancer patients out to a harsh labour market, robbing them of all benefits. An exaggeration that almost worked to ensure extended social benefits but enough voters were cautious of future economic crises and thought the alternative socialist and ecological coalition too weak.

The financial crisis of 2007-2009 in the world and later in Europe were well handled by finance minister Anders Borg and Prime Minister Fredrik Reinfeldt, both moderates. In neither crisis was Sweden at the center as the country and its financial investors did not have much risk capital in the failing US banks and corporations, nor was Sweden a part of the euro currency. The weak center-left leadership could not gain much confidence in handling national interests in these crises in the same way former socialist Prime Minister Göran Persson had done with admiration across the political spectrum, especially during his temporary EU leadership.

By spring 2011, after many months of ordeals, social democratic party leader Mona Sahlin was replaced with unknown Håkan Juholt who immediately made a fool of himself, politically and privately. He lasted for ten months and was replaced by former metal workers' trade union leader Stefan Löfvén. A change of three socialist guards in five years showed a party in crisis. Minimum reign for heads of Swedish social democratic party chairmen has been 10 years (Carlsson, Persson) and maximum 23 (Erlander, with Hansson close at 21 years and Branting 18 years).

---

[156]   Bengtsson ed. 2010

Many social democrats, especially old timers and workers, thought that the new finance minister Anders Borg, formerly a libertarian economist and bank consultant, was much more able to handle global financial storms than the socialists. He has been true to the new moderate program of compassionate and social conservatism, though these terms never were used and he has fiercely defended the Swedish model of high taxes, welfare state services and union rights. Since 2006 much has happened. Many taxes have been lowered, especially for low income earners, over 200 000 jobs created, pressuring people on long term sick leave to try work, over 50 000 less people in early retirement, cuts in defence budget and abolishment of draft, education reforms in schools to enhance studies, trainees in vocational schools, introduction of teacher certificate and a new grading system[157]. Popular reforms have been tax deductions on household repairs (ROT) and household help (RUT). However these market solutions for families and households continue the social engineering and government interference socialists started, but the center-right coalition chose these regulations instead of lowering taxes. The OECD gave credit to Sweden's ability to weather the 2008-2010 crises due to low gross government debt, a sizable structural budget surplus and good fiscal reforms from the domestic crisis in 1990s, even if more structural reforms are needed.

MORE TO REFORM

There is still need for further reforms of the social benefit and taxation systems to provide the right incentives for increasing working hours, the OECD warned Sweden[158]. But going by the mood of Swedes brought up under extreme welfare state propaganda, tactics of the new moderates since 2002 have worked well. If market oriented reforms had been more vocal and proposed from libertarian and conservative politicians,

---

[157] Alliansens vitbok 2010. Sympathetic observers to the center-right coalition like Engellau and Gür 2010 nevertheless reiterates ten unanswered questions to politicians in order to go further in the reform agenda towards a functioning market economy and legal government.

[158] OECD 2011.

of whom a few still exist in the moderate party, voters would have been scared off. The infiltration of the middle ground in Swedish politics by the former conservative party has gone so far that the new moderates get criticism from business people for being too weak on the unions. Labour ministers Sven-Otto Littorin, Hillevi Engström and finance minister Anders Borg, all proud new moderates, defend the Swedish model by reforming it they claim. The Confederation of Swedish Enterprise (Svenskt Näringsliv) mutters that too little is done too late by the party that used to be on the side of business.

Comparisons between USA and Sweden show that work pays less in Sweden, leisure is attractive and employing staff or hire services are expensive, whereas the opposite is true for US business and people. For a Swede it pays better to stay at home and fix household chores rather than work extra and pay someone. Due to higher taxes for a third of the workforce, higher education, more workloads and higher paid careers do not pay off and ambitions die. If an employee would want or need to work extra hours, these extra hours are taxed harder by marginal taxation. A tax law was introduced by socialists that gave government the authority to tax funds in companies according to the views of tax administration officers. The law simply stated that too much money in a private enterprise that did not seem to lead to necessary investments according to the taxmen, could be taxed, if the hard earned money was not spent on salaries (with income taxes, payroll taxes etc.). The law was abolished in 2010. No wonder growth in Sweden does not give more jobs compared to growth in US, and have few registered companies. In fact, Sweden has more people on early retirement than who own their business. With harsh tax policies for small business, a work of a lifetime that can be gone in a few months or weeks if the taxmen hit[159].

---

[159] Linder 2006. Melki 2009 tells the story of how the Tax Authority (Skatteverket) attacked his small business in cleaning services. After two years the taxmen lost their court case but continued to fight Melki but lost again after his strong defence for rule of law. His case is one of many where small businessmen are under investigation for tax fraud with no relevant accusations.

Most controversy has been around the labour market legislation on employment protection from 1974. Social democrats, left party members and activists, new moderates, nationalists, green parties and unions all want to keep the legislation while some in the liberal, center, moderate and Christian democratic parties and employers want a reformed and liberalized labour legislation. No one dare even to open a debate about abolishing the legislation that hinders employers to keep the best people or to hire youth and immigrants more easily. Even employers have given up on ruling their own company hiring procedures and have settled for a reformed legislation. In June 2011 employers and unions agreed to disagree in a joint report[160].

A paradox of the strange fact that new moderates defend the welfare state says that the social democratic party lost but the social democratic welfare state won. Political scientist and social democrat Stefan Svallfors has polled the attitudes towards welfare state among Swedes for decades. A growing proportion of the Swedes have become even more faithful to the welfare state since the neo liberal influence early 1990s. 75 % of polled Swedes by 2010 imagined themselves even willing to pay more taxes if the extra money went to government health services, a truly socialist tactics. A more liberal interpretation of this positive attitude to spend more private money on health care would be to channel the cash flow not to taxes but to private health services. In 1997 under socialist rule, 67 % percent of polled citizens held were willing to pay more taxes. From 2006 when center-right coalition government has been in power support has risen for government run welfare services, especially among middle class voters The new moderates and their coalition partners won because they were the new guards of welfare state policies. Center- right or center-left did not matter to a majority of voters that were loyal to the

---

[160]   Svenskt Näringsliv and Landsorganisationen 2011. Nycander 2010 claims that legislation is better than not since there is not a good order on the labour market since the employers left collective bargaining 20 years ago. But there must be a new reasonable collective agreement between unions and employers he states, alongside the controversial legislation. Sanadaji and Nyman 2007 criticizes the new moderates for being too weak.

foundations of welfare state policies as a majority of Swedes still are[161].

Internationally, liberal welfare policies stress the importance of equality of possibilities whereas socialist welfare policies also want to ensure equal outcomes through strong redistribution. Swedish center-right parties often share both of these policies with the socialists, which make them hard to distinguish for an outsider and for many Swedes too. But equality of outcomes give no reasons for anyone to work harder unless there are other incentives such as better values or employees' influence on management or other. The little income disparities that have risen since 1990s are being seen by many, including many center-right politicians, as harsh divisions in society that must be fought by more and new taxes. Taxation is a tool that if used too hard gives rise to an informal economy since people want to avoid high taxes. A black market of goods and services started in 1970s with around 8 % of GDP and by 2010 around 20 %. Avoiding taxes has become problematic since investigations from taxmen can lead to break of integrity and rule of law. Swedish tax authorities have far-reaching powers to intervene if they believe a case of tax evasion is at hand. In court the authorities have the advantage to rule over citizens and enterprises at their will. In the end, a high taxed country leads to fear, submission and control. What also destabilizes such a country is the introduction of new taxes in parliament by the ruling majority with little support that may be changed by another majority later. By legislating tax hikes only with a secure majority of 65 % or more, tax matters will be better judged and decided[162].

CENTER-RIGHT WELFARE STATE
The center-right governing coalition has a need to rewrite the Swedish history as nation building has been one sided by the domination of unions, social democratic, green and left sympathizers in research, educa-

---

161   Svallfors 2010 and Rothstein 2010.

162   Wickman 2010. The idea that egalitarian redistribution give better functioning societies, like Sweden, has been rebutted by Saunders (ed.) 2010 against authors of *The Spirit Level* with their admiration for large welfare states.

tion, media and many policy statements. But how may such a story sound where the social democratic welfare state is a parenthesis, not a start of the Swedish success story? There are new more liberal leaning interpretations by writers Anders Johnsson, Henrik Berggren, Lars Trägårdh, Johan Norberg, Svante Nycander, Andreas Edwardsson and many more on Swedish history but more will have to be researched without socialist and welfare state ambitions to defend.

The large Swedish welfare state of social democratic features is itself worthwhile to sustain and defend intact with no changes some radical socialists still argue, but they are few[163]. A way to get reforms implemented is to hide them. Most people do not notice the changes in welfare structures. Political scientist Anders Lindbom argues that changes have been quite large but invisible to the voters and media. The hidden changes of pension reforms, EU membership, budget cuts and a less ambitious rent-control system for housing were necessary as the Swedes probably never would have accepted an open mandate for such hard cuts. But the coming demographic problem of more elderly and fewer working adults may become urgent soon. To retain standards for care of the elderly would mean having Swedes working ten more years than now, to 77 years which few would like to[164].

A rewritten story of the Swedish welfare state is needed when the parties that used to blame the welfare state for all ills suddenly defend it. But maybe the welfare state is not socialist at all or to begin with. The hypothesis of social democrats as riding on an earlier economic and political liberalism, protestant work ethic and homogeneity is supported by some scholars that view the idea that the legal and social institutions in pre-social democratic Sweden were crucial to build the rich welfare state.

---

[163]   For left wing agitator Greider 2011, the large Swedish public sector is "embryonic socialism". Thus for example, the more municipally employed there are, the more socialist the country gets. He has no idea of how users of municipal services, elderly, students etc. can be addressed and satisfied with such municipal monopolies.

[164]   Lindbom 2011. See also Santesson-Wilson 2011 and Santesson 2012. Bergh 2012 and Fölster 2012a are not as pessimistic and think around 5 extra years will do.

Trust precedes the welfare state as no welfare services can work if trust is not there for all citizens to do their due[165].

Ulf Kristersson, moderate minister of social affairs, hailed in 2012 the 100 year birth of the welfare state in a commemorative article with a positive attitude unthinkable without the move towards the center of Swedish politics by his former right party[166]. But best support for non-socialist foundations for the rich Swedish welfare state that the new moderate party has found, comes from Henrik Berggren and Lars Trägårdh already mentioned concept of Swedish state individualism[167]. This concept both explains the particular Swedish contract between citizens and state but can also be used to defend such a contract, based on an ambitious welfare state with few civil society institutions. Just like the new moderates took the working ethics from the labour movement, state individualism has also become its ideological support.

---

[165]   Rothstein 2011a and Bergh 2009.

[166]   Kristersson 2011. He recommends social democrats to learn from their own history of non-extensive social policies, that is, pre- Palme. The birth of Swedish welfare state he argues begins 1913 with small government pensions. Another start would be the 1906 peace treaty on industrial relations in the labour market or foundations of "feudal capitalism", see Baker 2011. Three fundamental features in the welfare state model, or Swedish/Nordic Model are free trade reforms, the agreements on collective peaceful negotiations by strong unions and employers and some universal welfare benefits, such as pensions. Trade became free in 1850s under JA Gripenstedt making business more profitable and these other features occurred during liberal cabinets led by Karl Staaff long before socialists took power in 1932. See Nycander 2007. However, the Swedish social democrats have desperately launched a legal fight by seeking copyright to the word "The Nordic Model" in 2011, something that clearly shows how threatened they are by the new moderate move towards embracing the welfare state and claiming parts of its history too. The inter-governmental Nordic Council of Ministers, who do not like one country out of five and certainly not one political party having legal copyright to the popular yet vague term, have overruled the decision by the Swedish patent authority and the case will continue in 2013. See *Washington Post* 2012-03-13.

[167]   Lönegård 2011, Berggren and Trägårdh 2011.

The new moderate party spin doctor Per Schlingman, who was crucial in transforming by triangulation the losing old conservative party to its present successful new moderate party, has learned from Berggren and Trägårdh that Swedes have a complicated and strange but rational relationship to the state. In articles and interviews he greets Berggren and Trägårdh as two thinkers that have finally come up with how to analyze the Swedish welfare state and simultaneously praise it. Apart from viewing the state as being good, distinguishing Scandinavians from most world citizens, the state keeps us from ourselves. The proud independent farmer and modern urban Swedes do not need others and are willing to pay a high price and keep their voices quiet about taxes, child care, immigration, feminism, even the stifling conformism and correctness itself – just to be left alone. While accepting that this has been largely true, there are good and hopeful reasons to think Swedes will not continue along the path of state individualism paying its price with money and silence.

Spin doctor Per Schlingman's and the new moderate party's hailing of state individualism is the opposite from what the former moderate leader Gösta Bohman meant in his 1981 speech on the new individualism and new insecurity. Bohman meant that the state had become too powerful and making people dependent on its services with few possibilities to flourish as an individual. State individualism grants a kind of false freedom to the individual that Schlingman uses to lure voters successfully but will be fatal in the long run. Bohman was more realistic and liberating in his tougher stand against the state. The new moderates will have to do better than take over collectivist concepts like state individualism if they want to have chance in future political battles and meet expectations of substantive individual freedom, not nominal. To defend state individualism is not only to defend egotism and state repression, but also to be conservative in not wanting to change anything in the large welfare state built by socialists. Bohman was more open, principled and liberal 1980 than Schlingman is 2012.

Sweden has changed and will change even more. History will be remade and change the Swedish mentality again. The socialist war on traditional working class ethics, middle class values, family, education, culture and business was to some extent stopped in 2006, but the wounds are deep and will take generations to heal. With administrative-technical solutions and legislation much can quickly be restored by an able center-right government decisions, but getting less tangible areas of herd mentality and helplessness replaced with humanism and integrity are the real challenges as it involves not just socialist views but innate Swedish. Moderates and the other three center-right parties take the easy way out, which won two elections, but they have to do more to get away from the extremes of state individualism. There are totalitarian streaks in this concept that view citizens as unable to take care of themselves and to speak their minds. Protections of minorities, rule of law and separation of state powers have no place in such a relationship between citizens and their state. Meek as sheep, citizens are being guarded by a wolf-in-disguise.

The many socialist scandals after 1970 that has been told here are of different degrees and have had various impacts[168]. Of course many seem trivial but the sheer amount of scandals of a ruling party and its people is what outraged voters not just one time in 1976, taxing popular author Astrid Lindgren with 102 %, but many times later. The social democratic party had turned state functionaries into party bureaucrats. The ideal of neutral civil servants of Max Weber's style was replaced more with rad-

---

[168] Socialist scandals ended abruptly on Jan 21, 2012 when the erratic and incompetent party leader Håkan Juholt resigned and ended his ten month roller coaster ride of daily errors in parliament, television, radio and press. His last memorable impression was a laugh, when he stated he could not stand physically on the same side as nationalist Swedish democrats in a television studio. He insisted on another place in the studio debate but was rejected. His prompt decision lead to there being no socialist speaker in the debate at all, which of course was good news for the ruling center-right coalition leaders to have no opposition to talk to, except green and nationalist parties' chairmen. The charade continued in 2012 when the socialist block (incl. left and greens) in parliament refused to join the Sweden democrats in the annual parliamentary football match against ministers playing for the incumbent center-right cabinet. Their reason for not kicking balls together with nationalist Sweden democrats was that parties not in majority do not make up a joint parliamentary opposition to the ruling cabinet.

ical social workers and Mao's red experts[169]. The many opportunities to work the state system in party interests or even personal were tempting for many socialists, with or without powers, and for some non-socialist business people too. Scandals have been revealed were also of the kind where business interests were involved. Many municipal contracts from socialist mayors went to certain building contractors (BPA, NCC, SKANSKA etc.) without any market incentives[170]. Thus many entrepreneurs outside the labour movement profited from the extra democratic powers. To disentangle these secret networks will be hard but must start and it has begun. Gothenburg municipality has given a good lead but many other municipalities and counties should follow.

The Swedish economy by 2013 is going well. The Euro crisis and debt problems affect Sweden but there is a good growth forecast ahead unless something extraordinary happens in Europe, Sweden's largest business partner. Reforms of labour markets and service sectors are still needed but not possible since many Swedes including middle class voting center-right, still think against clear evidence to the contrary that a functioning welfare state needs certain restrictions for youth and immigrant employment. Business organizations, OECD, McKinsey, the center-right government own globalisation council and the ministry of finance long term report of 2011, all give same pieces of advice; deregulate the labour market, abolish rent control, liberalize the service sector, trim the public sector and introduce more market incentives, but the non-socialist co-alition is not yet planning any such reforms until pressed for[171]. Voters will punish anyone that will change the basic structures of welfare state planning and labour rules. Unemployed youth and immigrants will still be out of jobs by a fulltime unionized and well protected workforce.

---

[169]   Ahlberg 1975 and Löfstedt 1977.

[170]   Dagens Samhälle 2011 reported that the actual amount of public spending in Sweden on goods and services from private sector was $115 billion, not $70 as previously calculated. The difference of $45 billion equals six times the Swedish defence budget.

[171]   Recommendations stem from Globaliseringsrådet 2009, SOU 2011:11, Fölster and Kreicbergs 2011, OECD 2011 and McKinsey 2006 and 2012.

The everyday challenges of paying these costs are felt as disempowerment of personal strength. Swedish men and women work around 10 % more than average EU citizens, yet have the second highest tax revenue of GDP in the world at 46 %. Compared with the other OECD member states, only Denmark display a higher tax ratio, but this fact does not seem to bother the happy Scandinavian citizens much. More than half of Danes, Swedes and Finns said in September 2009 they were very satisfied with the lives they led, compared to 9 % in three south European countries (before the collapsing euro)[172]. But they do not know much about the future.

FUTURES 2030

Two economists have tried to picture Sweden in year 2030. Both are liberal and quite optimistic. Stefan Fölster, chief economist of Federation for Swedish Enterprise, maintains that there will be no demographic shocks of each adult citizen supporting too many young and old. The older will be able to work longer. There are possible improvements in the public sector that will be necessary. Fölster holds the broadly defined middle class and working class accountable for asking too much from the welfare systems. Their spokespersons in unions and vested interests have put the poor and marginalized in front of them. But the ones receiving better care and benefits have been the lower and middle classes, not the poor. In order to stay healthy, the state has to downsize to perform its more necessary obligations such as law and order, emergency and defence. Lower taxes are necessary since the welfare state cannot deliver just and efficient services, which already by 2012 is the case Fölster argues. With higher salaries left, citizens will start to pay for their services from private entrepreneurs in health care and education as the Japanese, Swiss and Australians do. Lower taxes of these countries have not affected their life expectancy, a good measurement of living standards. Sweden

---

[172]   2011 figures from EU Commission at www.ekonomifakta.se . For analysis of relations between large public sector, wealth, happiness and growth, see Henrekson 1996, Fölster 1998, Henrekson and Bergh 2010, Larsson 2011, Rothstein 2011a and Henrekson and Bergh 2011.

will transform into a welfare society instead of a welfare state, Fölster envisions[173]. But he adds that unless Sweden make reforms in business environment, the country will slide further down in standards of living and climate for entrepreneurs. Since 2007, crisis management has been prioritized by the center-right government, while focus on catching up with other Western economies through reforms has been forgotten. Sweden has turned into a fat lazy cat that did well once and still do somewhat well, but will not make progress with present status quo[174].

Liberal economist Andreas Bergh at Lund University and Research Institute of industrial relations (Institutet för Näringslivsforskning) defends the capitalist welfare state Sweden by 2030. Taxes may still be high at around 45 % of GDP because the needs in public sector must be met. He believes that public financed and administered welfare services are what the elderly, many of them 1968 rebels, expect, as do their children. The welfare state will still have massive support from political parties and voters. Possibilities to top up public basic levels of elderly care and other welfare services will expand. Higher education which now is free to all Swedish and EU citizens may be charged. A more flexible social security system may develop where for instance levels of sick leave benefits could be differentiated so each recipient could decide for a high but short level or a low and longer. The government welfare services will be inspired from solutions in insurance companies but remain the major security[175].

The center-right government has recently established two commissions with broad parliamentary support for planning future welfare services (Socialförsäkringsutredningen) and other long term challenges in environment, social cohesion and entrepreneurship (Framtidskommissionen). Both will present their reports by spring 2013. Longer time in the workforce, earlier entries to study and work for youth and shared private-public responsibilities for welfare services are some topics, but

---

[173] Fölster 2012a. See also Fölster and Kreicbergs 2011, Fölster and Wallen 2011, Fölster et al 2011 and Fölster 2012 b.

[174] Fölster 2012c. See also Svenskt Näringsliv 2009.

[175] Bergh 2012. See also Bergh 2010.

without reforms for a better business environment, especially for small business, leading to higher GDP growth, there will not be enough resources to pay within the end. Given the reasonably well functioning economy going in the right direction in the short perspective at least, other extremes are not. The next chapter will show some contemporary extremes.

Reforms 2000- 2012

2001   Postal services liberalized

2001   Reformed unemployment benefits

2002   Limit on municipal day care fees

2003   All privileges of nobility abolished

2003   State unemployment agency and welfare services coordinated

2005   Employers financing employees' sick-leave

2005   Tighter control of welfare benefits

2007   Reduction on income taxes for all

2007   Reduction on pay roll taxes for youth and long term unemployed

2007   Reduction on taxes for household services

2007   Reforms of sick leave and early retirement

2007   Deregulated labour protection legislation

2007   Abolition of wealth and real estate taxes

2007   Some public companies sold

2008   Choice in elderly care and health services introduced

2008   Labour immigration legislation deregulated

2009   More police officers trained and employed

2009   Sharper sentences for criminals

2010   Market for drug sales deregulated

2011   Grades from class 6 in primary schools

2011   Teaching certificate introduced

CHAPTER 6

Contemporary extremes

There are remaining extremes in Sweden that will surprise a foreign reader. People can fret hours over how a couple divides their parental care or if someone calls herself Swedish. Conformism will be the theme of this chapter with gender and ethnicity as the most debated topics with a distinctive Swedish twist. But what is actually Swedish culture and traditions besides being extremely conformist and dull? And how can that bring controversy?

SWEDISHNESS

Ethnologists agree with most Swedes and foreign observers on some national characteristics, of course with many reservations on viewing culture as living processes and not all Swedes having all features all the time.

Negatively, Swedes are somewhat clumsy and shy in public presentations, to the point (if not boring) and unemotional, stiff and private, unassuming and mediocre, melancholic, avoiding conflicts and formal in socializing, rather depend on welfare state than family and friends, scared of being excluded from groups if expressing uncommon views, attitudes or interests. In American folklore, Swedes are practical–minded but stupid. These are all negative features which some Swedes proudly say of some other Swedes. They themselves are different and un- Swedish. Being proudly un-Swedish is an extreme Swedish trait. Few Frenchmen or Americans would state that they are happy being un-French or un-American.

Positively, Swedes are straight forward, care for their closest family members, informal in working life, active (often outdoors) and sportive, value nature, honest and dutiful, humble, show affection (hugging people if under 50), self-confident, punctual, well organized and autonomous, modest, technologically advanced and rational[176]. Being alone especially in nature is valued highly in Sweden, which does not mean to be lonely. Swedes just do not always want people around or being bound to them. An extreme kind of individualism. The strong success of social media like Facebook, half of the population signed on in Sweden relates to this individual trait, which also brings in technology where Swedes are early adopters[177]. To be social yet not too close is perfect for the shy Swedes who can fiddle with gadgets and talk shop or trash, without any commitment. Some immigrants find Swedes somewhat uncivilized or use them as a mirror to understand themselves. Brits who come to Sweden feel Mediterranean since their stiff upper lips become loose when compared to the Swedish dryness. Finns claim the opposite and find Swedish men too frivol, gay even, in their quick and emotional expressions.

The reluctance to stand out from a crowd, bleakness and to express strong values has lead ethnologist Karl-Olov Arnstberg and economist Mauricio Rojas to claim that the distinctive trait about Swedish culture is its denial of any national culture[178]. Swedes seem to believe that their own culture is so rational and normal that they do not see it at all as a national trait. Thus they expect everyone else to do the same and view their culture as most rational and at least normal. The extreme position of Sweden in the World Values Survey as the most self-expressive, rational and secular country in the world is invisible to Swedes. Yet the Swedish culture may be to have a bland yet rational and somewhat rural culture. This vagueness clashes with being the most self-expressive country in the world, if one by self-expression means to actually express something. But Swedes may have another stranger notion of self-expression, being

---

[176]   Arnstberg 1989, Herlitz, 2003, Daun 2005 and Arnstberg 2005. Daun views Swedes as northern Japanese and Japanese as Asian Swedes. Saunders 2010 explains the good human development indexes of Japan and Sweden coming from its similar cultures and histories rather than income redistribution and equalitarian policies, p. 118-122.

[177]   Swedes score highest Internet usage 2012 in the world according to the World Wide Web Index, http://thewebindex.org/

[178]   Arnstberg 1989 and Rojas 1993.

the right to be alone, blend in groups or silent in languor. Whatever hides behind these values, Swedes are extreme.

Swedes survive their rational and somewhat inhibited emotions with their certain rural and romantic kind of melancholia which is valued more positively as languor (vemod). By keeping silent and protecting feelings inside, Swedes may look bored or sad but may be content, just resting with a bittersweet and romantic feeling of being lost in urban and administered life. Sentimentality is close but the Swedish languor is valued for its deep roots. Troubadours, writers, filmmakers, music orchestras and actors keep dwelling on these sentiments that stay with Swedes even today with successful interpretations and expressions over centuries[179]. Yet languor is a price paid for these repressed emotions. Taken together with other mental disorders which will be explained below, the land of extremes suffers badly with little insight into its disease. The culture of languor, a diagnosed national panic syndrome, self-censorship, infantilisation and a sociologically defined spiral of silence all breed frustration, depression, anxiety, temporary outbursts of temper and inability to lead normal adult lives. National schizophrenia rules under visible patterns of everyday neurosis and mild hysteria. Being normal according to Swedish standards yet knowing these standards to be extreme give rise to parallel values, views and ways of living and lying. Staying normal in Sweden demands oneself to stay extreme.

Qaisar Mahmood, born in Pakistan but raised in Sweden and a well-placed government officer, travelled around Sweden on motorbike to find traces of a distinctive Swedish culture with little success. Sweden is like an onion with layers and layers and no inner core was his conclusion which is similar to what Arnstberg and Rojas say, but has some unfortunate consequences as the multicultural left shun all definitions of Swedish cultural identity. The Swedish cultural left and supporters of

---

[179]   CM Bellman, August Strindberg, Greta Garbo, Ingrid Bergman, Ingmar Bergman, Evert Taube, Monica Zetterlund, Lars Gullin, Cornelius Vreeswijk, Blå Tåget, Ulf Lundell, Kebnekajse, Träd-Gräs-och Stenar, Kent, Sofia Nordenstam, Gunnel Mauritzson and many more including recent Nobel laurete Tomas Tranströmmer.

multiculturalism view his negative findings as victory and claim therefore that anyone who claim to be Swedish or define Sweden as a cultural or historical notion are implicitly xenophobic or even racist. This is
nonsense and not what Mahmood wanted to say, nor did Arnstberg and
Rojas. There are certain traits in Swedish life styles, culture and history
that define Sweden, among them being modest. That should not be taken
as a mere anything, but something with certain features including vagueness. "Bleakness is all", Christopher Hitchens wrote in a review of Stieg
Larsson's bestselling crime fiction *Millennium* trilogy:

> "If a Larsson character wants to show assent, he or she will
> 'nod'; if he or she wants to manifest distress, then it will usu-
> ally be by biting the lower lip. The passionate world of the
> sagas and the myths is a very long way away"[180].

American writer Susan Sontag spent seven months in Stockholm 1969
and wrote back a letter to the alternative, new left and hipster magazine
Ramparts in San Francisco, telling of her experiences in the cool socialist utopia. Even if four decades date her impressions, most of them
are still true. She viewed Swedes, including the so-called hipsters and
bohemians at the time, as being prudent and nice, expressing a child-
ish self-centeredness and always in tight self-control. The most severe
policing of aggression are done by each Swede himself. Silence is the
Swedish national virtue with strange exceptions. She noted that they

---

[180]   Hitchens 2011, p.402. Two other comments on Swedish boring1970s are by American literary theorist Stanley Fish who wrote a brilliant essay on "The unbearable
ugliness of Volvo" and the British punk rock/new wave music group The Stranglers
with the song *Sweden (all quiet on the Eastern Front)*: "Let me tell you about Sweden.
Only country where the clouds are interesting. Big brother says it's the place to gogo.
Too much time to think, too little to do (repeated). 'Cos it's all quiet on the Eastern
front. Fluctuations at a minimum. Hypochondriac tombstone. Sense of humour has
gone astray somewhere. Cumulus nimbus floats by.." The lyrics were created when
band member Hugh Alan Cornwell did his PhD 1975 in biochemistry at Lund university in southern Sweden, before he was charged with possession of illegal drugs
and did time at Pentonville prison.

always tell if they are going to the bathroom, and what they are going to do there. Being with people is like work for them and many complain of being tired of people and having to talk. Something a New Yorker like Susan Sontag simply did not understand and noted further that the city of Stockholm is the anti-thesis of a melting-pot. Drinking makes all the difference and young and old behave silly and wild, just the opposite of their behaviour before intoxication. "The Swedes want to be raped", she wrote reflecting on their sexual behaviour while drunk. She does not believe for a moment that social democracy or the welfare state is responsible for the profounder defects in the quality of Swedish life, but rather the rural traditions and lack of the self-confidence in human interactions. The Swedish shyness is almost pathological, Sontag sighed. Extremely shy. Yet she hung out with the most laid back flower power people and radicals in Stockholm 1969.

Another true story of Pär the Swede and Mauricio the Latino from 1978 will further explain the extreme Swedish modesty and honesty. Latin American economic historian Mauricio Rojas travelled with a Swedish friend to the UK, a few years after he had escaped Pinochet's Chile. In Sweden they had gone out for drinks and food together and split the bill, each paying for his due the Swedish way. Rojas told his friend Pär that now when they were going abroad, he would like to pay the bills as he had somewhat more cash and wanted to live more the Latin and European way. Pär agreed after some doubts and drank on the behalf of his friend at the English pubs. On the flight home however, Pär could not stand the pressure from his self- inflicted duty to relieve himself from any bounds to anyone, not even his friend Mauricio. Pär exclaimed that he owned him 150 Swedish crowns for all drinks and foods during the visit, as he has been counting every pint and fish n' chips. Mauricio had to take the money and learned how hard it is for a Swede to be dependent even on friends[181]. Or just normal.

Another view on Swedish values and culture comes from Nima Sanandaji, liberal writer with origins in Iran. The success of Sweden is not due

---

[181]   Rojas 2004.

to the welfare state Sanandaji asserts. Rather, it is the result of cultural and demographic factors, as well as a favourable business environment throughout most of Sweden's modern history. Three arguments support his analysis:

First, Sweden showed higher rates of growth and had a model society well before the start of the social democratic era in 1930s.

Second, descendants of Swedes who migrated to the North America in the 19th century are also today characterized by favourable social outcomes, despite not being supervised by a caring welfare state. This indicates that cultural factors such as Protestant and rural hard work ethics have played an important role in the success of Swedish society. Migrating Swedes were even more Christian and puritan.

Third, starting in the 1990s, Sweden has scaled back the size and scope of government services and welfare program, which was followed by a recovery of the earlier strong growth rate. The period characterized by the most extensive welfare state policies, around 1970–1995, is associated with low growth rates.

It is true that Sweden maintains a high standard of living, despite steep taxes, but at the same time, it is wrong to assume like center- left politicians and some economists do, that this proves no effects of high taxes on economy. Strong values are the foundations upon which the welfare state rests Sanandaji states. "Rather than being the cause of Sweden's social strengths, the high-tax welfare state might have been made possible by the hard-won Swedish stock of social capital"[182].

---

[182]   Sanandaji 2011, p. 24 and Sanandaji 2012. See also Bergh and Bjørnskov 2011. Saunders 2010, p. 122 states, "Like several generations of left-wing Utopians before them, Wilkinson and Pickett [authors of The Spirit Level] think that America or Britain could be made to look just like Sweden, if only the income distribution were changed. As Marx nearly said, change the economic arrangements and the rest will follow. But Sweden and Japan have the income distributions they have because of the kinds of societies they are. They are not cohesive societies because their incomes are

But the hard-earned trust, hard work ethics and civic participation that make up some of these social capital gains have been eroded. With the expanding welfare state, the number of Swedes who agreed to saying that claiming government benefits to which they are not entitled to is never justifiable shrunk from 81 % in 1981 to 61 % 2008[183]. A fourth of the polled Swedes had lost the traditional Swedish beliefs in honesty and duty, if the survey was to be taken seriously. Trust takes centuries to build and a decade to erode. The many socialist scandals have led to distrust since socialists themselves portray themselves as better and on higher moral grounds than ordinary sinful Swedes.

Hardworking, trustworthy and silent Swedes expect able fellow citizens to contribute as universal welfare state services cannot carry many free riders. The welfare system is for all without distinction. In other selective welfare schemes, recipients are investigated and questioned[184]. But not all Swedes are trustworthy.

SECURITY ADDICTS AND WELFARE ART TRICKSTERS

With eroding trust, free riders and helpless people become frequent. Phenomena such as welfare art tricksters emerge. Psychiatrist David Eberhard has many reports from his inner city clinic and has written books about what he calls the particularly Swedish system of so-called security addicts in a country with a severe mental disorder as nation. His diagnosis of Sweden as a mental patient is based on the psychiatric disorder called panic syndrome. Being afraid of normal hardships, preferring to stay on benefits than to move or try a new job, not appreciating but rather devalue competition, even for small children, are all symptoms of Swedish helplessness, resulting in an extreme national panic syndrome. Swedes are also more anxious about inequalities in society than Amer-

---

equally distributed; their incomes are equally distributed because they are cohesive societies."

[183] Sanandaji 2011. p.19, adapted from World Values Survey. See also Lindbeck 2006 discussing moral hazards in Swedish welfare policies.

[184] Rothstein 2011a.

icans are, even though Sweden is among the most equal societies in the world and USA is not.

Eberhard has met many young men and women who come to the emergency room late at night, crying because their boyfriend or girlfriend had broken up or wanted a proof of sickness to stay off work. An extreme example but not rare. One night a 27 year old woman came to the emergency room, claiming to be put on sick leave. She had worked for six months as a waitress and was tired of drunken men, her back ached and she needed a rest. Her family was well but she wanted government services and doctors to fix her problems. Dr. Eberhard said **no** and told about her story along with the other hundred such stories in his books about the security addicts[185]. By not learning to cope with normal situations, which may include some insecurities, Swedes deem themselves to depression, stagnation and in need of total security. Every small discomfort must be ruled out, cured or banned. He has for instance criticized the idea of banning attending football matches for kids less than 15 years which a third of polled Swedes supported. Banning young teenagers on football arenas would keep them from being recruited by football hooligans. But not watching any football.

What happened next to Dr. Eberhard was beyond his imagination. Late one night in 2009 police was called to a bridge where Anna Odell, a young woman, was trying to jump to commit suicide. The police officers took her into their van after some fighting where she violently protested against their care. At Dr. Eberhard's emergency clinic she continued to try to break away, spat and fought and was finally put to rest with sedation and strong belts around her arms and legs. Odell then revealed

---

[185]   Eberhard 2009, p. 60. See also Erixon 1999, Eberhard 2006 and Heberlein 2008. Another psychiatrist with similar experiences and views, William Dalrymple, notes "For most of the British population today, the notion that people could solve many of the problems of society without governmental *Gleichschaltung*, the Nazi term for overall coordination, is completely alien", 2008, p. 121. Lindbeck 2003 shows that 40 % of Swedes accept staying home on sick leave without being ill, but because the work is tough or if one has family problems. See also Engellau and Rossander 2004.

that she was not suicidal at all but an art student. The attempt, police custody and emergency psychiatric treatment were all parts in her final graduation thesis at the University College of Arts, Crafts and Design of Stockholm, a government institution. The art project and her academic thesis was called Unknown woman 2009-349701 (Okänd, kvinna 2009-349701) which was her reference number at the hospital records. Health services and police forces were used in order for her to show what she called hidden power structures and victimization of mental patients. The police, hospital staff and Dr. Eberhard were furious and said that they tried to help her and save her life. Putting violent and self-destructive patients to sleep is rarely used but sometimes necessary. The intentions were no other than to treat her like any other desperate suicidal person, but that did not get across. The cultural left and most of state media defended her as well as her government-run art school which hailed her as an icon of breaking into new frontiers of concept art and provocations. She was eventually sentenced to pay $1400 which her teachers collected in her support. Extreme support from government funded art college teachers[186].

A similar welfare art trickster was graffiti artist Magnus Gustavsson (tag name NUG) that a few months after the fake mental breakdown art project revealed his thesis from the same University College of Arts. In the 2 min video "Territorial pissing", he is shown breaking a window of a

---

[186] For a valuable theoretical critique of artistic nonsense disguised as provocation, see Stjernfelt and Thomsen 2007. Combining art, politics, mental illness and crime was not new for the cultural left and radical therapists. In 1999 playwright Lars Norén involved three hard criminals while in prison to participate in a play at National Travelling Theatre, a socialist popular movement supported with government funding. Their contribution while rehearsing a play on repressive legislation for prisoners, resulted mostly in yelling racist remarks to the actors and everyone else. The criminals who were out of prison at the time and under surveillance managed to get away from the theatre. While away they robbed a bank and killed two police officers. One of the murderers, Tony Olsson, escaped later in 2004 to Costa Rica and so did several other extremely dangerous criminals same year from the most secure prisons in Sweden. Socialist minister of justice Thomas Bodström did not resign.

metro train, spraying paint all over while scared travellers watch him run around with cans and then leave. The metro train office tried to have him arrested and sentenced as cleaning trains afterwards had cost them around $10 000 but in vain. Same spring in 2009 art student Yonas Millares sprayed the marble statues of the University College of Arts entrance as his thesis, incidentally also a protest, but this time against the white male middle class repression in Latin America. Yonas Millares comes from Chile where such statues are symbols of repression he argued, but this time the art college refused his thesis, dismissed references to Latin America and demanded him to pay for restoring the sculptures.

CLIENTELISM AND VICTIMIZATION

Being victimized or feeling hurt due to discrimination is a common phenomenon among dissatisfied members in many welfare states but is taken to its extreme in Sweden. Court cases abound with trivial problems or sometimes real social issues but twisted, where a claimant is looking for a reward[187]. Religion but also ethnicity, food, clothing, attitudes and sexual orientation including transgender identity discrimination of toddlers in nurseries, are all legal grounds for discrimination. Laws give rights to anyone feeling hurt or discriminated to try for money. Such as wanting to try for $10 000 (attending an introduction meeting at a cooking course with pork and not shaking hands with prospective employer) or $2 000 (a lesbian couple referred to another hospital clinic specialized in same sex fertility treatment)[188]. The Swedish Ombudsman of Discrimination Agency states that it is the feelings of victims that are grounds for discrimination. Thus, the accused so-called discriminator has the burden of proof, a procedure more common in totalitarian states.

---

[187]　　Schultz 2008

[188]　　Diskrimineringsombudsmannen. 2011 and Arbetsförmedlingen 2012. In 2007 the Discrimination Ombudsman lost a case defending the rights of a female Muslim dentist not to wear short sleeves at work, a hygiene routine at most hospitals and dental clinics. The Ombudsman contested this routine and urged health care management to arrange for working conditions where this effort to prevent contamination was not necessary, but failed.

Demands from citizens in soft welfare states like Sweden give rise to expectations that when not fulfilled can lead to much frustration. The last decades of cutbacks in public services and introduction of market mechanisms in the public sector have led to resistance from angry parents, patients, youth and people on social benefits. The number of medical staff, policemen, teachers, judges, social workers, politicians and social insurance officers threatened with violence from angry welfare recipients have risen. The staff at Social Insurance Agency (Försäkringskassan) have reacted to threats from dismissed welfare clients by blaming government cutbacks and demanded that the cutbacks should stop since they as staff have to take the heat. These social welfare staff was used to administering rights to sick-leave and early retirement mostly by handing out what people asked for, but has lately had to say no. Earlier socialist governments had used the social security system to hide unemployment, but from mid 1990s under Göran Persson and with stronger force under moderate Fredrik Reinfeldt, the recipients of benefits were much harder scrutinized. Clients of the Social Insurance Agency had been on sick-leave for years without seeing doctors or having to prove their possible inability to work until Reinfeldt and the two social ministers Ulf Kristersson and Göran Hägglund reformed the failing system. But the recipients fight back supported by the socialist, left and green party busy-bodies.

Stones thrown at buses, ambulances, police cars and fire engines in immigrant dominated suburbs since 2000 have been excused by left leaning social scientists, activists and journalists (called group C below) as caused by racism, repression and marginalization. It is logical if the welfare state promises to do everything for its citizens, but does not deliver that welfare recipients react with the few weapons they have. Being penniless without jobs there are not much else to do. Some people on long term sick leave threatened with suicide attempts launched blogs, media sensations and actions to defend their rights to support. Much hard work is done by such disease struck activists who viewed themselves incapable of working at all. If the structures are to blame, fight the representatives of Swedish state, e.g. social workers, doctors, teachers, who are middle class anyway and supposed to be kind and nice. If the state can do everything for you it can also take away everything. By having few resources on their own like strong family ties, savings or defence from a robust civil society, Swedes are logically victims of their own struggle for total security and trust in government rather in themselves.

The extreme extent to which Swedish media and left politicians could feel sympathy for perpetrators as victims, not the actual women and men assaulted, happens all the time, but two events stand out. In 1994, three young men tried to enter a night club at fashionable Stureplan in Stockholm but were rejected. They wanted to get back at the security guards at the club and went home to get a machine gun which killed three people. One of the killers, Marquez Jara, had Latin American origins, a harsh life while raised in Sweden and was deliberately excused by some leftist media and anti-racist activists, claiming that his hard upbringing as marginalized youth had led to his violent actions. Left wing singer-song writer Michael Wiehe wrote a song about Marquez Jara, asking listeners to understand "how much it takes before it is too late" to protest like Jara did with his gun. The album sold 15 000 CDs immediately in 2000[189].

In 2000, a young Swedish girl was gang raped in a garage in the Stockholm suburb Rissne by seven young men of foreign descent. Instead of focusing on the raped girl, some left leaning media and anti-racist activists blamed the background and hardships of the rapists causing the horrible act. In the end what had caused the gang rape were not these young men, but the Swedish welfare society that had not given them their rights due to racist discrimination they claimed. In fact the opposite was true. These raping immigrants had been influenced by an anti-Swedish racism that devalue Swedish young women and define them as easy sexual targets, Swedish whores (svennehoror)[190]. In the press after the gang rape, many immigrants were ashamed of the actions and other young immigrant men who even afterwards claimed that raping Swedes was

---

[189]   Weihe's earlier songs in 1973 about the communist martyr and Chilean singer- song writer Victor Jara lead people to believe that he was related to the murderer Guillermo Marquez Jara. Victor used music however, not machine guns, to defend himself.

[190]   Bäckman 2009

more acceptable than immigrant girls. Nevertheless, the rapists were sentenced and lax left media had trouble explaining their stand to socialist minister Ulrika Messing, who finally intervened on behalf of the real victim, the girl.

Being a recipient of Swedish social welfare benefits is by comparable standards not difficult and some stay on welfare for many years. Besides rights to basic goods, food, clothes, shoes and rent for two- bedroom apartments, a single person on social welfare will get support for television, telephone, newspapers and internet. The right to a fair (skälig) standard of living is ensuring that recipients are not living poor lives[191]. If a young woman lives with her parents and gets pregnant without having a steady relationship with the father or being married, she will get an apartment as there is strong support for independence. The man can stay in the background if she wants to as the government will pay his alimony if he does not. Neither of them has to take responsibility for their child's wellbeing and welcoming to the world. The social services in the major cities keep access to hard guarded apartments for such cases as is well known and much used since there is an immense lack of rented flats due to government rent control monopolies. With a baby, a single parent sidesteps all waiting lines and the child may be the only means to an apartment for decades.

Incentives to work are low as welfare to a family with many children gives more or the same as from two parents' salaries and often more than a family with one working parent. Some local social services tried to put pressure on the welfare recipients to make them accept work training 30 hours a week, but that was ruled illegal by National Board of Health and Welfare (Socialstyrelsen). *Nihil* rather than *quid pro quo*. A report to the

---

[191] Rivère 1998. See also Rivère subsequent writings online on welfare moral hazards. A woman in Strängnäs town with fear of other people and spaces (agoraphobia) needed the internet to be social and thus had huge electricity consumption. The local services rejected her demand but was overruled by court. Computer with internet connections are given by routine to families on welfare support in Eskilstuna town to make children keep up with school work, thus leaving parents with little incentives to accept work and pay for their computers.

center-right government itself supported the verdict and wanted to ban all possibilities demanding the 500 000 welfare clients to make themselves more eligible for work or training[192]. Workfare reforms of the kind Bill Clinton and Tony Blair introduced 1990s have not yet reached the Sweden. Such incentives exist, but are weak and leave recipients with the choice of not working.

MULTICULTURALISM AND IMMIGRATION

Sweden received many immigrants after 1945 that wanted to leave their war torn countries and were in demand from booming manufacturing industries. They became a part of working life and Swedish society. With no racial streaks from bounds to former colonies or imported slaves, Sweden seemed like a hospitable country with a homogenous but quite bland population. Boredom, cold winters and small language were manageable obstacles. Since the mid 1970s when borders were closed for migrant workers, Sweden has received mainly refugees from countries in internal conflicts, dictatorships or victims of catastrophes. Some refugees were more motivated by social and economic reasons to enter Sweden, than political, but questions were few, especially during the Balkan crisis 1992-1995, Somalia 1991- , Iraq and Afghanistan wars 2003 and many other regions in disorder or chaos (Middle East, north and central Africa and Latin America).

Lack of strict regulations from government and social authorities to push immigrants to provide for their own livelihood has led to harsh living conditions in certain suburbs around the major cities, lower employment

---

[192]   SOU 2011. Bilaga 11. " I [Eva Mörk] think that is necessary to remove the clause in the Social Services Act, which gives municipalities the right to make demands on recipients (4 § 4 of the Social Services Act)." Minister of integration Erik Ullenhag wants harder demands on recipients, especially newly arrived immigrants, who when been given residence permit can have 3-4 years financial support from parental leave funds if they arrive with 3 children. Each child yields 1,5 years and with a universal welfare policy, there are no exceptions, even if the arriving recipients have not contributed a single day with work and taxes to the social security system.

rates, parallel cultures to the Swedish and a division in society between the native Swedes and the newly arrived. With seven years on average for a male immigrant to provide for his or her own living, restlessness stir from both immigrants not feeling accepted and Swedes paying for their livelihood.

Outspoken racism is rare but exists in small white supremacist groups, usually disgruntled young males in rural areas. The Sweden Democrats party are often portrayed as racist but are more of a traditionally nationalist nostalgic party similar to True Finns with 20 % in Finland, Fremskrittspartiet with 23 % in Norway and Dansk Folkeparti 12 % in Denmark. In the 2010 election, the Sweden democrats entered parliament for the first time as the 6th largest party (of 8) with 5.7 %. The lack of a representation of nationalist parties before 2010 is due to the well organised socialist working class structures absorbing all opposition. The anxiety of media and establishment to acknowledge any problems with immigration backfired in 2010, when the Sweden democrats could portray themselves as martyrs of Swedish political correctness and gain votes, especially from traditional workers living in areas with many immigrants, where few journalists would enter voluntarily, not to speak of living there.

Liberal party Folkpartiet gained many votes in 2002 by arguing that a language test should be a requirement for citizenship. Sweden is unique (along with a few Western nations) in having no demands at all, besides living for four years and being reasonably non-criminal. But ruling Folkpartiet ministers have not dared to bring its own 2002 idea to parliament due to its unpopularity in the left leaning media and self-proclaimed anti-racist leagues. The party gave anti-Islamist Somali-Dutch activist Ayaan Hirsi Ali its Demokratipris in 2005, but has since turned away from any views that could endanger the anxious party priggish stand on immigration. Islamophobia is the word used when racism is not applicable to any proposal that can be interpreted as sign of racism. A view of native Swedes as intrinsically racist has become an accepted point of view, when two other disrespectful racist views are probably more prevalent. Primary view, one ethnic immigrant group negative to another immigrant group and second, immigrants turning negative towards Swedes (as the gang rapists did and their backers). Few Swedes dare to speak openly outside small groups they trust about this, but some books exist outside mainstream media[193].

Immigrants are often more outspoken, also about their fellow faulty countrymen and can discuss what goes on around them without fearing harassment, censorship or censoring themselves. Swedes are starting to understand what a laughing stock they have become among immigrants but usually keep quiet. Journalists who have a job to write about these kinds of events and issues, such as illegal immigration, welfare frauds, plans for terrorism or criminal immigrants, do not do their work well. Stories and actual documents from illegal or dubious immigration cases at the Migration Board are available in print on the 466 pages collected by writer and migration activist Merit Wager and online everywhere except in print, television or radio. Each story would be possible to cover respectfully with regard to ethical guidelines by Union of Swedish Journalists. Readers would get useful information, politicians would discuss policies and an open debate would follow. Or a media hunt. Journalist Jan Guillou tried already in 1980s to present Romani gypsies living in Sweden as true as he could do, which is quite well since he disclosed the Swedish intelligence service IB in 1973 and served one year in prison for doing it. Even his sober presentation was interpreted as implicitly racist[194].

---

[193]   Karaveli 1997, Arnstberg 1998, Björkman et al 2006, Arnstberg 2008, Eriksson and Rennerfeldt 2009, Caesar 2010a and 2010b, Wager 2011, Arnstberg and Sandelin 2013. Wager's book contain reports from civil servants at the Migration Board who want illegalities, irregularities and mistakes to be known but dare not blow the whistle, thus all of them are anonymous. A pattern repeated since Huntford 1971 interviewed high placed government officials anonymously.

[194]   Guillou 2010. Being an independent minded and hardworking journalist and former Maoist, now still left of the left party, he does not care much for feminism or silly mulitculturalism but defends working class values, harassed immigrants and personal integrity. Together with other independent socialist writers Leif GW Persson and Jan Myrdal, he has much influence in contemporary debates. Mostly for the better. Persson always, Myrdal rarely.

Given the Swedish tradition of being silent, doing what is right and being kind and nice to people in dire circumstances, it is no hard guess that many Swedish authorities were and still are taken for a ride by clever immigrants of all kinds. Or not so clever as the Chilean travel agency in Valpariso which sold the same four stories named A B C D along with a single ticket to Stockholm in the 1980s. The so called political refugees from the Chilean dictatorship were regular criminals, acquitted from prisons by general Pinochet just like President Fidel Castro had done with the reality behind the film character Tony Montana of *Scarface* and his compañeros about the same time. Same shady mechanisms would work in transition to Sweden involving fake passports and ages, smugglers, making up stories and identities along the way. Many refugees that has come the last 30 years are hard-working and honest people who had to leave their countries with more or less decent reasons according to international conventions in Geneva or to amendments due to humanitarian, subsidiary protection or otherwise in need of protection. But migration policies are not an exact science. Norway and Finland who have signed exactly the same conventions and protocols allow much less immigrants into their countries.

Contrary to official statistics, a fourth of accepted refugees have by UN, EU or domestic legal agreements right to stay, the rest do not. 96 % of all asylum seekers do not carry passports so the frustration of civil servants at the Migration Board and among police officers is boiling[195]. Receiving 100 000 people a year in a country of 9 million, Sweden is given high ratings and praise from UNHCR and EU. 20 % of residents in Sweden have now foreign background. The costs of immigration are around $7- 14 billion due to higher unemployment, retraining many without education and higher expenses. The argument that sparsely populated and aging Sweden needs more people does not hold as the immigrants get old too and work less than as much as the Swedes do. Only a huge rise (15 %) of more employed immigrants would make Sweden break even in costs and benefits, which is less likely to happen and though utopian official policy,

---

[195]   Sandelin 2011.

seldom discussed sensibly even by economists[196].

Why Sweden must receive twice as many immigrants than Norway and Denmark is usually answered that Sweden has to be more open. But if the majority of the refugees do not have legal right to stay or a workplace waiting, why must Sweden accept them? With a view of Sweden as an exceptionally decent country, a world champion in morals, it follows logically from the preceding chapters that Sweden must do what no one else does because it is the best alternative. Calculations of resources spent on housing, livelihood, education, administration and security in receiving immigrants give that resources spent in neighbouring countries (Kenya, Pakistan, Turkey etc.) are many more times effective. But even these conclusions are brushed away as implicit racism as much else. With few frank and open discussions, strange discussions start online and racism grows. Real racism, not the kind directed to minister of culture Lena Adelsohn-Liljeroth, who accidentally cut a cake consisting of a black naked woman with the black artist Makode Linde laying under the serving table screaming in spring 2012, causing world attention and critique. The Museum of Modern Art in Stockholm had invited her and led her to the table with no intention to make an implicitly racist scene nor did she know what was happening when someone gave her a cake knife. Yet the Afro- Swedish Association blamed her as racist since she was cutting up a black woman and between the legs. The issue blew all over the world and the mad connection of the cake with female genital mutilation was forgotten. Artist Makode Linde was not forgotten and his sensation gave a boost to his art sales. Minister Adelsohn- Liljeroth apologized. If this welfare art trick is racist, there are no words left for the real thing.

The tradition of exceptional Swedish openness in spite of even Swedish evidence to the contrary has a recent history. During the Balkan crisis summer of 1992, more than 30 000 people entered from Kosovo, the Albanian part of the failing Yugoslavian state. A few percent of them had legal status but the majority was out of work due to conflicts in other parts of Yugoslavia and in Switzerland. The minister in charge, liberal Birgit

---

[196]   Tullberg 2011.

Friggebo, did not act but told the Migration Board, who were putting up tents when renting expensive hotels was not enough, to do the necessary. Diplomatic and UNHCR reports confirmed that the leaving Kosovo Albanians were better cared for where they were and faced unemployment rather than political repression, but to no avail. The socialists who had closed borders to some extent while in charge in 1989 brought Integration Minister Friggebo, Prime Minister Carl Bildt and head Christina Rogestam of Migration Board to the Constitutional Court at Swedish parliament. Bildt was ruled as "not able to fail critique"[197].

This was the last time the socialists criticized their center-right opponents for being too open with immigration policies. Following decades, socialists would compete with left wing party, green party and liberals in being most open to immigration. The minority cabinet of Fredrik Reinfeldt does not have majority in parliament after the 2010 election and has been forced to seek support from the green environmentalist party. In exchange for support, the greens have gained acceptance for receiving around 15 000 Somalis without legal documents, no restrictions of proofs of identity and support for free hospital treatment to immigrants residing in Sweden illegally, that is people residing there after their cases have been rejected in asylum or other courts and with a verdict to leave the country immediately.

Further, fears of terrorist attacks have grown since Sweden became a target for Islamist terror. It was not always so. Osama Bin Ladin actually mentioned Sweden in November 2004 around the George W. Bush re-election campaign. Bin Ladin explained in a grainy video why Al-Qaeda "attacks USA and not Sweden for example". Another leading Al-Qaeda ideologue, Al- Abu Mus'ab al-Suri, supported also the Scandinavian countries due to their lax security and generous welfare systems[198]. Since then much has happened which has lead Al-Qaeda to put Sweden as No.

---

[197] Sveriges Riksdag. *Konstitutionsutskottets Granskningsbetänkande*, 1992/93. KU: 30. Del 1, p.104. See also Björkman et al 2006, p.66-73.

[198] In Sandelin 2012, p.39

1 enemy in their glossy terror magazine *Inspire*, summer issue 2010.[199] The enemy Sweden sent forces to Afghanistan under NATO and UN supervision and the artist Lars Wilks had portrayed the prophet Muhammed as a dog. These actions resulted in two aborted terror attacks, one in Sweden and one in Denmark but done by Swedes or residents of North African and Middle Eastern origins.

10 December 2010, Taimour Abdulwahab al-Abdaly accidentally blew himself up instead of his target, Christmas shoppers by a pedestrian street in central Stockholm. He sent messages to media and police before the fatal incident, mentioning Swedish troops in Afghanistan and the artist Wilks and called "all Mujahedin in Europe and Sweden" to follow his fight. 19 days later on December 29, 2010, five men of Middle Eastern and North African origins were caught in Copenhagen by Danish and Swedish secret police before they could execute their plan. They had prepared to kill journalists and others at the Danish daily *Jyllands-Posten* that five years before had published cartoons of the prophet Muhammed, which had ignited more than 100 deaths and violent storming of Danish embassies in Muslim countries. Four of the terrorists reside in Sweden and three are Swedish citizens. An attack was also aborted in Bosnia in 2005 where Misrad Bektasevic, a jihadist Swede of Balkan descent, almost succeeded to blow up a bomb in central Sarajevo in collaboration with the real Al-Qaeda network. Artist Lars Wilks has had several attempts on his life, been attacked twice at universities (Karlstad, Uppsala) and at his residence including arson. Then in July 2011, white supremacist counter-jihadist Anders Behring Breivik killed 8 government employees in central Oslo, Norway and 69 youngsters at Utøya Island from the socialist Workers' Youth League. The three aborted jihadist attacks would not even combined have ended in so many casualties.

Keeping these attacks in mind and many other incidents where immigrants were victims or perpetrators, falsely using Swedish welfare and fooling migration authorities but also being under attacks from Sweden

---

[199]   Sandelin 2012. p.15.

democrats, has led to no possibility of a normal debate about immigration in Swedish parliament, municipal councils and certainly not in the press. There have been small streaks of racism before World War II, but since 1945 Sweden has made many efforts to keep all such concepts out of discussion about foreigners. The opposite view that Swedish racism has been severely overestimated is rather true. Tendencies in mainstream media and policy discussions accuse normal native Swedes of racism and find racist structures in government, labour market, culture, health and schools. Insisting on respect for cultural traditions from other mostly Muslim countries, such as separate times for men and women at public baths, divided classrooms according to gender or carrying of female dresses of niquab and burqua while in school or work, divide Swedes and immigrants into unfortunate groups blaming each other for racism in a cacophony seldom heard in public debate before.

The very idea of being Swedish versus of immigrant origins, has turned many discussions sour, as some vocal defenders of multiculturalism want to have it both ways - respect for identity of people born abroad or with foreign parents and respect for their Swedishness. Even the word *immigrant* is not used much as it may exclude or harass people who have been born in Sweden but look foreign. There are fuzzy lines if one goes beyond the mere fact of Swedish citizenship as what counts as Swedish, but people calling themselves Swedish and some others immigrants are not inherently racist. Reference to Swedish culture, Sweden as nation and Swedes are ridiculed, mostly by priggish Swedish journalists and grounds for victimization, hurt feelings and claims of rewards. A state television reporter was surprised in 2009 when musicians played the national anthem and asked whether the song might not be viewed politically right-wing and nationalist. The Swedish flag has been center of similar bans as schools have asked pupils not to wear t-shirts or wave the yellow and blue flag as it could be interpreted as racist. The only ones who wave the flag and celebrate the national holiday with pride are immigrants who are happy to be in a free and decent country. Unlike in 1930s when nationalism went right in Europe under Mussolini and Hitler, but left in Sweden, the socialists have abandoned any affirmation of nationalism as at worst racist, or at best parochial. Per Albin Hansson was able to transform feelings of patriotism using the neologism folkhemmet cleverly and turning Swedish social democracy into an exception[200]. Contemporary left leaning leader shun all such references in favour of EU and globalism, thus losing all patriotism to the nationalist party Sweden democrats.

The situation of identifying criminal immigrants can be labelled racist. Lund University had problems of theft in 2010 and a security officer sent out a mail to staff at computer labs to look out for people with Indian or Asian features. Soon the mail was reported to the university bureau of discrimination and media and had to be rephrased so no one could identify any thieves. Stockholm police office published a report on heroin peddling and found out that many Gambians were involved. Whether this was true or not was not analyzed, but the mentioning of this particular immigrant group was and the report was labelled racist. The last extreme story comes from the commercial television network TV3. In their talk show on wanted criminals, a clip from a surveillance camera was shown of man with non-Swedish features robbing a store, but with his face mostly blurred with a white square. A police asked viewers if they could identify this man and the studio host repeated the message, "If you recognize this man, please call this number". Faces of Swedish criminals are shown though. Stories like these make people frustrated and distrustful of media and establishment. Doctors protest against proposals from Migration Board on medical examinations of young people who claim to be minors under 18 years and entering easily. The doctors believe such measurements of skeleton and teeth examination are racist. Et ad infinitum.

Most immigrants find these discussions futile while some other vocal immigrants (Group D below) defend normal and universal values among Swedes and other civilizations. They defend Swedes against attacks from other immigrants (Group C below) with their agenda of multiculturalism, often aligned with radical leftism and feminism[201].

---

[200]   Berman 2006.

[201]   A potent mixture where the attackers' respect for religious and cultural patriarchy lead to tolerance for misogyny, as in debates over honorary killings where the mentioning of the concept of honour being related to feudal traditions in East Africa and

Intersectionality is the latest PoMo/PC buzzword but may have gone stale already. These self-proclaimed anti-racist attackers who are researchers, activists and media people are mostly funded by the Swedish government and act as spokespeople for all immigrants, telling them that Swedes do not like them, want them to leave and keep all jobs to native Swedes. In that way, they claim Swedes to be racist and themselves to be on the anti-racist side, but the opposite is sometimes true. Sociology professor Masoud Kamali of Iranian descent and his subordinates pushed out other researchers from the 2004 parliamentary commission on integration because they were native Swedes and thus by default could not do research on structural racism in Sweden, a fact that was taken for granted by Kamali but not by other social scientists[202]. Socialist minister of integration Mona Sahlin obeyed his call for absolute powers over the commission, enrolled almost only of immigrant scholars and dismissed the Swedish professors.

Sadly the idea of Sweden as a racist country prevails within the left, socialist, green and in multicultural advocacy groups with the result that some easily fooled immigrants give up hopes of being integrated and start hating Swedes. A change in labour policy that may give work to

---

Middle East immediately lead to accusations of racism. It took at least three lives of young people (Fadime Sandahl, Pela Atroshi and Abbas Rezai) and ten years until these traditional views could be discussed somewhat sensibly by Swedish politicians, researchers and journalists. Sweden has around two known honorary killings per year. Discussions on the merits of receiving immigrants that kill their own family members are heated and calling participants racist for discussing horrific traditions among immigrants rise the temperature to boiling point. Same mechanisms apply to debates on female genital mutilation, halal meat in schools, sharia law, Swedish identity, forced marriages and ethnic strife. Given the Swedish insistence on being kind and nice to all, especially downtrodden strangers, many native Swedes feel uncomfortable when facts are presented and conclusions drawn that imply stricter rules also for immigrants. See Rothstein 2006b for lack of constitutionally based social cohesion in multicultural Sweden and Johansson Heinö 2011 for overview of Swedish immigration debate.

[202] Borg 2006.

jobless immigrants is attacked for being inherently racist. No jobs are better than low wages the multiculturalists argue. The left wants to have even stricter rules for employers who now have to make diversity plans each year for ethnic and gender equality. Still the labour market is over-regulated and Swedish employers behave very well in hiring people of non-Swedish origins[203]. But being dragged to court because you asked a prospective employee to shake your hand and fined $10 000 for doing so do not make employers happier to hire strangers. This happened to an employer who had a female manager that was rejected by a Muslim trainee who preferred to hold his had close to his heart as Muslims do in Muslims countries[204]. She was fined for asking.

Most immigrants do not care about such nonsense and they are luckily in majority. A simple and imprecise but useful way to understand the field of discourses on migration and integration is to divide all immigrants residing in Sweden into four groups:

A – Overwhelming majority of honest, working or work searching immigrants

B – Disloyal minority, violent, trouble makers, fraudulent behaviour, criminal[205]

---

[203]   Zaremba 2006, Rezania 2007, von Bahr 2011 and von Bahr 2012. In her latest report, von Bahr shows that Swedish employers are less likely to prefer hiring their own citizens than employers in Denmark, Norway, Canada and Germany.

[204]   Diskrimineringsombudsmannan 2010.

[205]   According to BRÅ 2005, the national Crime Prevention Agency, immigrants are twice as often sentenced. The 2005 report is for 1997-2001 and the agency has not done same report after the large immigrations from Iraq, Afghanistan and Somalia since. In spring 2013 Group B made riots in Husby suburb by Stockholm and in other cities, defended by Group C and criticized by Group D, much to the embarrassment of their parents, Group A. Similar predictive media and activist relationships occurred about the same time 2013 when police tried to nab illegal immigrants in the subway when travelling without tickets. Even the immigration minister did not back the law enforcement and the much hailed writer Jonas Hassen Khemiri vitnessed in *New York Times* about the horrible treatment he had experienced in racist and xeno-

C– Self chosen spokesmen for all immigrants, multicultural and self- proclaimed "anti-racist"

D – Immigrants that insist on universal rights and duties for all, yet proud of their foreign origins

A do not care much for C, who are defending B against A and D. Neither does A care much for D, but they are very concerned over B, their mostly younger family members who attack Swedes or other immigrants, throw stones at policemen and behave badly in school. Some of B also are on welfare while working illegally somewhere, but that is a tricky area as there are some in A who are proud workers too, even if illegally. The possibility of someone from D starting a discussion about how badly B behaves may lead C to appeal to Godwin's law and replace Hitler with Breivik and then the discussion and sanity ends. Godwin's law states that anyone that can relate any political discussion to Adolf Hitler by using the trick of guilt by association has won. It is a joke abroad and online but reality in Sweden. Months after the horrible Norwegian tragedy, any sensible discussion about problems around immigration lead C to attack D and all Swedes for implying support for Breivik and thus the meek Swedish journalists were silenced. As a result of silenced discussions on problems with immigration in the left leaning media, Swedes have highest distrust of media reporting on immigration in EU. 60 % of all polled Swedes do not think they get reliable information from media compared to the average 40 % in EU[206].

Group D exists and does not form a homogenous group of journalists and intellectuals, but they are usually in favour of universal human rights and respect for individuals, against silly forms of multiculturalism and soft headed arguments[207]. When Swedes back down and do not take a

---

phobic Sweden. Alas.

[206] European Commission 2011.

[207] Nima and Tino Sanandaji, Harry Schein, Tomas Gür, Nima Dervish, Nyamko Sabuni, Maciej Zaremba, Dilsa Demirbag-Sten, Merit Wager, Bhareh Andersson, Mauricio Rojas, Hanif Bali, Alice Teodorescu, Boris Benulic, Sakine Madon, Arhe Hamednaca, Jasenko Selimovic and Sara Mohammed among others, and globally, for example Salman Rushdie and Kenan Malik. This group D and the anonymous

fight, they defend Sweden, civic humanism and same rights and duties for all. Sometimes they are called racists, home niggers (husnegrer), Oreo cookies (brown outsides, white insides) Uncle Toms and islamophobes by C. Group A and B exist but not in media. The vast majority of vocal immigrants either working in media or as activists/ politicians belong to C and are too many to mention. They have vast support in state television and radio, in academia and in the cultural pages of all newspapers including them with liberal- conservative editorial pages. Swedish radical academics and journalists use group C as an alibi for their identity politics and hip radicalism, much like Palme and his generation used fighters in the anti-colonial struggles in Asia, Latin America and Africa, to make them feel the heat and strife of hardships for a while. On an American scale, the Swedish group C stand for old identity political multicultural world of Jesse Jackson, while group D is more with Barack Obama, who told black teenagers to study hard and their parents to shape up.

The cultural left and nationalists have more in common than they know. The cultural left is repressing every dissent by using the most Swedish of traits in public discourse, conformism. The nationalists want Sweden to live up to its cultural heritage which include conformism. By insisting that everyone should share the ideals of multiculturalism (and a certain kind of feminism, share their income with others through high taxes, wear helmets when biking etc.) and keep quiet about problems related to large immigration, the left is being utmost Swedish. The more conservative Sweden democrats have found a secret ally in the public debate as they openly declare nostalgia for the 1930s Swedish socialist folkhem conformism and consensus seeking ideology. Besides conformism, the Sweden democrats defend economic protectionism which parts of the illiberal left does too. What distinguishes them is immigration.

Immigration to Sweden is hailed by the UN but that praise is for the legislation, not for the reality which is another game. It takes as mentioned on average seven years for male immigrants to land a job. Sweden receives

---

group A will be part of making Sweden normal and actually save the nation along with more sane, hardworking and aspiring immigrants.

more immigrants than similar countries. Laws for entering and staying are very lax, but firm to adhere to international conventions when immigrants have committed a crime, their application for residence permit has been rejected or they have unclear national status. Sweden keeps sentenced criminals who have done their time in prison because no country wants them back, especially people coming from Africa and Middle East. Still Swedes have high acceptance for new cultures and want to keep borders as open as possible, polls show. But acceptance is not enough. The combination of large immigration and lax legislation is problematic and will not be solved until all facts are on the table and open for discussion. Every sixth inhabitant in Sweden has foreign roots, some of them negative to more influx of immigrants, some accepting. Socialists have usually strong support in the immigrant population, but that has started to change, which also happened to workers who left collectivism and socialism for middle-of-the-road parties or more right leaning parties in 1976, 1991, 2006 and 2010.

CULTURAL LEFT, LEFT MEDIA

What has been said above about cowardly Swedes and some brave immigrants is a product of the domineering left wing discourse in media, education and government policy. Historically, socialism, and subsequent socializing structural explanations, has been a tremendous success in media and state propaganda since the post war period. Very few intellectuals opposed the hegemony 1950-1960s under Prime Minister Erlander, apart from Vilhelm Moberg and Sven Rydenfelt. But by 1980 the time was ripe for a debate on the dominance of leftist culture and media. Four writers, Sven Fagerberg, Sven Delblanc, Lars Gustafsson and Jan Myrdal, attacked the middle class left leaning media establishment as being not only corrupt but also a new semi-totalitarian power. The last three had been or were at the time socialists themselves, but the analysis went far beyond politics. The dominance from the social democratic party, corporatism and loyal journalists had led Swedes to depend of welfare systems and absence of free thought, the angry writers argued and faced massive accusations of being reactionary[208]. Gustafsson left for Austin, Texas and Delblanc packed his suitcase for Copenhagen but changed his mind and wrote a dystopia of Swedish future, *I Moria land*.

Since then the phenomena of a leftist dominated media has cooperated with higher education and research, into something unlike anything similar in other open Western societies. The 1968 radicals which entered public sector, universities and media in the 1970s have been followed by younger successors, who take the Cultural Revolution further in all aspects, with no areas untouched by left leaning messages. Until 1970 journalists could defend established middle class values that were not socialist, but 30 years later they defend the socialist establishment against any critique. Examples could be the textbooks in primary education on foreign aid and books for adult immigrants learning Swedish that have strong partial views in favour of socialism[209]. According to polls made by Gothenburg University in 2011 but with same trends since 1980, journalists have sympathies for the green and left parties far beyond the average Swedish voters. 70 % versus 40 %. In 1999 and ten years after the Soviet Bloc fell, 31 % of Swedish journalists supported the ex-communist Left party (Vänsterpartiet) that had started in 1917, hailed Stalin and supported Soviet communism until 1989.

Today the green environmentalist party is overrepresented among media professionals. 12 % of average voters support the greens versus 41 % among journalists. At Swedish public radio and television more than a half of editorial staff supports the green party[210]. Few journalists dare go

---

[208]   Frenander 1999 and Norberg in Tribell ed. 2012. Enzensberger 1987, p.13, would give the four angry writers in 1980 credit in his writing two years later in 1982 later, noting that "It looks like the perennial managers of this [Swedish] culture, the social democrats, had successfully and completely realized a project that all other regimes, from theocracy to Bolshevikism already had wrecked, namely to domesticate the humans". Even the left criticized the new media left, in Hultén and Samuelsson 1983.

[209]   Andersson, Sanandaji and Segerfeldt 2006, Rojas 2007, Mattlar 2008, Braw 2009 and Segerfeldt 2012.

[210]   Asp 2012.

against the mainstream and those who do pay a price, sometimes even with threats to their lives but usually they get harassment, ridicule or neglect[211]. Factual debates are rare which is strange in a nation that prides itself of a pragmatic, rational and factual tradition of politics and policy making. Yet around migration, gender, drug use, child rearing, Swedish culture and alcohol etc., many journalists and intellectuals cannot keep cool. Political correctness has value no doubt as there are some values that should be cherished and some criticized, but in the Swedish establishment since 1980s, these areas have seldom been well understood and discussed with respect to facts and of people trying other perspectives than the ordinary Swedish extremes[212].

The large Swedish public sector dominated by 1968 rebels, domineering socialist culture, repressed middle class and lax welfare state together with the Swedish traditions of consensus and conformism were in the 1990s joined by another influential lines of thought and cultural trends. Postmodernism and political correctness came from the American cultural left, taking European trips over France to pick up post-structuralist philosophy, over Germany to grab critical theory and copy cultural studies in Britain. Journalists and activists (Group C is well represented) now quote Michel Foucault, Gilles Deleuze and Félix Guattari whom they may have read or not[213]. They feel rad-

---

[211]   Sandelin 2011, Sandelin 2012, Carlqvist 2012 and Per Gudmundsson all write bravely about immigration and Islamic terrorism in Sweden.

[212]   See Ellis 2000 for reasonable political correctness, Egonsson 2007 for valuable nuances, Boekhout van Solinge 1997 on Swedish drug policy seen from the Netherlands, and lack of factual debate on foreign aid Segerfeldt in SILC 2012. Kullbom and Landin (eds.) 1998 is sadly still applicable and Friedman (forthcoming) too.

[213]   If they had read all about these subversive yet brilliant and exciting thinkers, they would also find that Foucault supported Ayatollah Khomeini's Islamic revolution, Deleuze supported the German left wing terrorist group Baader-Meinhof gang and Guattari Italian left wing terrorist groups. All three extreme thinkers and activists can be studied at Södertörn University College. There is at least consistency in the left romanticization of left wing terrorism. In 2011 Swedish art and academic institutions (Konsthall C, IASPIS, Södertörn) invited former Palestinian hijacker Leila

ical in lecturing Swedes on their presumptive conservative behaviour when Muslim women's clothing are discussed or how certain names of food items are parts of intrinsic racism. Just like the 1968 rebels did in 1970s children programs on state television and with the same condescending tone.

What Susan Sontag called radical chic in 1965 has become staple food for all these young and not so young middle class radicals. Their fondness of queer politics, feminism, ecology, leftism, post-colonialism, norm critical discourses and multiculturalism is simply bewildering but true to the rise of a new radical middle class. In the US, this cultural left has long ago left connections with working class and middle class people, preferring identity politics, rainbow alliances and its own miniscule agenda, usually relevant to a minority of victims and their own self-congratulatory selves. Reproduction rights of transsexuals has led to a media hype 2011-2012 and the cultural left was outraged by legal experts pondering over the consequences of giving new legal identities to people changing sex, but not their genitals modified and their possible rights to have children. Principled discussion yes, but marginal to most people like most caus- es the cultural left drown themselves in and forget everyone else. The American pragmatic philosopher, former strong leftist and now social democrat Richard Rorty was quite concerned and pessimistic when I met him in 2001 and talked of how white working class men had few spokes- men that understood them[214].

FAMILY LIFE

Another unique sad feature of Swedish social policy is the legal right to

---

Khaled as lecturer and hailed her as a feminist violent heroine ("political icon", as Che Guevara). Support for Colombian terrorist guerrilla FARC, Lenin, Hizbollah, Holocaust denial, RAF/Baader-Meinhof nostalgia, anarchist group Reclaim the Street, Subcommandante Marcos and silence on jihadist terrorism is legio.

[214]　Sjunnesson 2002. Rorty was brought up in a Trotskist Communist family and joined later the Democratic Socialists of America, hoping to unite the Old and New Left and admired Sweden for its welfare ambitions. See Rorty 1998 and Lasch 1994.

take children from parents that are suspected to be maltreated by them. These actions of social services are needed when there are actual, real problems, but repressive when not and when applied to families not conforming to welfare institutions or routines. Former judge Brita Sundberg-Weitman saw many mishandled cases, children and court decisions and decided to write about them[215]. She investigated over 150 claimed cases from angry parents to the parliamentary ombudsman JO and found few legal grounds for taking children away. JO only checked the routines, not whether the cases seemed sound and neutral which also are reasons for JO act apart from mere administration. Instead JO always took the side of social authorities. Swedish parents have little power against social authorities as there are few ways to question their decisions.

Families wanting not to have their children in nursery or kindergarten are often suspect in the eyes of social authority[216]. Some, very few Swedish parents even keep their school children at home and start home schooling. The center-right coalition does not appreciate this exception and freedom of choice for parents. With a liberal government, freedom for parents has become even more restricted. A law in 2010 that practically forbids home schooling makes Sweden the only EU country besides Germany to ban parents that keep their children off schools. The German law is from 1938 as the Nazi party did not want anyone else to school the young. Groups of home schooling parents are leaving Sweden for Finland and other more tolerant nations. Fines of $30 000 have been imposed on a family with several children and social workers have told

---

[215]   Sundberg-Weitman 2008. See also Alopaeus 1983, Warnling – Nerep 1995 and Hammarberg 2011. The German magazine *Der Speigel* did a news story in 1983 that spoke of "Kinder-Gulag". See Brown 2009.

[216]   Seven year old Dominic Johansson was kidnapped by social authorities in Visby while boarding a plane to India in June 2009. Uniformed police grabbed him from his Swedish father and Indian mother who had not put him in kindergarten nor wanted to have him vaccinated. These reasons, tooth cavities and suspicions of the father not being mentally well led to the custody. The father was declared mentally sane by a doctor, but with no result. The case is registered at European Court of Human Rights but no release of Dominic Johansson yet (July 2012).

them that the security of their children cannot be guaranteed. This implies that the social authorities planned a police encounter but wanted to warn this middle class family from Uppsala. Late one night in February 2012 they left their house and stole away to Åland, a Finnish island in the Baltic Sea where more home schooling parents from Sweden reside[217]. The extreme position on home schooling in Sweden is seldom discussed or understood as the very idea to question compulsory education for any Swede seems deranged. Yet other Scandinavian countries manage to uphold the duty to educate children without insisting it should be done by teachers at schools. Compulsory education yes, compulsory schooling no.

Public child care is a foundation of welfare states that want both parents to work, to emancipate women and to stimulate young children to learn and develop. Of the three reasons for organizing day care and early childhood education, the last one is seldom well understood in Sweden for the youngest children, 1- 3 years old. Sweden has probably the highest number of children under 3 years in municipal (or administered by municipality) day care, 85 %. Nowhere in the world have so many so young children been away for such long time. It is an experiment with small children of enormous proportions that Plato dreamed of his authoritarian opus *The Republic*. State controlled child rearing is also central in Orwell's and Huxley's dystopias. The very young are of interest to all state propagandists of all ideologies for political streamlining as family influences then can be counterbalanced. Democratic totalitarianism is no exception, a concept that will be explained below.

For some toddlers day care may work, but not for all of the 86 % of small children under 3 years. Yet there is little discussion and research about how these youngest children actually fare outside home and little is known about results from other countries. What is known is that long hours in large groups are not good for small children. 30 hours a week for two year olds is normal in Sweden, but there are even longer hours

---

[217]   Talk by Jonas Himmelstrand at Freedom Fest in Stockholm May 2012. See www. mireja.se and www.rohus.nu

for some. 25 % are away for more than 36 hours and 13 % more than 40 hours per week[218]. For small children, large groups can be tough to cope with, but the number of adults per child has gone down while the number of small children in each group of small toddlers has risen. In 2003 groups with 17 children or more for 1- 3 year olds were 8 %, but doubled in 2010[219]. Swedish preschools have no restrictions on the total number of children per adult, only recommendations unlike in the UK and some US states where legislation set strict rules.

The quality of day care and early childhood education can be divided into cognitive and learning development on the one hand, and socio-emotional development on the other. Swedish and Scandinavian early childhood education is called educare which sums up the combined idea well. The caring aspect is more important for the youngest children under three years. But even the Swedish National Institute of Public Health (Folkhälsoinstitutet) cannot find research that supports any advantages of socio-emotional development for toddlers. Cognitive skills are enhanced for the small ones, but ability to attach to new people, social interactions or emotional stability are not substantiated by international and Swedish findings[220]. Small children, or any children, should not be treated collectively. Some children below 3 years catch infections more easily; some are more attached to their parents. UN Convention of the Rights of the Child, Article 3 states that the best interests of the child in singular. Swedish pre-school and gender policy favour children as col-

---

[218] Kihlbom in *Psykisk hälsa* 2011, p. 59. See also Kågesson 2006, Himmelstrand 2007 and Kihlbom et al 2009. Paediatricians Lars H. Gustafsson and Hugo Lagercrantz, child psychologist Eva Rusz and child psychiatrist Magnus Kihlbom do not recommend child care under 2 years.

[219] Skolverket 2011.

[220] Folkhälsoinstitutet 2009, p. 30, "The results from the literature review show that children who attend day care centers perform at a higher cognitive level in comparison to home care children. This suggests that young children benefit in the long term from center-based day care arrangements. However, this review does not settle the debate of socio-emotional development because, here, the literature is inconclusive." See also Drugli 2010.

lective entities, not individuals by an early forced entering age to the day dare system.

Small children have a need for social interaction apart from their family members but this does not imply meeting 15- 20 other toddlers 6 – 10 hours/ day. If there were open play schools where parents could bring their children or other families at home, being a house parent would not be so lonely. But with strong pressures, social, financial and cultural, some parents go against their conscience and start working. Diversity of various kinds of preschools exist since 1980s deregulations and parents may choose from municipal, private for-profit, cooperative non-profit and with profiles in culture, language, science, outdoors or Reggio Emilia and Montessori pedagogies. The quality is usually very good, even if there are some low quality preschools that will be detrimental to the future of certain children in need of good care due to their dire family conditions. But there is little choice for parents to choose not to use preschools at all for whatever long time or reasons or use them as an option for visits.

The day care system is geared to make both parents work. Paid parental leave is very good for 18 months and lower another year. Parents have a legal right to work 6 hours/ day until the child is 8 years old. Day care is subsidized with 92 %, a fact known only by 12 % parents[221].

Since family responsibilities for their own children have been under attack from education authorities and government child care, many parents believe that child care outside home better take care of their young just like Alva Myrdal said in 1930s. By registering almost all children in day care early, staying at home or find a child minder or relative (who also works fulltime) are no alternatives. Given the high taxes and low level of savings relying on one income, it is a challenge for parents to stay at home. The working parents keep on paying taxes and get noth-

---

[221]   Johansson 2009. Parents may consider staying home if they were given the total sum of costs per child/months, $ 2000 per month. Lower taxes would also enable more parents to decide, organize and pay for their daycare themselves.

ing in return while if both parents work, and pay taxes, they get child care almost totally subsidized. One reason Swedes argue so much over day-care benefit levels between the parents is that families have few other reasons to support themselves. With little or no money in the bank, they are at the mercy of Social Insurance Agency (Försäkringskassan), the most used agency and the first term immigrants learn when entering Sweden.

There is a deep divide between public opinion in Sweden and establishment on child care. Here are the most supported views that do not get any political interest or support in media:

8 of 10   mothers would like to stay longer at home.[222]

8 of 10   parents want a subsidized benefit for parents staying at home available nationwide [223]

8, 5 of 10   parents want to divide the parental leave among them. [224]

State is all, family nothing. Elsewhere in the world, where the majority of world population live, the opposite is true. Family is all, state nothing. The majority of states in the world are not well trusted by their citizens, while the Swedish state is and by all measures has reasons to be viewed as such. Still the road to hell may be paved with good intentions.

The division of parental leave between father and mother is a heated issue in Sweden. Standard parental leave runs at 480 days and 60 of those days are reserved exclusively for dads. All parties to the left and some of the right go against their voters and propose that the parental leave should be 50 / 50. Such attempts are almost political suicidal from the party establishments, but show themselves to be strong feminists, nice do-gooders and active busy-bodies. The majority of Swedish parties call themselves feminist, but not even these party establishments can go against the massive opinion. Instead persistent and often unsubstantiat-

---

[222]   Familjeliv 2010

[223]   *Svenska Dagbladet* 2010-04-24

[224]   Santesson 2011

ed state propaganda and media campaigns for feminist issues are done in
ways that go beyond imagination.

FEMINISM AND THE POLITICS OF BODILY FLUIDS :

1. Social democrat politicians in Stockholm have proposed installing
   gender-neutral restrooms so that members of the public will not
   be compelled to categorize themselves as either ladies or gents,
   thus supporting transgender people.
2. Left party chairman Lars Ohly said in parliament in reply to practical problems with a mandatory 50/ 50 division of parental leave
   between men and women that there are breast pumps available for
   those who need mothers' milk to their newly born.
3. Local left party politicians have proposed regulations to make
   men not to stand and urinate[225].

Another sample comes from preschool policies and is functioning in

---

[225]   The ability of men to urinate standing may also be analyzed as repressive for women
        and get governmental support. This story about the project Pussy Pants (Fittbyxor)
        by an independent feminist education NGO is luckily untranslatable but sadly true:
        "Malmö Fria Kvinnouniversitet betecknar sig som en feministisk organisation för
        konst och kunskapsutbyten och har tidigare gjort sig känt för att 2007 ha anordnat
        workshopen 'Fittbyxor', vilken presenterades med orden: 'Att ståkissa kan tyckas
        självklart. Om man är man. Med workshopen 'Fittbyxor' står Malmö fria kvinnouni-
        versitet upp för kvinnans rätt att kissa upprätt. ' ('Seminariet avslutas sedan med
        en gemensam kissstund i det fria för dem som vill.– Vi kommer att duka upp en
        vätskedrivande buffé bestående av öl och te. Sedan går vi ut och kissar tillsammans').
        Året 2006 beviljades 'universitetet' 280 000 kronor i bidrag ur stiftelsen Framtidens
        kultur." (quoted from the NGO:s official website http://mfkuniversitet.blogspot.
        se/2007/08/fittbyxor.html). The $40 000 in government support, which support-
        ed a workshop on letting women urinate standing and thereby liberate themselves,
        came from the former wage earners fund transformed into a foundation for future
        culture. The funds were allocated from working people's wages and used to present
        cultural and feminist events where women tried to transcend their anatomical inabil-
        ity to urinate standing.

hipster areas in central Stockholm. There some child care centers have a policy to devalue the concepts of boys and girls altogether in order to be gender neutral, thus including all sexual orientations, gender identities and break down the old female/ male distinction. If small children hear talk of boys and girls from their teachers, see different toys (cars, dolls) for each sex, get cuddling from teachers if girl or play football with other boys if boy, then the gender distinctions will continue. According to these preschools, behaviour from adults and environment should be neutral from early years to keep the whole preschool experiences free from repressive gender identities. By not being geared into the doll corner if girl, each girl may develop her inner identity more free and start kicking balls instead. But the program is impractical and in the end totalitarian. One preschool removed free playtime from its schedule because when children play freely, teachers saw that stereotypical gender patterns were created and cemented. Boys chose balls and girls dolls if left to themselves which was not intended. Maybe their parents or friends still influenced their gender identities or worse, biology.

In research, gender studies are popular and get much support, but can also lead to biased results. Ten doctoral dissertations were studied by journalist Susanna Hakelius-Popova. These were presented as best practices by the National Secretariat for Gender Studies at Gothenburg University. Nine of ten were about women, eight used feminist terminology and jargon without any definitions. All took for granted a research program of gender structures that cannot prove anything unless these structures are empirically verified. Few conclusions were substantiated in the studies. Most of the studies had already decided their result before any investigations took place[226]. What is more alarming is that the National Secretariat makes the same problem. This research institute has as its aim to do research about how men and women are made as social and cultural beings, thus disregarding other research specialties such as medicine or psychology. Science is not welcome to understand the relations between

---

[226]   Hakelius – Popova 2006. See also Rothstein 2009 who argues that the simple and politically naïve distinction of a leftist social constructivism and a rightist biology concerning gender is unscientific and ideological.

sexes. The Swedish government has the same policy in education at all ages and public services. Gender is made, biology is secondary[227]. Men bear already from preschool collectively the sins of earlier patriarchal generations. Boys cry when they hear how bad they and their fathers are and men always have been. Students in secondary schools are shown a play based on the bizarre SCUM manifesto (Society for Cutting Up Men), which urges women even if only fictionally to cut up men, eradicate the men from earth and establish a matriarchy[228].

Millions are paid to gender research project that give little or no results back that make sense. Eva Lundgren, former professor in sociology and gender research, made a career based on two unfounded studies. First she wrote a thesis on murder rituals of foetuses and babies among deeply misogynist and patriarchal Norwegian Christians and then a study which showed that almost half of all Swedish women have been assaulted by men. She was hailed as a prophet of new research programs on gender and a feminist ideologue used by socialist minister Margareta Winberg. But none of this was true. Police investigations in Norway went in vain looking for the hundreds of lost children and responsible families that had let their newly born be sacrificed in manly religious rituals. Her second study was not true

---

[227]   Robert in Kullbom and Landin (eds.) 1998 and Abrahamsson 2006, especially her interview with Annica Dahlström, professor in histology and neurobiology, and the ensuing media hype.

[228]   The playwright Valerie Solanas was a mentally deranged drug addict, victim of child abuse, prostitute and writer in late 1960s and is hailed by the cultural left as a heroine. Her attempt to kill Andy Warhol almost succeeded. The TUR Teatern (Theater without reactionaries, Teater Utan Reaktionärer) in Kärrtorp which gave the play to students during school hours gets support not only from the media but also national agency Kulturrådet, municipality and county council of Stockholm, and sales from schools who require students to partake in the controversial messages. The TUR Teatern official website present themselves in English: "Theatre without Reactionaries promotes an experimental, border-crossing and political theater for children, youth and adults. We want to be a theater without conventional boundaries, where the high and low culture are mixed and where our strongest guiding principles is [sic] lust, disrespect, and love."

either. Uppsala University did an investigation of her study Hit Dame (*Slagen dam*) and concluded to the contrary that certain men are more violent towards women (drunk, unemployed and young), not all men as Lundgren had maintained in her theory on male normality and minister Winberg had supported. The process was called normalization which meant that all men secretly believe that assaulting women is normal.

Swedish women have good conditions for work and family and so do men. But there is no use to divide them into two halves yelling at each other. Neither to uphold one interpretation of feminism and research on gender over any other in the way Swedish media, academia and government has done. Some progress towards reasonable views on gender has been made last decade and that is thanks for some brave and bright women and men outside regular feminist movements[229].

REPRESSING FREE THOUGHT AND SPEECH

In a democracy there are still ways to repress independent thinking. The obvious Swedish silent conformism has become an interest to anthropologists as the country becomes even more conformist and silenced[230]. Utterances that were heard of 25 years ago are silenced by media, education and government propaganda. Government staff and officials are afraid to speak to media if immigrants have behaved badly or any harassment case may be coming for whatever reasons, gender or sexual identity. A spiral of silence has rooted, using the sociological concept of Elisabeth Noelle-Neumann, where silence of one repressed group gets more repressed with each silent period, reinforced by fear of exclusion and maintenance of social order by the perceived major public opinion. When no opposing views are heard, people do not believe there are any

---

[229]   Kurtén-Lindberg 2001, Rothstein 2006a, Ström 2007, Östergren (ed.) 2008 and Persson 2010.

[230]   Friedman 1999 and Friedman forthcoming. Other Scandinavian anthropologists take interest in Swedish political correctness as typical of Swedish consensus seeking culture and mentality Friedman tells,

even if they themselves dissent from public opinion and thus the spiral of silence continues. The reason why dissenting expressions that at least existed before has gone away is due to the victory of leftist and welfare liberal thinking no matter what elected cabinet ruling. In domineering public policy and thought since 1980s with ever new generations with their agendas, there is little space left for dissenting groups and individuals. If heard they are called extreme and thus of little relevance. The official norm is normal, dissent extreme. Yet the reader knows that Sweden is the land of extremes so the normal is extreme there.

Repressing free thought can also be done by allowing repressive thought and cultural expressions inciting violence to political opponents who do not share left wing politics or current immigration policies or want welfare art tricksters to be sentenced or at least not have their art college degrees granted.

Here are two samples of many similar violent actions expressed as works of creative radical art and thus excused. In rap music, rage from frustrated youth of immigrant background is excused to the extreme as when named politicians are threatened to death. This happened twice recently. First, national public radio Sveriges Radio broadcasted in 2011 a song in which four singers urge listeners to sharpen their knives. Then they named a member of parliament for the nationalist Sweden democrats as target. Studio hosts declared while broadcasting the song that it was their favourite song but did not mention the incited violence, rather enforcing it. The song was reported to the government broadcasting board with no result.

Next example is from poetry. The poet Johan Jönsson received the prestigious Eyvind Johnsson prize[231] in literature 2012 for his work *med.bort. in* in which he described his will to kill prime minister Fredrik Reinfeldt

---

[231]   The prize money and decision came from cultural council at municipality of Boden, i.e. taxpayers. Eyvind Johnsson was born there as poor young man, became a writer, fought against his colleagues who were loyal to Stalin in post-war Sweden, taught himself medieval French and Latin, became a member of the Swedish Academy and a Nobel laureate in literature himself in 1974.

("how his brain is smashed. breaks up. from inside." and spread his genital herpes to a rich family by using their bathroom towels to his crotch. The poem was read at the national Royal Theatre Dramaten in Stockholm to a cheering audience of journalists and cultural elite, who afterwards explained themselves, declaring that poet Jönsson expressed class hatred in such new and interesting ways.

The two examples above together with the SCUM manifesto of leftist violence in music, theatre and poetry are hailed by the cultural establishment and media as are the welfare art tricksters. Criticism is viewed reactionary, racist, bourgeois, anti-women and against natural youthful rebellion. The results of such repression of free thought are two: powerful majoritarian journalists and powerless dissenting citizens. The journalists think they know better and have no fear of telling people to shut up. Usually media wants to be on the side of the victim and thus portray the dissenting citizen as master. If the victim is a blond girl being raped by seven immigrant teenagers, the media tries to have it both ways, giving both the credit of victimization. But when the cake gate exploded in 2012 with a black artist and a white minister, there was only confusion.

What is more serious is harassment of people who speak out. Since the 1980s when open white supremacist gangs were hunting immigrants around Sweden, there have been anti-racist gangs fighting them with sticks and stones. These free ranging left wing fighters are now present at public meetings with the Sweden democrats who won 340 000 votes in 2010, at pro-Israel manifestations and at any open meeting that criticizes the left or official immigration policies. The police have earlier looked away and left leaning politicians justified the violence, but that has changed for the better. The autonomous communists, anti-racists and anarchists believe in the strategy of independent violent free corps gives them the right to interrupt public meetings. At first, meetings are disturbed with whistles, songs and yelling, trying to overtake any speaker they do not like. If that does not work, violence is used. Since very few dare to gather under placards saying "Less immigration - Scandinavian levels", the opponents are always in majority. Before winning German elections in 1933, Adolf Hitler used the same tactics with his Nazi Sturm-abteilungen fighting the Stalinist Proletarische Hundertschaften. Right and left violence were accepted on both sides at beer halls and gatherings with batons and knives. After the collapse of Weimar democracy, Hitler rose and Stalin sealed his dictatorship.

The Swedish Left party, and sometimes the green and socialists, excuse these actions and join by making their political opponents less human and worthy only of spit, threats and punches. If this is not enough, opponents can be harassed at home with doors knocked in, axed or house set on fire, having their children being told at pre-school or school that their parents' houses are known, victims of internet frauds, raped, beaten or even killed. Losing jobs and being thrown out of unions and other organizations are also results for speaking out dissenting views. My career will most likely be affected by publishing this book, even if done by private money and print-on-demand publishing. Some politicians participate in this, albeit in the background, but not always. Some members of the Left party support openly the semi-military Anti-Fascistisk Aktion (AFA) and so does the anti-racist magazine *EXPO* (which is where Stieg Larsson worked, *Millennium* magazine). AFA was earlier present at public meetings with the Board of Integration and much used by schools to campaign against racism, being more cool and younger than regular teachers. Government run anti-racist museum head and media analyst Birgitta Löwander called them "heroes of our time"[232]. AFA breeds the spiral of silence with sticks and stones.

With internet blogging and online forums providing new forms of freedom of speech, more facts have become accessible to more Swedes, but there is fear of being traced and hit at your home even when using in-

---

[232]   Arnstberg 2005, p. 252. She now works at the Living History Forum (Forum för Levande Historia) in central Stockholm, a museum that exposes children, youth and adults to facts of the Holocaust but also to the phenomenon of political correctness. The exhibition P.K. (PC in Swedish) wanted to foster tolerance among pupils through psychological methodology, not facts. Demirbag-Sten 2009 is a relevant exception.

ternet. Fictional character Lisbeth Salander has many likeminded young angry women, which may be good, but Sweden is not a male chauvinist rightist dominated nation as Stieg Larsson and his fellow left leaning Swedish crime fiction writers try to tell the world. Rather the opposite.

Left politicians use the state apparatus to cancel dissenting opinions, quite openly. In 2004 Fox News reporters went to an immigrant suburb of Malmö, which since has become infamous internationally for murder, anti-Semitism, poverty, radical Islamism and stones hit at firemen and postmen. The American reporters interviewed policemen, anonymously of course, and a school principal. The story was broadcasted via the Swedish network TV8 and caused uproar in media and politics as being racist, exaggerated and untrue. The Left party and independent parliament member Gudrun Schyman accused the Swedish channel for not obeying to agree to the rules on impartial broadcasting[233]. She registered a case at the Board of Broadcasting Inspec-

---

[233] Gudrun Schyman contains all and more one can imagine from a feminist leftist with attitude, personal problems and humour. She was active from 1970 in Marxist-Leninistiska Kampförbundet supporting revolutionary violence. In order to show the benefits of natural delivery and empower women, her naked body was shown in a film documentary while she was giving birth. She then joined the left party (Vänsterpartiet) and became its celebrated chairman until her alcoholism became public at an official film event where she urinated in her seat and were drunk at subsequent press meetings. She resigned as chairman but kept her place in parliament. Then she was caught with fraud concerning reimbursements from parliament, sentenced with fines, but was still active and in new ways. She started the new party Feministiskt Initiativ, but kept her place in parliament as independent as she had left the left party after proposing a special tax for men. In 2010 she burned Swedish bills, cash that is, worth $13 500 at a political event as a protest against income disparity between men and women. Sweden is the most equal nation in the world according to UN and Swedish young women will in a few years be better paid than young men, as they already are in USA, Norway and UK. The ombudsman for gender equality did a survey of 750 000 employees and found an income disparity of 0.6 % between men and women, see Jämställdhetsombudsmannen 2008. See also Rothstein 2011c for the coming female dominance in labour market and education.

tion (Granskningsnämnden) in order to shut down broadcasting of Fox News in Sweden. Closure happened anyway but the mere action of a political party member to interfere with commercial broadcasting dissenting political views or comments would be unconstitutional in other countries. Fox News, or any other commercial channel apart from the Swedish, could make a difference to the dominant media if there is enough courage among network managers and editors. Strangely the commercial channels are just as repressive as the public. The liberalizations of broadcasting radio and television brought only freedom of commercialism, not thought and expression. Socialist Sweden supported consumerism rather than freedom to broadcast new editorial content when the rules were changed in 1987 and broadcasting television was freed but editorial content left unchanged.

In academia, actions of repressing thought are more subtle and many academics fear to do anything that may dissent from mainstream university grinding, even if there are a few exceptions, among them Bo Rothstein, Svante Nordin, Karl-Olov Arnstberg, along with some (ex) members in the Swedish Academy, brave editors (*Axess*, *NEO*) and a few free spirits. Universities are not autonomous in Sweden and were for last decades ruled by non-academics who outnumbered professors at the boards. Socialist trade union LO was well represented and still is but to lesser degree. In order to receive funds for research, academics have to follow the current ideological trends at government donors and agencies[234]. If done so well, resources may be received for something which is not research at all, just pure ideology, or even fraud, but with the right ideological buzzwords. Gender is one. Marianne Laxén granted in 2006 as head of government gender equality project funds of $80 000 to a feminist organization she was a member herself and later mismanaged funds for gender research with little relevance. At her unit another strange issue happened the year before when a male official got $200 000 by using the right trendy words in gender research for complete fake feminist projects.

---

[234] Rohtstein 2009. His chapter VI includes samples and analysis of insular and cowardly features in Swedish universities. Yet he is a staunch defender of the welfare state and a social democrat.

He was sentenced and fined but other dubious recipients of funds for gender research are not[235].

Since the welfare state relied early on expertise in urban and family planning, dirigist macro economy, government administration of health, social and cultural issues and practically all areas of citizens' lives, research is an important factor to control. By referring to scientific results, soft paternalist government agencies will with campaigns, ideology, and sometimes biased science try to persuade citizens to make the right consumer choices, exercise and keep good diet, support countryside development, youth activism and anything (un) imaginable concerning gender and ethnicity.

The governmental agencies have the last decades been at the forefront of ideological production as government ministries have been downsized and regular parliamentary commissions axed. Political scientist Bo Rothstein has analyzed the Swedish phenomena by using Marxist theorist Louis Althusser's concept of ideological state apparatuses[236]. The corporatist features of Swedish welfare state foundations and the Swedish consensus culture breed acceptance to instructions from enlightened and kind masters above. Instead of channelling voices and aspirations from the people to the state, the state constructs opinions which are then forced to the people. Democracy backwards. The efficient state machinery is tempting to use for any political party and the center-right government since 2006 has not been much different. The moderate party establishment in particular has spin doctors, focus groups and market strategies using the same government apparatus.

Repressing academic thinking and exchange of ideas can sometimes be blatantly obvious. In 1997, Karolina Matti, a young PhD candidate in

---

[235] Abrahamsson 2006, p. 59-60. See Rothstein 2009 and Hakelius –Popova 2006. Bergqvist 2009 revealed that $70 000 was given to a research project for finding gender perspective on the musical instrument trumpet. The hypothesis was that the trumpet was (too) phallic.

[236] Rothstein 2005 and Rothstein 2009. See also Rankka 2005 and SOU 2007:107.

sociology at Umeå university made the headlines. She did her graduate research on right wing activism and racism and gathered 8 other graduate students for a meeting. Her idea was to investigate what would happen if other sociology students would be informed directly by a representative of right wing activism and racism rather than through any mediator or scholar. His talk would be useful to understand his ideology but also to understand his self-image, she argued afterwards.

She spoke to Dan Berner who was an active Nazi and agreed to the speaking terms. She introduced him using a written manuscript and let him speak for less than an hour about his views. Afterwards the group split but a few students felt ashamed and worried. They had listened to a real Nazi without any restrictions and decided to report Karolina Matti to the University Board. She was given a suspended sentence with fines and lost her status as graduate student by order from the university dean and socialist minister of education Carl Tham. The Nazi speaker Berner was jailed for one month on charges of inciting hate against certain groups, among them Jews and immigrants. The main question was if the meeting was a propaganda meeting for a violent and undemocratic ideology on university premises or an academic attempt to understand how such views rise and may be understood scientifically. If the latter was the case and Karolina Matti had made a distinction between herself and the invited speaker, the case would be closed. But so did not, the court, nor academics and minister Tham reason at all. Tham wanted even more restrictions on academic work[237].

Another case concerning immigration and academia happened same year in Lund. Associate professor of anthropology Kajsa Ekholm Friedman was invited to a meeting to give a talk about global systems anthropology, which she and her husband Jonathan Friedman, also professor in anthropology at Lund University, specializes in. The inviting organization was a group of mostly elderly people who were disturbed by the influx of immigrants but generally open to immigration and not openly xenophobic or racist. She talked to them and they asked her

---

[237]   Nycander in Kullbom and Landin (eds.) 1998.

about multiculturalism which she answered as truly as she could, being an anthropologist with experiences from Africa, Polynesia and Latin America. She then wrote two articles in the main daily *Dagens Nyheter* about her research and doubts concerning multiculturalism and hell broke loose. She was blamed for talking in front of racists and making statements that could be interpreted as leading to racism or hate speech against certain groups. The dean of Lund University, Boel Flodgren, was strong in defending her professor even if she wrote that had she been asked if Ekholm Friedman should go to this kind of meeting, she would have advised her not to[238].

Last example of repressing freedom of speech comes from Chancellor of justice (Justitiekanslern, JK) Göran Lambertz and socialist Minister of Justice Laila Freivalds. Because of the violent uprisings around the world and attacks on Scandinavian embassies in 2006 after the publication of Muhammed cartoons by Danish daily *Jyllands-Posten*, an official at foreign ministry, Stefan Arnér, shut down web servers that were hosting sites in Swedish with samples of the controversial cartoons. The decision to close the websites was done in cooperation with minister Freivalds, which she denied but proved wrong. Freivalds had to leave office. This was her last scandal (1970 supporting car theft, 2000 real estate and 2004 tsunami catastrophe). Göran Lambertz who had granted the website censorship continued his defence and explained his views on the "global crisis for freedom of speech" later same year. He wrote that Western media should not "unnecessarily" violate feelings and opinions among Muslims. With his action and defence in print, he had proven that freedom of speech means little in Sweden[239].

VALUES AND VIRTUES

The relaxed attitude towards traditional values since 1970s and more tolerance for new life styles in later decades have given Sweden an advantage as a country with citizens who are quite open and non-interfering in

---

[238]   Friedman 1999, Ekholm Friedman and Friedman 2006 and Friedman forthcoming.

[239]   Lambertz 2006

public spaces. A diversity and openness similar to what can be found in the well-educated and liberal East and West coasts in USA dominate the major cities, especially university towns. Immigrants are surprised and often happy about how the Swedes are tolerant, relaxed and chilled out at all ages. The stiffness Susan Sontag detected during her 1969 visit is gone. Middle class cultural traditions have been replaced with middle class materialism. Church life is replaced with new age or violent secularism and teachers are told by pupils rather than the opposite. Anyway the poorly trained teachers cannot always spell and send weekly newsletters home that make some parents wonder how their children are taught. Or maybe the parents do not detect the misspellings or do not care.

What sadly went with the Swedish stiffness and tight-assed bourgeois traditions was also a division between ages. Infantilisation has replaced maturity as the generations between 30 and 60 still try to behave like their children or grandchildren. Neotony, juvenilization, is the ideal look, meaning to look young forever and live like Peter Pan. The immigrants who come from countries with more traditional values start to wonder if the Swedes are alright and if they like Swedes at all. Given the stories so far, any reader should at least give them the right to question what an extreme nation Sweden is. They may talk to some older Swedes who shake their heads in their homes for elderly care with few family visits. The immigrants would then go back to their cramped apartment with granny, cousins and uncles and continue to ponder over why they ever left Diyarbakir, Mogadishu or Bagdad. Next day they go to the mall which is warmer than the winter cold outside and meet shopping Swedish parents looking like their teenage sons and daughters.

Values are the foundations of every society even in strict neutral Sweden. But it is probably the closest the world has ever seen to the dry dream of John Rawls' strictly political liberalism with an overlapping consensus of strict practical socially engineered values and behaviours[240]. Value neu-

---

[240]   For Rawls' concept overlapping consensus, see Sjunnesson 1991 and for weakness in the Swedish constitution to support a national and multicultural consensus, see Rothstein 2006b.

tral liberal states do not uphold any specific beliefs for its citizens, other than minimal restrictions as codified by laws. Any debates on integrity, moral actions, natural rights, responsibility and other values are brought down to whether it is illegal or not. Not to act when someone is in need of immediate help is not illegal in Sweden but the idea of introducing such a law has been discussed. Other Scandinavian countries, France and Germany have laws that put legal pressure on those who walk by an emergency doing nothing.

Most Swedes feel uncomfortable with such legislation and refer to their privacy and payment of high taxes so why should they as private neutral citizens help someone else. The fear of getting involved and become a victim oneself is well founded; so many Swedes have reasons to pass fights in the subway or around their houses. People have been kicked to death in central Stockholm with no one around reacting, sometimes 10- 20 people watching skulls being kicked in. But it is not a decent society. Tony Blair initiated a legislation called Anti-Social Behaviour Order that for some years worked against threats to public order and decency (urinating on subway platforms, abusive behaviour, threats to passers-by etc.). Sweden is the last country to even consider it, but the first country that needs it or at least acknowledge the need to act as adult citizens and decent human beings.

Sexual debut for teenagers has gone down in age and is now around 17. Contraceptives are given free from school nurses and sex education is geared towards getting young people used to the idea of consensual sex with whoever wants to. Teenagers who do not want to have sex are not well supported and if their parents intrude to defend sex abstinence, suspicions arise. If the parents are Christian or Muslims or just have immigrant background, questions on honorary cultures and abuse may lead to rumours of repression and neglect of children's rights. A father and mother from Sülemaniyah, Addis Abbeba, Lima or even Stockholm, may still want to keep their teenagers to come home at 11 pm from school dances or not letting them join school trips with two adults responsible for a class of 28 teenagers. Or maybe girls do not want to have sex, but feel such pressure from school, boys, adults and policy statements that they have sex anyway against their will. These pressures are harder for some frustrated working class girls, who have sex earlier than for boys and middle class girls.

If Sweden is such a tolerant and liberal society with little emphasis on values for citizens, how come some families and individuals with traditional family values are portrayed as potential murderers and sexually repressive? There are legal boundaries of locking youth inside their rooms, keeping them indoors or following them around outside. But there are no restrictions on what a parent can tell his children and urge them to follow without forcing them. In most cultures and for at least 6 billion people, it is normal for an elderly family member to speak out of judgment and experience. When coming to a new country one should adjust and try to understand the values, but if these strongly go against one's own, there are situations when most adults would like to have a word with their children. Advantages and disadvantages of actions and attitudes must be calculated for by family and if not, then that is also a stand of permission, which many Swedes take. In Sweden discussions on virginity, honour, shame and sexual freedom are open and should be able include traditional and firmer family values as well. If society and culture are to be tolerant, there should also be tolerance for values that question tolerance in all matters and all areas of life including family privacy. Some people may argue that family matters are private and do not understand or accept Swedish attitudes towards sex and find them extreme. They are not aware of the deep historical roots of the Swedish sin.

In some northern rural regions, young men have for centuries actually gone collectively to young women at night. The young men parted and visited each a girl at night time to speak and maybe hug in order to see if the two could make a good couple. Sex was not always the result but occurred and also led to babies who mostly were treated well. This rural tradition continued until 20th century and met in 1930s with legendary socialists Myrdals' ideas on regulating sexuality and welfare policies for a larger and better population. Being quite uninhibited while taking baths, swimming and mixing sexes, Swedes were not much embarrassed when nudity was shown in films and pornography followed in 1950s and 1960s.

Women's liberation in 1970s, gay men dying in aids on state television in 1980s and tolerance for sexual orientations of all kinds after 2000 have led to a chilled out attitude that is hard to get a grip on for a father from Pakistan or mother from Somalia. Expecting them to do this journey in months from landing a residence permit is simply inhuman and impractical. Where most people come from who enter Sweden, the state, if there is one, is evil and useless. Not good and useful. People born here may also benefit from having traditional perspectives on human relations and sexuality. Swedes are extreme in sexual matters but usually do not reflect and question their stand. Instead Swedish authorities and citizens seem to know what is best for everyone, human reproduction and how to deal with relationships all over the world.

Meeting a Swede on a walk in the woods does not produce any greetings even as people almost touch walking narrow paths. Same when entering a store or asking a sales clerk. On the British Isles or on the European continent, people greet each other with a short Hello, Bon Jour or Grüss, and same politeness reign when entering a store or asking for help there. Swedes are to the point and if there is no need to interact, they seldom act out of politeness or kindness. They rather silently bump into strangers than speak to them. In stores they approach clerks fervently with no signals. In this sense, Swedes are known to be uncivilized people, unused to exchanges outside their small groups.

Virtues are practically nonexistent entities in Sweden and even less public debate or awareness of this extreme lack[241]. Yet Swedes believe in some of them (prudence, justice, temperance, thrift, contentment), but have no language whatsoever to reflect on virtues Inhabitants in the land of extremes live *After Virtue*. Philosophy in Sweden is known for three things: the aforementioned mentioned death of French 17th century founder of modern philosophy René Descartes, the Uppsala school of analytical philosophy in 1920s and rejecting the PhD thesis *Histoire de la folie à l'âge classique* by the French historian Michel Foucault in late 1950s[242]. The fate

---

[241]   Engelau and Gür 2012 is a welcome exception.

[242]   Department of history of science and ideas at Uppsala university, rejected the thesis

of the two Frenchmen is most known worldwide, but the middle tradition of logical positivism is more interesting and influential on Swedish welfare state foundation and constitutional law.

The Uppsala school of analytical philosophy around 1920 was empirical and logical in its attitude towards ethical judgments and legal reasoning. Their argument was that words such as right and duty were basically meaningless as they could not be scientifically verified or proven. Natural law and ethics based on human rights or human dignity were abandoned for a flexible utilitarian approach, labelled value nihilism by the press. The consequences of scientific and philosophical reasoning for not respecting natural law and human rights were strong as the early founders of the modern welfare state, students with social democratic sympathies (ministers Gunnar Myrdal, Östen Undén), were disciples to the Uppsala professors Axel Hägerström, Anders Wilhelm Lundstedt (socialist parliament member) and the more freewheeling Ingemar Hedenius, a sceptic secular whig and wit. The Uppsala philosophers cleared up a lot of old German idealism and domestic bizarre thinking, but paved way for an unlimited attack on universal human rights. Dubious means were justified by valuable ends if well applied utilitarian calculations said so. Virtues and values have little place in this tradition even if the Uppsala philosophers would support them. Being nice to people is good because it gives oneself good feelings of oneself, reciprocal actions and makes relationships smooth. The idea of duty, self-respect and human dignity play no role. Incidentally this coldness fit well with the Swedish culture of privacy, non interference and independence. State individualism again.

A simple test to see where use and discussions of virtues and values would have a more important role is order in school classrooms. Every parent,

---

due its wild theorizing and unreadable style (which Foucault himself realized later). However, the three years were well spent as Foucault could sit at the Carolina library and read, the at that time unknown collections of medical and scientific books from mid 15th century in the Erik Waller donation. These findings of the earliest printed books would become the base for his history of madness from medieval time in Europe to 19th century. No Uppsala archives, no Foucault fame.

teacher and pupil knows that to be able to learn, there has to be a certain order around the students, young and old. Levels of small talk, comings and goings, appropriate clothing and much else can not be left to the most vocal and strong pupils. Yet that is often the case. The international education Programme for International Student Assessment (PISA at OECD) found in 2000 that Swedish students had less favourable attitudes in terms of disciplinary climate. Head of Swedish School Agency Mats Ekholm and the socialist school minister Ingegärd Wernersson defended unruly students by saying they had creativity and if exposing bad behaviour, it was not their fault but social factors[243]. Since then the left has tracked back on school policies and the center-right government has been able to implement some weak measures for teachers and principals to give sanctions to misbehaving students. But the students themselves do not see much difference, rather the opposite. In 2009 the National School Agency did a survey and found that

- 50 % of students in class 4–6 have order around them sometimes in class
- 66 % of older students have order
- 22 % of all students are disturbed at all or almost all lessons (14 % in 2006)
- 60 % of all students trust the teachers ability to keep order[244]

These views come from students aged 10 to 19, not from hell-bent right wing politicians. Yet there is little public support for implementing strong values that would help students focus on their studies. Some families may want to but an increasing number of parents support their children and believe whatever they say, attack teachers and school management. Virtues and values of good behaviour along with stricter rules and sanctions would make a difference, but the defence from some parents, the cultural left and school establishment at higher levels, is massive and in favour of freedom and learning as espoused by Rousseau, Dewey and

---

[243] Aspelin 2003, p. 7. OECD 2000, p. 68.

[244] Skolverket 2009.

progressive education[245]. Teacher trainees are told that some students call each other "you whore" or "you Arab" out of mutually accepted signs of affection, and should not be corrected. Which students have these bonds of foul language is unclear at any school, but some students' language use have been researched Fanny Ambjörnsson and Richard Jonsson, whose well written PhD theses are used as syllabus in teacher training. Their findings are interesting but useless for prospective teachers who want to know how to keep order, not make mental lists of who calls who by which name in which class and whether these actions should be tolerated or not[246].

Swedes had strong values and virtues especially around work and justice. The labour movement was built upon doing one's duty and demand one's right (gör din plikt, kräv din rätt). Strong work ethics prevailed but were eroded by the moral hazards of a kind welfare state and a sly market that would tempt with consumer goods and credit cards. As Nima Sanandaji expressed above, a strong Protestant work ethic was an important factor in Swedish culture no matter where in the world Swedes went. It was these ethical guidelines socialist Prime Minister Göran Persson appealed to when he brought Sweden out of the economic crisis in late 1990s. And again insisting on doing one›s duty was the base for center-right victory in 2006, as the four party alliance had managed to steal the idea of strong working ethics from the socialists, by then mostly supported by people who either worked in government or received welfare benefits. That is, either living on and giving away other people›s money or receiving them.

Virtues imply efforts and build character. People need self-respect, but self-respect must be earned. It cannot be self-respect if it is not given by others. Else it is just infantile attitude. The only way to achieve respect

---

[245]   Swedish educationalists have been extremely reluctant to express any criticism of the social democratic founded school system and produce relevant research. Important research and writings were instead done by journalists Maciej Zaremba, Hans Bergström and Gunnar Ohrlander, political scientist Karin Hedenius, ethnologist Jonas Frykman and language scholar Inger Enkvist. See Sjunnesson 2012.

[246]   Ambjörnsson 2004 and Jonsson 2007.

is in the face of the possibility of failing. For the young, there should be incremental steps to learn to cope with failures, but Sweden has gone the other way and abolished both grades and mild sanctions when misbehaving until to age 13. Freedom is only meaningful related to responsibility of actions and consequences from actions. Instead Sweden has built a system for people young and old not to take responsibility and not to even understand the consequences that follow from undesirable actions. This leads to lives that are with no dignity or aim. Knowing that we have responsibility for the consequences of our actions is a major part of what makes life worth living. Dr. Eberhard tried to say this in his analysis of the pathological need for security among Swedes and their lack of endurance when confronted with the possibility of being hurt, suffer or failure at any small challenges.

What makes contemporary Sweden extreme in its development of values and virtues is the acceptance of fate and not seeing any alternatives to the present predicament. If some contemporary values and virtues are simply dysfunctional, Swedes excuse them by referring to the inevitable process of change, no matter in what direction. There is little awareness of any idea that processes can be turned to other goals, stopped or even reflected upon. The left dreams of socialist utopia, human innocence and faith in modern welfare state solving all problems are gone. Without socialist hopes and views of all human as all good, or the conservative tragic view of mankind liable to fault, the more depressing –isms of nihilism, pragmatism, infantilisation and consumerism prevail. Earlier belief in Swedish folkhem modernity and optimism is now replaced by fatalism and immediate satisfaction of desires with no regard to the past or future. If such satisfactions are questionable in the long run, they are excused with the quick relief of suffering or instant happiness. Since history is outdated and the future uninspiring, present is all. The real existing condition of post-modernity has replaced the real existing project of socialist modernity. Fascination for youth culture add more to the hedonism of many adults as they themselves behave under their age and are treated as such from their children. Youth is admired in Sweden unlike anywhere else in Europe.

Immigrants and foreign visitors do not always understand why adult Swedes behave as they do. The weak links to European traditions which got even weaker after World War II has opened up for a semi-American youthful culture. Now Sweden is connected by a bridge to Europe via Denmark, but culturally the country is closer to Disney Santa Land which may be located at the upper right corner of the World Values Map.

But morality in Sweden may be more complicated than just put in one corner. Political scientist Gina Gustavsson has shown in analyzing the World Values Survey that the positive values in Swedish tolerance and acceptance for individualism may imply strong values nevertheless. A long quote explains her findings that use Isaiah Berlin's two concepts of liberty:

> "However, Swedes are often portrayed as the epitome of freedom-oriented people (Berggren and Trägårdh, 2006; Schwartz, 2006). Inglehart and his associates [at World Values Survey, JS] even speak of a 'Swedenization', as opposed to an Americanization, of the world (Inglehart and Welzel, 2005: 65, 87). The Swedish data may thus also tell us something of a more general interest. They suggest that valuing freedom need not, as previous research often assumes, be incompatible with strongly condemning certain choices, or even favouring their restriction by law. In fact, it is not entirely unlikely that the positive Swedish attitudes towards prohibitions are to some extent an *effect* of valuing freedom; not in the sense of doing what one pleases unhindered by others, but in the sense of realising one's authentic self (Berggren and Trägårdh, 2006: cf. 213; Gustavsson, 2010).

> Yet, existing research tends to assume that the ethos of valuing individual freedom /. . . / is by its very nature devoid of moral fervour for or against any one way of life. Some empirical scholars lament what they see as a weakened commitment to following any moral constraints and clear moral guidelines in life (Flanagan and Lee, 2003), while others

welcome what they see as the natural decline in moral abso-
lutism and closed-mindedness (Inglehart and Welzel, 2005).
Both sides essentially agree, however, that valuing freedom
brings along a general permissiveness towards different behaviours, for better or for worse[247].

The peculiar Swedish kind of individualism seems not to support something eccentric, but rather let other people be and respect their individual choices in important matters (family, relationships, life styles), while
still keeping to strong moral values of freedom. These values are popular
among Swedes and intended to liberate everyone. Nevertheless, they are
interpreted with little reflection, often domineering and contribute to spi-
rals of silence and political conformism. Swedes have for instance little
tolerance for other perspectives on sex work, drug use, parent-at-home and
home schooling than the established paternalistic and maternalistic views.

CIVIL SOCIETY AND DEMOCRATURE
With an expansive and expensive welfare state, there is a risk that civil
society gets squeezed between individuals demanding welfare services
and the state trying to keep up, using measures against civil liberties and
civil society. The modern Swedish welfare state has many such features,
but was built on strong popular movements and crafty people from all
classes and regions. These movements have been transformed into municipal or government agencies giving similar services. Democracy, individual voices and civil participation were overruled in many areas and
civil society diminished to museums.

Since the Swedish constitution do not have many limits on government

---

247   Gustavsson 2011, p. 12. Her analyses using empirical methods from World Values
        Surveys of romantic liberalism and repressive liberalism are relevant in discussions
        on multiculturalism and political conformism. A repressive liberalism forces liberal
        values upon non-liberals with illiberal means, such as in the Mohammed cartoons
        controversy but also in the repression of free thinking in Sweden. See ibid, essay III
        and Gustavsson 2012.

actions nor protect parliamentary minorities well, a cabinet can rule with no limits backed up by parliament. With a majority backing, or making a minority cabinet get enough support, socialist governments have turned democracy itself into a soft dictatorship. Already by 1965, the clearheaded writer and popular agitator Vilhelm Moberg used the word democrature (demokratur, combining Swedish terms demokrati + diktatur, dictatorship) to describe a state with a dictatorship by the democratic majority. Such a state is nominally a democracy but lacks respect for freedom of speech, an ability for dissenting groups to speak on their own terms, do not follow rule of law for all groups, where careers are endangered if dissent is voiced, where political violence could follow from voicing dissent while the police looks the other way and laws are not followed by the state itself. A totalitarian democracy[248]. Citizens do not realize this and believe that they are hearing factual objective information from media and live in a substantial, not a nominal democracy.

More than 40 years later and with three shifts in government power from left to right, the analysis by Moberg is more relevant. Acceptance of alternative lifestyles, of market solutions in welfare services and deregulations of broadcasting have contributed to efficient services and more varied entertainment but not to serious and factual debate. The cultural left and welfare liberal policy regulations rule more than ever since Palme. The pressure not to voice dissent is harder now than when he reigned. Swedes can choose from a variety of services and since 2006 get lower taxes and buy more goods, but they cannot speak up in public and definitely not outside trusted groups at work or with friends.

The ruling majority in parliament leading to such consequences has roots that go back a few centuries. Medieval king Gustav I in 16th

---

[248]   Svensson 2000, p. 16. See also Hayek 1960, p. 5, "The powers which modern democracy possesses would be even more intolerable in the hands of some small elite. Admittedly, it was only when power came into the hands of the majority that further limitations of the power of government was thought unnecessary. In this sense democracy and unlimited government are connected. But it is not democracy but unlimited government that is objectionable".

century and Lord High Chancellor Axel Oxenstierna in the 17th century had built a centralized state with firm administrative powers and strong royal rule. During the 18th century, parliament brought more power to itself and did not set any limits to its executive ambitions. When a new constitution was formed in 1809 there were some influences from ideas of checks and balances with inspiration from Montesquieu and the 1776 American constitution but not enough. Whether the king ruled or parliament or the Realm of the Estates, they ruled without separation of powers of execution, legislation and judiciary. Parliament elected or not, ruled over the state as sovereign. Rule of law protecting citizens against the state and parliament, as in Anglo- Saxon traditions or French constitutional traditions, were less important than inspiration from the German legal state, Rechtsstaat[249].

With a party ruling from 1932 to 1976 as sovereign, execution was all. Party, cabinet, government, society – all intertwined. Prime Minister Tage Erlander often spoke of the strong society, when he meant the state. Socialists and unions campaigned for more powers to society by which they meant the state and its branches in counties and municipalities. But society consists of three divisions; state, market, civil society. Individuals take various roles in each. But with the specifically Swedish version of state individualism and a strong executive governmental power, there is only the state and its individuals. Civil society has little place and even if Sweden has a market economy, legal defence of property is not as strong as many cases of arbitrary taxation and unions interferences show. The 1974 constitution that replaced the constitution of 1809 has little protection for private property which was convenient for a socialist government in favour of high taxation and socializing private property with wage earners funds. The facts are there for anyone to see. Socialist Minister of Justice Carl Lidbom argued against individual civil rights and Prime Minister Ingvar Carlsson set security over human dignity, as done before by socialists and Soviet communists[250]. Social democrats

---

[249]   Thelin 2000.

[250]   Zaremba 1992, p. 73-74.

have always defended the strong state against the center-right parties that somewhat half-heartedly reformed the constitution when in power, the last time in 2010.

The Swedish constitution is principally based of the sovereignty of the people rather than a separation of powers. What is politically decided is right by law, not by any other common law, natural law or notion of individual human beings worthy of respect. The independence of courts from parliament and cabinet is still weak[251]. With a closer integration with the European Union, the Swedish constitution has to make more amendments for separation of powers and rule of law, just as the Court of Justice of the European Union earlier had helped citizens against the strong Swedish state. Technocratic powers and social engineering combined with long reign and majority rule have proved to be detrimental with respect to human dignity. When the state has grown so strong that it can give its citizens all they need, the state is also powerful enough to take everything citizens need away, as the US founding father Thomas Jefferson used to say. If citizens become liberated by the state from each other and all associations, they have nothing to defend themselves with against the state. Freedom changes into weakness. Independence into dependence.

The French 19th century political thinker Alexis de Tocqueville saw these mechanisms clearly and his ideas have been discussed lately in Sweden[252]. For Swedish government ruling, the idea of individuals in need of protection from the state is purely wrong, as the state always is good. All talk about courts protecting citizens against the state was sign of an "undemocratic and dangerous thought. The uttermost guarantee for human rights is the relevance of democracy to the opinion of the people", said socialist Minister of Justice Lennart Geijer[253]. What the majority in par-

---

[251]   Hirschfeldt 2009 and 2011.

[252]   Zaremba 1992, p. 80-82. See also Ehnmark 1994.

[253]   Zaremba 1992, p.78. Socialist minister of justice Lennart Geijer supervised the 1976
         committee on sex crime which proposed lax legislation on pedophilia and underage
         sex, while he himself went to prostitutes to such an extent that the head of secret

liament decides is right, even in matters where there are little relevance or knowledge, such as which psalms to sing in the Swedish Lutheran church or when life begins in the womb.

Civil society, market and state make up society. Swedish civil society with roots in the 19th century popular movements, voluntary self-help associations and in middle class traditions has been replaced with government mechanisms at national, regional and municipal levels. Family structures do not have same importance as before and care for old and young are administered by professionals. Religion that influenced the labour movement cherishing altruism and brotherhood has withered away. Values rooted in tradition, learning and strive for excellence have been replaced by mediocrity[254].

Social democrats have wavered in their favour of civil society. As long as popular movements dominated this third share of society, civil society was reduced to these movements, especially the ones dominated by the labour movement, such as Folkets Hus, folk dancing halls, lotteries, co-operative and other socialist corporatist entities. The intermediate kind of 19th - and early 20th century associations where poor workers put $10 a week into a bucket and after 5 years bought a plot and started to build a small shared house was tolerated but not more. Churches were frowned upon, their hiring procedures were regulated to maintain gender equality and bishops in the state church were appointed by cabinet. The self- governing folk education movement that I have been trained in, folkbildning with folkhögskolor and studieförbund, has been overregulated into a bureaucracy with little democratic and free independent education as existing goals.

New suburban utopias were designed to make new kinds of communal life possible around the major cities, but created more misery in the high story buildings, smaller three story houses and endless fields of townhouses. With the enormous influx from the countryside in 1960s, social

---

police was concerned and informed Olof Palme. See Mattsson and Rauscher 2004.

[254]   Zetterberg 2011, Zetterberg in Tribell 2011 and Gür in Tribell 2012.

engineering methods could not cope well with social ills such as anonymity, alcoholism and rootlessness, especially in the functionalist one million apartment project 1965-75. Physician-turned-writer PC Jersild wrote the novel *Children's island* in 1976 that tells of a pre-pubescent boy being left alone in Stockholm city and affected by other lone urban strangers[255]. One of the main aims behind the planning of these residential areas was to create good democratic citizens. To achieve this aim, decent housing projects were erected, with a good range of services, including schools, nurseries, churches, public spaces, libraries, and meeting places for different groups of households. A principal aim, although ultimately unsuccessful, was to mix and integrate different groups of households through the spatial mixing of tenures. But civil society is not created from above and many such areas are now outdoor museums, socialist utopian suburbs, Årsta and Vällingby in particular.

In the socialist utopia, history is dead, traditions boring and hierarchical. Modernity and future are all that matters. Not everyone agreed and by 1976, a romantic view of rural Sweden along with criticism of industrial waste and care for environment brought the center-right coalition to power. The new middle class after 1945 made new voluntary bounds between them, some more equal, some more hierarchical. The latter was fought in every possible way as socialists wanted no equalities to emerge. A good example is the anxiety of meritocracy in education. But as Tocqueville noted, these hierarchies could also defend people's interests against the state and market. Such entities could become harmful in welfare state expansion but good in defending civil and communal freedoms. The liberal self-help associations and charities of 19th century, traditional bourgeoisie and professionals based on middle class values were to be reduced to smallest possible units and replaced by larger collectives and government institutions.

Folkhem foundations and ideology ruled from 1930 to around 1970. But with rising wealth and more knowledge at end of 1960s, some of the

---

[255]   Jersild 1986. The book became also a popular film about Swedish anonymity, modernity and pre teenage life.

new middle class started to vote for the center-right parties. When poor people eventually got richer and bought independent houses, started to try out upper class sports such as tennis, golfing and sailing, making trips abroad and enjoyed life as they wanted, ruling socialists did not approve. The socialist establishment tried to direct the emerging new middle class with rural and working class roots as they had done successfully with the labour movement, but people started to behave more independently with rising living standards.

Some socialists were also recent members of this new middle class and became loyal to the welfare state, some more loyal than rising workers were. Thus the cultural left of 1968, the vanguard Maoists that had the right class consciousness, was born: a middle class telling workers that in the interests of the working class (and adding later immigrants, women, environment, and sexual minorities), it is best you let us talk, give us your money and keep quiet. We will liberate you if you give us power and hegemony. Interestingly, in the 1970s as an effort to give voice to workers and downtrodden people (addicts, criminals, and patients), radical journalists interviewed the oppressed and sometimes got the wrong answers back. Some workers wanted to keep more money and pay less tax. Some addicts liked their lives. Some people wanted less immigration. All housewives were not feeling repressed. Young men said they like to fight and get drunk. Media learned and the openness from 1970s was replaced later by a moralizing and self-censoring climate where few dared to speak their mind.

In 1982 filmmaker Ingmar Bergman come back to Sweden from German exile and showed his masterpiece *Fanny and Alexander*. In this film saga and family drama, Bergman had the main actor repeatedly refer to the little world of arts and family in contrast to the increasing chaos of life outside. Socialists viewed Bergman as a petty bourgeois who wanted to disclose himself from the real and larger world. Civil society was that small little world that socialists themselves wanted to escape from. With the conservative sociologist Hans Zetterberg's research and prolific writings in defence of a bourgeois definition of civil society, the left found its target and attacked anything smelling of charity, free community and separation from universal welfare state ideology. But the left misunderstood most of what the new debate on civil society was about and had little connection with other left bent sociologists at the time who also wanted to cherish civil society. The American debate on the value of community, the communitarian debate in 1990s, was in similar fashion misjudged by the left[256].

One of the left leaning proponents of civil society was Robert Bellah in USA, another Jürgen Habermas in West Germany who launched the two concepts of life world and system in his 1981 treatise on communicative action. For Habermas, the concept of life-world explained the communicative actions of individuals in civil society and relationships, whereas the concept of system was described as external means coming from bureaucracy and market, colonizing the life-world of human interactions. These nuances passed with no notice from the socialists in Sweden as they continued the attacks on community life, middle class traditions and voluntary services. The socialist union of municipal employees wanted in the 1980s to ban parents that helped out at cooperative day care centers which were owned by parents themselves. These parents sometimes joined the employees when needed and cleaned the center every fortnight, but these contributions were deemed privatizing collective areas and replacing municipal workers with volunteers.

Civil society need not be defined to organized community but also communal feelings and empathy for people, strangers and clients even, displaying normal compassion and altruism. In 1992 two home helpers were subjects in the court of Bollnäs town, accused for showing affection to their clients, elderly men and women, in order to receive money in exchange. The helpers claimed innocence. One of them had after many protests received $400 from an old male patient and put the money in an envelope not to be used. The other helper was selected as only heir of a

---

[256]   I edited and translated essays by John Rawls, Charles Taylor, Michael Sandel, Michael Waltzer, Alaisdair McIntyre and others for left leaning publisher Daidalos but they were never published except for a few in *Res Publica* later. The book may be published by print-on demand as well though.

house where an old woman wanted to stay and thus give it to the helper as private donation. One of the helpers was kept in police arrest for nine days with no legal grounds and later tried to commit suicide. The other was set free but both their lives were ruined. Two middle aged uneducated women with good hearts was trying to do more than was asked from them professionally but as humans.

The strangeness of the cases was the intimidating investigations of the helpers' actions, feelings and display of affections towards their clients. Their manager told the court that it was not the responsibility of municipal care services for elderly to be so helpful, especially off working hours. To do so must imply a sly attitude to gain profits for personal use. One cannot simply help people out of compassion, the manager of social care argued. From the police investigation: "The first hug was given by Easter/.../The accused use to read the paper for the client". One accused helper seem to think too much of herself. Her colleagues reported that "Many colleagues has felt that she thinks too well of herself and she has many times uttered 'People are so happy when I come'"[257]. Civil society is built on friendship, shared happiness and voluntary actions, but these normal human traits were suspected and ridiculed. Zaremba had again found the extreme results of modern welfare mechanisms, two decades after seeing naked old ladies being run through hospital corridors and collectively cleaned with water hoses without any ideas about human dignity among staff or doctors.

Civil society organizations are strong in Sweden where people keep themselves active with little or no importance to welfare services or real importance to their personal freedoms. Over 80% of adults are members

---

[257]   Zaremba 1992. The title of the essay is "Den obarmhärtige samariten" which is a pun on the Good Samaritan, the Swedish word for home help (hemsamarit, a job I have had too) and the unkindness shown by the leadership at the municipal care for elderly in Bollnäs, who said "It is not our duty to deliver compassion". The essay also tells about a priest being too religious, an official at refugee center too kind when drinking coffee with asylum seekers and teachers who spend too much time out of office hours with their students.

of organizations and 50 % of all Swedes spend their free hours working within some organized non-profit activity. Besides the Dutch, Swedes are the most active people in the world with regard to voluntary member-ship. But civil society do not take over the strong relationship between the state and individuals, the structures of state individualism that let Swedes be supported by the strong welfare state to realize their freedom. Civil society comes second and any support for a more communitarian society as the Red Tory project in UK seems undesired and quite im-possible[258]. The center-right coalition won not because they wanted to replace welfare institutions with voluntary associations and enhance civil society as communal morality, as some moderates had tried earlier (Hans L. Zetterberg in particular in the 1990 moderate party program). Rather it was the acceptance of the welfare state and trust that center-right pol-iticians could outdo the socialists with that paved way for the victory in 2006. Swedes love their state. But the state is a dangerous friend and its overwhelming kindness may turn cold, leaving citizens with nothing on their own and no one to turn to.

NORMAL POLITICAL IDEOLOGIES AND PEOPLE

Political ideological debate beyond current affairs and parliamentary politics has risen somewhat the last decades, but are nothing impressive so far. Parties produce little ideologically motivated proposals and refer seldom if ever to political ideologies or thinkers. The ruling center-right government has put the foot forward in execution and some policies but little in ideology and principles. Pragmatism has ruled Sweden since the left leaning 1970s and right leaning 1980s. Governments earlier led by Persson and Reinfeldt now are closer to each other than any other rivals ever have been before. With that in mind and the usual Swedish reluc-tance towards ideological debates, there has not been much of an ideolog-ical discussion the last decades but that may change. Conservatism was done with 1945, socialism 1991 and liberalism has ruled itself do death as

---

[258]   Trägårdh 2011. Research on and advocacy for civil society are being done at Stock-holm School of Economics, Ersta Sköndal foundation and Sektor3. See also Wijk-ström et al 2006 and Jacobsson (ed) 2010.

all parties are welfare liberals of some sort, from left to right.

The Swedish parties to the right have been under such dominance that their own self-image and labelling have been thwarted. In 1976 the victorious three party coalition called itself sometimes non-socialist to distinguish themselves from the socialist block of social democrats, greens and communists. To use the opponents' label and reverse it makes oneself into a pure negative reaction to the dominant view. Liberal and agrarian parties have most reluctance to use any references that that could lead to defence of traditions, except intellectual and rural traditions possibly. Both parties had at various times during the long social democratic reign supported minority cabinets and did so off and on until 1998.

Culture broadly defined has been dominated by the left as has been shown earlier. But the press is predominately liberal, center or moderate, so there is a strange division of labour in the press. Editorials may speak against socialism whereas the cultural pages support government initiatives or review left issues and events positively. Cultural pages in Swedish newspapers have since 1960s also dealt with social and political issues. The Swedish non-socialist press owners and editors have not cared enough about culture since 1970. Now they may regret this decision, but there is a long tradition of left activism on these pages to fight[259].

The Swedish word borgerlig is sometimes used for right of center politics and attitudes. It comes from the German bürgerlich, French bourgeois and the middle English burgeis, later burgher, i.e. the urban dwellers behind walls in small towns, later middle class and professionals. Sweden went through such a deep transformation into a state dominated by the working and lower middle classes that the idea of borgerlig seemed outdated, sedated, boring, middle class and smelled of old conservatism and irrelevant traditions of culture or manners. Today the term borgerlig can be applied to somewhat insular middle class life and materialism without political connotations. Thus a worker in his townhouse may have a materially better and more borgerlig lifestyle yet vote socialist.

---

[259] Haage in Almqvist and Gröning (eds.) 2011. See also Lagercrantz 2011.

Borgerlig is often replaced with liberal. Few openly express conservative values. Since the fight against wildcat strikes and wage earners funds in 1970s, employers gathered large funds to be able to use their lockout weapon if needed. These funds and other business and private contributions helped to create borgerliga think tanks, publishing houses, journals and educational institutes which mostly function: Timbro, Ratio, Ohlininstitutet, Den Nya Välfärden, Smedjan, City Universitetet, Studieförbundet Näringsliv och Samhälle (SNS). Lately Fores, Captus, Kebnekaisegruppen and Liberalerna have joined the liberal- conservative camp. The middle of the road think tank Global Utmaning is not quite liberal, but not old socialist either. Rather pink green. None of these think tanks and initiatives can measure up to the massive propaganda in government run media, union and socialist corporatist organizations.

Using borgerlig in book titles is not frowned upon anymore as last years' publications show[260] and there is an interest among youth and academics for other ideologies than leftist. Principles of freedom have come to the forefront through discussions on internet regulations, citizens' right to information and reluctance to pay for digital material. A political party only based on internet issues, Pirate Party (Piratpartiet), was 2009 voted into the European parliament with two members. The intense discussions and wide support for illegal downloading of copyrighted products give Sweden an extreme position, but very close to current trends in internet technology and lax attitudes towards legislation.

Some rare thinkers try to bring in liberal and conservative ideologies and policies in a country dominated by pragmatism and left politics. Caution: Remember that what is considered classical liberal and conservative in Sweden is just right of center on a world scale. Thinkers mentioned below may share ideals of welfare liberalism which make them stand apart from traditional Tories and Republicans. They do not make up a group with an agenda, but stand clearly apart from the cultural left and most center-right party establishments.

---

[260]   Almqvist och Gröning (eds.) 2011, Tribell (ed.) 2011, Tribell (ed.) 2012.

Mattias Svensson and Johan Norberg are two liberals that question the Swedish idea of a large state as foundation for democracy. The smaller the state, the lesser democracy, Svensson maintains, has been the Swedish welfare state argument. But the large state can bring its opposite, less democracy. A totalitarian democracy like Sweden was about to become in 1970-1990 has now been avoided, but there are still strong egalitarian tendencies among people. Those with such tendencies may blame other families for their child care solutions, their mode of transport or any other distinction that other families lack. They are busybodies not minding their own business. Svensson has continued his libertarian critique of Swedish paternalism in his book about regulations of drinking, dancing and enjoying themselves[261]. Ayn Rand has been an important inspiration.

Johan Norberg is senior fellow of Cato Institute and member of Mont Pelerin Society, both classical liberal institutions, with a range of political, economic and historical writings as well as a column in the free daily *Metro*. He was a libertarian anarchist but turned classic liberal and defends vigorously open immigration and free markets. Since then he has devoted himself to world economy as well as a treatise pursuits of happiness, films on global economy, defended Milton Friedman against Naomi Klein and much else[262]. The Swedish government used his talents and energy in the first report of the Globalisation Council after the center-right victory 2007. His early historical writings on Swedish liberalism and the freedom loving popular writer Vilhelm Moberg give him a backing in debates on finance crises and economic policy that few in Sweden have.

Isobel Hadley-Kamptz is another young liberal writer with few attacks on welfare state mechanisms. Her book *Frihet & fruktan* (Freedom & fear) is influenced by the American liberal theorist Judith

---

[261]   Svensson 2011.

[262]   For a collection of his process from wilder libertarian past to established liberal scholar, see Norberg 2010. Publications including two celebrated books in English at www.johannorberg.net

Shklar. With critique of military-industrial complex, gene modified foods, attacks on internet integrity and universal rights, she writes in a liberal and more pessimistic American tradition of Hobbesian political theory.

Conservatism as a political ideology has not been much supported by writers but a few exist and has taken steps further since Staffan Burenstam Linder, Torgny S. Segerstedt and Hans L. Zetterberg cleared some ideological paths after 1950. Fredrik Haage, Thomas Idergard and Stefan Olsson are new conservative thinkers, but none of them are much heard of in ideological discussions. The latter is the most prolific with a decent handbook of modern conservatism in Swedish, which was unthinkable a decade ago[263].

Johan Tralau and Roland Poirier Martinsson are scholars in the conservative tradition. Tralau is an erudite political scientist with studies in German idealism, radical conservatism (Jünger, Schmitt) and ancient Greek tragedy. His contributions to conservative ideology are mostly academic, while philosopher Poirier Martinsson tries to reach out. He is openly conservative and Catholic, both rare in Sweden. Using the think tank Timbro and moderate daily *Svenska Dagbladet*, Poirer Martinsson debates Swedish extremes from a standpoint outside Sweden, often American and unmistakably Texan. He is daring and gets much ridicule and hateful responses not just from socialist editors, but also from public radio and liberal press.

A forecast on ideological contributions from right of center in coming decades is hard to do but there is some hope. Two liberal but politically independent people with enough clout that could make a difference in decades ahead are the editor PJ Anders Linder and Johan Norberg. Together they cover history of ideas and literature, entrepreneurship, small business, taxation, political ideologies from classical liberalism to compassionate conservatism, global markets and European finance cri-

---

[263]   Olsson 2011. See also Haage 2000, Söderbaum (ed) 2011 and Idergard in Tribell (ed.) 2011.

ses. Their popular and serious writings feature wit, no nonsense, clarity and often tongue in cheek expressions that carry far into the center of Swedish politics[264]. The more normal Sweden gets, the more Norberg and Linder will be heard of, understood and appreciated.

CHAPTER 7

Normal Sweden

Making Sweden into a normal country is the aim of this book. If any reader has come this far, something might happen. But I am quite sure that Swedes in general, believe themselves to be normal, whereas all features and incidents shared in this book reveal the opposite to be true. They are extreme. In fact I do not believe Swedes can make their country normal by themselves. They will need help from four groups of foreigners, Groups A, D, E and F. The first already mentioned two groups, A and D, are already residing in Sweden and contribute to a better and more normal nation[265]. The latter two will also help and some need not even enter the country to help the Swedes become more normal. Reasoning below explains the four groups and where you as reader fit.

The first group is the aforementioned Group A, normal people immigrating to Sweden for all sorts of reasons. They are the vast majority of hard working inhabitants with immigrant background, some citizens, some not. They often espouse values that are shared by most people in

---

[264]   Linder has not written ideological treatises, but is an effective organiser and proponent for sanity and centre-right politics. His work and optimism is hailed in Tribell (ed.) 2012 and at a much attended June 2012 event at Federation of Swedish Enterprise for his 50th birthday. A great event which I enjoyed.

[265]   Sjunnesson 2008.

the world. These shared values are in contrast to the Swedish extremes which are fostered by 0.00000000013 % of world population and isolated in the upper right corner of World Value Survey map. These immigrants on the contrary support family values, do not think politics should meddle in their lives too much and want to make a career and good money. The larger this group becomes the more normal will Swedish politics become, especially with more well educated people from Muslim and Asian countries. If the parties understand this, voters usually voting on Christian democrats, Sweden democrats, Moderates and Social democrats would go to the party with the most normal values.

Swedish politicians usually have called Group A conservative but these immigrants are normal. The Swedish politicians are extreme and even more so than the Swedish citizens who privately often criticize the extreme nonsense but remain silent in public. Given the proclaimed tolerance from welfare state liberals and the political establishment, these conservative Swedes with immigrant roots, and other conservative or just apolitical Swedes, must be given a fair place in debates and participate in elections.

Another immigrants group saving Sweden will be Group D. These intellectuals defend universal values and stand up against the welfare state free riders, jihadists, welfare art tricksters, troublemakers, and the silly multiculturalists and post-colonial immigrant intellectuals calling Sweden racist, Group C that is. Without Group D, Swedes would succumb to silly multicultural projects and remain ridiculed suckers and wimps. Many females of Group D have more balls than most immigrant men and certainly all Swedish males.

To help Swedish innovation and business, Group E, consisting of one million new immigrants from India, China, Africa and Latin America, will come for work and studies, carefully selected with strict immigration procedures inspired from Canada and New Zealand. They will, and some already are headhunted and working in Sweden, take all necessary jobs, from service jobs to technical industrial careers and qualified professions and make new links with their old countries. Brain gain. After settling down and starting families in Sweden, they will find the Swedish preschools, primary, secondary and tertiary education not up to their high standards. Chinese and Indian schools will start along with private universities and colleges. Swedish teachers will be in minority there, but may apply for headship. Swedish students that do not prioritize nor master science, engineering, technology or medicine will be replaced by these quick and clever immigrants and their children who are more eager to study than unambitious and playful Swedes[266]. Group E will benefit from the decent infrastructure in Sweden, start new companies and make innovations. They will also use the decent welfare system, but hopefully downsized to normal OECD levels.

Group F are you, the readers of this book. Since the Swedes cannot develop their country into a normal nation by them, this book has to be written in English. If you have come this far, you will know what to do and I appreciate your patience with all details and stories of extreme proportions.

> "A Swede cannot imagine himself apart from his welfare
> state without having to redefine his self-image and his own
> national identity".

This sad quote from *Vat land -den sensual socialsstaten (Our country - the Swedish welfare state)* by Hans Zetterberg and Carl-Johan Ljunggren in 1997 states succinctly what has been told so far that the country of Sweden is the welfare state, nothing apart. Swedes have no home but the welfare state and no identity outside its yarn. State individualism seems to reign from left to right. I cannot accept this predicament and many Swedes would agree with me. Most people do not put up with all the nonsense from the cultural left, too many free riders on welfare services or being told what to think, but they do not voice their dissent being caught in a spiral of silence. The establishment left to right can continue with extremes that

---

[266]   My forthcoming novel *Sara Sarasvati* will picture how a young Indian comes to Sweden for engineering studies.

are truly astonishing. Considering that the Swedish identity does not only rely on the welfare state but also on the promise of modernity, technology and progress, it makes sense for Swedes to try to keep to their identity as progressives since it has a good ring. To any question about problems and complaints around the world, Swedes would continue to listen first silently, then shyly smile and proudly state, in sing-song melody, that "In Sviiiden, we have a syyystem . . ."

The National Swedish Institute states that being a progressive nation is the core of perceptions on Sweden abroad. And of course Swedes want to stay progressive and view criticism such as mine as unfair. Adding to their unease in questioning progressivism is that according to authors behind World Values Survey, the world seems to be going more in the direction of Sweden with raising living standards and modern values so why bother? A reply would be, if so many countries head in what may be the wrong direction, the better if someone tells them. The earlier the better.

One question is whether Sweden is a truly progressive nation with its repression of thought and its helpless citizens, or rather the most extreme country in the world due to its own history. But granted that Sweden is progressive in the common sense meaning of the word, what would happen if Sweden tried to take a step back and not try so hard in being the most progressive country in the world? A slide down on the World Value Survey map would make Sweden closer to Norway and Denmark, similar progressive countries with same living standards and high taxation but more normal. Would not that be possible? Can Swedes imagine another less inhuman interpretation of being progressive or are they nothing worth without being extremely progressive? Being progressive includes high hopes and experiments with future but the costs are severe if reality clashes with hopeful yet extreme attempts. The Swedish progressive way applies only to Sweden, hopefully this book argues. Other countries heading towards modernization and progressivism will lead to other interpretations without a long history of medieval centralized administration, social democratic hegemony, totalitarian tendencies, conformism, rampant state individualism and a victory of the cultural left since 1968.

Sweden should, according to my advice not try to be as madly progressive and extreme, which the nation tried its best in, 1970-2000 but ended in humiliation. Rather than experiments and extremes, Sweden should try to develop into a normal nation and draw respect from other normal nations as being one among others, not The Big Sister of the world / UN /EU always knowing best and trying for world moral championship[267]. Normality does not mean to go backwards, but in this case to reduce welfare state promises, which my reports on demography and taxation limits already have shown is necessary, support civil society and give freedom of expression back to its people. That would be real progress and make Swedes less angelic, but more human. Less demonic in my opinion. The question the state individualism proponents Henrik Berggren and Lars Trägårdh asked in their 2006 book title *Is the Swede a human being?* will then be answered positively. Yes the Swedes are humans and thereby fallible.

Swedes are content with paying high taxes of which most they have no clue of, the first of the two barriers to normal nationhood I stated in Chapter 1. Myself I do not want to, but the overwhelming majority of Swedes are willing to give away at minimum 60 % of their salary to welfare recipients, state do-gooders, extreme projects and a large government sector. Expansive welfare states with overregulated labour markets such as Sweden lead to slower growth, ineffective service sector and many people on benefits, but these effects are brushed over by the Swedish majority who want to be progressives at any costs. Going from no 4 in the world economy ratings in 1970 to around no 15 in 2012 does not bother them, nor the prospects of sliding down further due to lack of well educated professionals and science and technology students. Sweden is a fat cat sleeping its way into oblivion from and of the world. The contract with the middle class and government which gave support for high taxes in order to get high standards in return is broken. Middle class in Sweden pay a lot but do not get enough back. Yet they keep trust in the welfare system.

The second barrier is the silence and conformism which both are rooted

---

[267]   Arnstberg 2007.

in Swedish history from centuries of bowing down, welfare state engineering, totalitarian democracy and the last decade's massive repressions
of thought and speech. I want to be able to speak my mind, call a spade
a spade and hear all arguments in all discussions without being called
extreme. Sweden is. This book is my attempt to remain normal in the
land of extremes.

Afterword by an extreme Swede

I am extreme in Sweden, but normal abroad. Then how did I become extreme? At first I was like any normal Swede, which is extreme on a global scale as I have tried to show, but that is seldom acknowledged and well understood in Sweden. My development has gone in the opposite direction, towards the values and views of most people in the world, towards normality, but this stand is considered extreme in Sweden.

How the story of modern Sweden came about has been my interest since youth. I wrote my graduation essay (specialarbete) at secondary school Lundellska in Uppsala in 1978 on the rise and fall of social democracy in Sweden. Two years before on 19 September 1976, I had been celebrating the fall of 44 years of social democratic party rule. The celebration took place at the Moderate party election night, but I was soon the leave center-right politics for leftist politics. The long reign of social democracy is unavoidable in any writings on Swedish 20th century politics and will be covered here along with other and deeper national roots to the successful welfare state.

For the next 25 years I was a left wing activist, elected and sometime writer. After finishing school in 1978, I worked at the left leaning and alternative music scene Musikforum in Uppsala, joined the communist party VPK and started a study circle on Marx *Das Kapital*. Marxism was not the only influence as I was involved in anarchist and libertarian socialist groups. My early libertarian influences would keep me steady though, going from libertarian socialism to libertarianism by 2000.

Keeping to the ideals of the new left and counter culture, I wrote in small journals and magazines, but also in the regular leftwing press, as freelance journalist and news reporter. I started a local monthly alternative magazine. When the left party needed a member of the board of culture in, I became an elected member of Uppsala municipality. My libertarian leanings led me to anarcho-syndicalism, autonomist Marxism, support for sex workers' rights and harm reduction drug policies. The last two areas were not well liked by the regular left establishment. But I could not sustain a living and had to support a growing family and needed to work.

I had a BA in philosophy which was useless on the job market, but gave me the idea of continuing with graduate studies for a PhD. My supervisors were not interested in my fascination for subversive French thinkers like Foucault and Deleuze and I did what I could to be a pain in the ass for them and Uppsala University[268]. Attempts to find compromises between their stand for analytical philosophy and logic and my post-structuralist and post-Marxist wilder ideas did not yield any results.

Academia and journalism did not pay off so I became an adult education teacher and graduated with a teachers' diploma as folkhögskollärare. Folkhögskola is a residential community college for adults in need of a secondary education or wanting to expand their knowledge or skills in some particular field. Myself I had been to one for media studies and quite liked the idea of self-directed learning. Folkhögskolor and study circles are parts of Scandinavian civil society as an egalitarian and formerly rural alternative to academic and urban educational institutions. I worked for such schools for adults in Brunnsvik, Biskops-Arnö, Wik and Rinkeby. Later I quit the folk education career and shifted to teacher education and school leadership, but continued to follow my intellectual interests at home and abroad.

Europe was considered conservative and rigid from the more modern Swedish point of view after World War II. But I was eager to get to know more about something other than bland and insular socialist Sweden. The left leaning yet open minded publishers Bo Cavefors and Brutus Östling were helpful to bridge the gaps to continental Europe for me and other dissenting leftists. The American influence of Sweden is strong. I had spent 1975-1976 in high school in the Ozark Mountains, Arkansas, and another six months hitchhiking from the East coast to the West in 1979. Anything but Sweden. In 1982 I moved to Denmark, hung out with squatters and tried to support myself on free-lance writing but had to

---

[268]   See Sjunnesson 1998.

move back. Later I moved again but now with family to Switzerland for a year of child care, probably being the only house husband there. Then I moved to USA again in 1993 as graduate student at New School for Social Research in New York.

The stories of extreme Swedish policies and the many embarrassing scandals of domineering socialist party has given readers a picture of Sweden as extreme in the chapters are picked from media. But I have similar experiences from various work places and everyday life that give me enough confidence to say that Sweden is certainly a strange country. From the age of 13, I have worked along with manual workers in my father's small construction business and later as home help and orderly at old folks' home and hospitals. Taking odd jobs as a young middle class man is common and I was no exception. The excruciatingly inhuman treatment of elderly that Polish born Swedish writer Maciej Zaremba talked about in the first chapter were common at elderly care homes where I used to work, such as Kungsgärdets Sjukhus and Akademiska Hospital. Zaremba was shocked as he had seen better care in poor communist Poland but I had not.

My work as reporter at local newspapers and free-lance gave me access to ordinary people in small towns. Their country views were less extreme but often ridiculed by the priggish left leaning establishment in urban areas. But my most important experiences that drive the work behind this book are my years working with immigrant youth and adults. Nowhere are the Swedish extremes more visible than concerning immigration, with feminism and family life at shared second place. In schools all these areas come together and sometimes collide as shown below[269].

As deputy principal of a primary school with 99 % children from immigrant families, I got many stories that would fill another book but here is a selection. This particular school, Hjulstaskolan north of Stockholm, did barely function with only 30 % of students getting grades in all sub-

---

[269]   This school section has been translated into Swedish and published in Arnstberg and Sandelin 2013.

jects and another 50 % enough grades to continue to secondary school. Yet it was hailed as a leading model for multiculturalism from National Agency of Schools, the principal was awarded and visiting groups of teachers and staff from more white areas came regularly to watch all the brown students. A human zoo with fights and loud laughs, exotic beautiful creatures and lots of teenage energy and rage. Fun but wild. I was responsible for organizing teachers in 30 languages as the Swedish policy on secondary language learning demands good knowledge and thus teaching of the first language. Newcomers had to learn their own language upon arrival, sometimes also new non-Latin scripts which were mostly useless outside their former nations. When immigrant families protested and asked for more Swedish teaching instead of classes in their own languages, there was no possibility. Teaching of the family language is strongly enforced policy and granted by law, even if parents or students do not like it. I quite enjoyed speaking Hindi, Spanish, French and English with the hardworking immigrated and settled teachers of all these languages. The Somalis in particular.

As I received the new students I saw bright young people that behaved well, listened to the teachers and studied hard. After six months they had changed into normal Swedish students, albeit with the immigrant cultural twist at this particular school. Normal Swedish student behaviour means misbehaving, not paying attention to studies nor respecting adults. Not all did and girls were better students than boys. But the socialization process into Swedish extremes was apparent and should lead to more than shrugs and smiles as the former shy students started to walk in and out of class or shout loudly in the canteen. Swedish teachers are extremely accepting of bad behaviour and viewed the new students' development as normal. I did not. At canteen, food was thrown at me and other teachers with little response. I got hit but could not see by whom and no one cared much either. Next episode was more troubling.

A 15 year old student of Somali origin that was known to be violent had accidentally broken a window in the girls' bathroom. As he was seen, there was no denial. He was pushed into my office by his mentor, a special education teacher, as was the routine not to be alone with misbehaving students. I told him that the window would cost him $100 in repairs but he had the option to work a few days in the school during summer if there was no money at home. His family was on welfare, a single mother with 8 children. He looked straight into my face and spat. End of story and a police report of the window and the spitting. My superiors did not like to report the incident to the police, but I did anyway and had to appear in court. The young man grinned when he was sentenced to have weekly talks with the social services. He had had many such talks with little effect.

There would be more visits to courts, police stations and social services. One day a gang of 20-30 young thugs from rivalling immigrant dominated suburb Rinkeby attacked the school with chains, fists and metal bars. Windows were smashed, people hit and panic erupted before the police came. Some student in the school may have invited them to stir trouble, but the school wanted to keep quiet. So did all involved students at the school as no one dared to speak of what they had seen. There was an informal local order in Tensta demanding absolute loyalty that was higher than school management and laws.

This school in Tensta suburb had a system of ethnic groups that revealed a pecking order according to various influxes and generations. On top were the Turks, Kurds, Iranians and some Middle Eastern countries. Their parents had come in late 1970s to 1990s and ruled Tensta-Rinkeby suburbs for a generation, replacing the hard working South Europeans and well educated Latin Americans who had come since 1960s - 1970 for work and asylum. This group on the top had their own representatives employed at a café and leisure center in the middle of the school who spoke Arabic, Kurdish, Turkish and Persian. When a conflict arose between a student speaking any of these languages and management, the instruction was to use this staff as mediators. They did not have any formal training apart from primary school often at their own former countries, at best. The students who got caught or were suspected of theft, harassment or disturbance were supported by these café employees and conflicts were to be solved with no Swedish involved, although the students could be born in Sweden and with good speaking ability before the conflict. Sometimes a *Qu'ran* was used where the student put his hand to ensure telling the truth.

After such meetings stolen goods could appear, expensive jackets, phones, keys and bags but there was no mentioning from where. The staff would hand over what was given to them by young intermediaries who learned how to deal with conflicts and issues within their ethnic group and outside any laws. Since there was no registration of which students had actually stolen anything, neither family nor police or social services were involved. Only the café staff may know but kept quiet as the ties to the youth were more important than keeping to the rules, laws and informing family. Whether theft was done by same or new students was never known as no records were kept and no follow up possible. Loyalty to local informal ethnic networks was crucial to make it in this destitute suburb.

If students were not from any of these Middle Eastern groups, they had to go by the regular Swedish rules which involved talking Swedish and have other adults informed. Somalis in particular were a large minority that did not get any help from the café staff, rather the opposite. Swedish students were rare. Other ethnic groups were also subject to regular school procedures. In this way, segregation was imprinted every day at school; one kind of treatment for Middle Eastern students, another for other students and distantly, a third kind normal regular treatment in Swedish primary schools. 2 km away were schools with predominantly Swedish students that obeyed normal procedures and many immigrant parents put their children there as my school was the last resort with a very bad reputation. Teenagers from this school had a few years before gang raped the Swedish girl in nearby Rissne which has been mentioned earlier here.

I worked also with unemployed young immigrants from same destitute area north of Stockholm, trying to get them interested in theatre and become social entrepreneurs but with little success. The Latin American theatre association I cooperated with was mainly a setup for channelling government funds for private purposes. Often despair and violence were used as an argument for getting more money, since without this theatre project according to this blackmail logic, the desperate young men and women would turn into criminals and cause trouble. Same reasoning was used at a secondary school where youth could study rap music for three years in a special arts program. I was deputy principal there and saw same kind but faulty logic. Without the rap music program they would turn into criminals, troublemakers or be unemployed. But after studying rap music they could not enter higher learning nor get a vocation and most probably not support themselves by rapping. Same logic was used for other studies such as skate board, basketball and floor ball. With these leisure oriented secondary school programs, students would not get anywhere. My argument would be that with these programs neither geared towards higher education, nor to vocations or a possible employment (demand for paid fulltime rappers and skaters is rare), students were fooled. Floor ball and skate are great activities after school, not during. I have stories of drug arrests, plastic bags with urine thrown from roof tops and much else. None of my experiences as school manager and for teachers in similar areas are exceptional.

My middle class upbringing that had led to leftist activism and rebellion was comfortable with three sisters, mother at home and hardworking father. My father came from meagre background. His land labouring father was single with six children in southern Sweden. He was bright but was not allowed by his father to go further than 7th grade. My father got mad, went to sea and joined the military which gave him a short engineering diploma which he used for further private studies in construction and road coating. He started his own construction company and became a self-made man. My mother came from more business family origins and was a fiery woman who went to New York and San Francisco for two years as a maid. She had a Mediterranean temperament and was quite courageous, as when she went alone to Iraq in 1973 for two weeks, a single pale red headed lady. My family had been hosting family to foreign students in Uppsala, among them an Iraqi nuclear scientist working for the rising Saddam Hussein regime. He had invited my mother after his years with us in Sweden. She took him by his word, went visiting his family and was probably the only white red haired single female tourist in Bagdad. No visits at any nuclear plants though.

I have tried to leave Sweden at least six times but always come back. India has been the last destination as I have family there. In New Delhi, I was associate director of the School Choice campaign at Center for Civil Society, a liberal think tank trying to implement school vouchers and deregulate the Indian school system[270]. With six years in USA, Denmark, Switzerland and India, I have gotten used to feeling normal in the rest of the world. Why I have such an ambivalent feeling for my country is because I feel extreme in Sweden, but normal outside. What is normal outside is considered extreme in Sweden. The country of extremes does not view itself as extreme but given all parameters as has been revealed, it is the most extreme country in the world in the sense of being extremely secular, rational, individualistic and paternalistic with radical egalitarian social policies supported by government and propagated by a left leaning media. Independent thought and expression in art, journalism, research and politics are discouraged and sometimes fought with violence by extra-parliamentary groups and activists who share same opinions as the left leaning media and political establishment.

Not only by standards from World Values Survey, but by all human measures and from all the extreme stories and scandals, is Sweden extreme. Only by acknowledging this and letting a million or more people migrate to Sweden will the nation become normal. Swedes are incapable to solve their problems as there is no self-awareness of being at fault. The patient is sick but does not notice. Psychiatrist David Eberhard gave the nation the medical diagnosis of panic syndrome. If Sweden was a patient, it would suffer from episodic paroxysmal anxiety due to its citizens' incapability to cope with everyday frustrations, anxieties and small challenges. Other countries have citizens who live much harder lives with no such symptoms. I call these countries normal and would like Sweden to become one too. In this I am optimistic but quite rare. As you have gathered I put some hope into the new Swedes, the immigrants, who are sometimes more patriotic than the original inhabitants. I would like all Swedes to become like that, normal citizens in a normal nation.

---

270   See www.ccs.in and Palmer 2011 for overview of CCS' political and ethical thinking on free markets in India and beyond.

Acknowledgements:

Thanks to Richard North, Parth J. Shah, Rajyasri Rao, Inger Enkvist, Jacob E:son Söderbaum, Patrik Engellau, Nima Sanandaji, Janerik Larsson, Mie Josefson, KO Arnstberg, Svante Nycander, Brenda Geise and Anders Edwardsson. A special thanks to Fredrik Segerfeldt, Subramanya Rao, Graham Siebert, Nicolas Bredefeldt and Jonathan Friedman for help with editing and publishing. A great thanks also to all known and unknown contributors who generously supported the printing through www.crowdculture.se .

I dedicate this book to my parents, Hans and Margareta Sjunnesson, the rock and spirit of my life.

Stockholm and New Delhi, summer 2013

Jan Sjunnesson

sjunne.com

Governments in Sweden 1876 - 2014

1876 – 1932	Various conservative, liberal and socialist minority cabinets in coalition. Prime ministers Lindman, Staaff, Branting and others.
1932 - 1976	Social democratic labour party. PMs Hansson, Erlander and Palme
1976 - 1982	Center-right coalitions. PMs Fälldin (thrice) and Ullsten
1982 - 1991	Social democratic labour party. PMs Palme and Carlsson.
1991 - 1994	Center right coalition. PM Bildt
1994 - 2006	Social democratic labour party. PMs Carlsson and Persson.
2006 –2010	Center-right coalition. PM Reinfeldt.
2010 - 2014	Center-right coalition. PM Reinfeldt.

Parties 2010 - 2014

Left party (Vänsterpartiet)   6 %
Social democratic labour party (Arbetarepartiet Socialdemokraterna)   31 %
Environmentalist green party (Miljöpartiet de gröna)   7 %
Center party (Centerpartiet)   7 %
Liberal folk party (Folkpartiet liberalerna)   7 %
Moderate party (Moderata Samlingspartiet)   30 %
Christian democrats (Kristdemokraterna)   6 %
Sweden democrats (Sverigedemokraterna)   6 %

References

* Available online and found by search engines

Abelin, Matthias. 2012. *The Swedish 1997 – 2011 sterilization debate*. Stockholm: Vulkan.

Abrahamsson, Maria. 2006. "Feminism i det svenska medialandskapet" in *Samtida feminism*. Stockholm: Axel och Margaret Ax:son Johnsons stiftelse.

Aftonbladet. 2005-12-01. "Interview with Inga-Britt Ahlenius".*

Ahlberg, Leif. 1975. *Revolution på tjänstetid*. Stockholm: Ahlberg.

Ahlmark, Per. 2003. *Vänstern och tyranniet*. Stockholm: Timbro.*

Ahlmark, Per. 2011. *Gör inga dumheter medan jag är död!* Stockholm: Atlantis.

Allians för Sverige. 2010. *Alliansens vitbok de fyra första åren.* *

Almqvist, Kurt, ed. 2008. *Betydelsen av revolutionsåret 1968*. Stockholm: Atlantis.

Almqvist, Kurt and Gröning, Lotta (eds.) 2011. *Den nya borgerligheten*. Stockholm: Axel och Margaret Ax:son Johnsons stiftelse.

Almqvist, Kurt and Glans, Kay (eds.). 2001 *Den svenska framgångssagan ?* Stockholm: Fisher & Co.

Alopaeus, Marianne. 1983. *Drabbad av Sverige*. Stockholm: Brombergs.

Ambjörnsson, Fanny 2004. *I en klass för sig*. Diss. Stockholm: Ordfront.

Andersson, Patrik, Sanandaji, Nima and Segerfeldt, Fredrik. 2006. *Välkommen till Sverige. Om politisk snedvridning i kurslitteraturen för SFI – svenska för invandrare*. Stockholm: Timbro. *

Andersson, Jenny and Hilson, Mary. 2009. "Images of Sweden and the Nordic Countries" in *Scandinavian Journal of History*. Vol 34: 3.

Anners, Erik. 1975. *Den socialdemokratiska maktapparaten*. Stockholm: Askild & Kärnekull

Appelgren, Sofia. 2008. *Wild'n fresh : min berättelse om salladsbaren*. Stockholm: Ekerlids.

Arbetsförmedlingen. 2012-02-27. *Pressmeddelande. Arbetsförmedlingen förlikas med DO angående arbetsmarknadsutbildning.**

Arena Idé and Timbro. 2010. *Vi har råd med framtiden – men då krävs en långsiktig och sammanhållen politik för välfärdens finansiering*. Rapport från kommissionen om välfärdens framtida finansiering. Stockholm: Arena/Timbro. *

Arnstberg, Karl-Olov.1989. *Svenskhet: den kulturförnekande kulturen*. Stockholm: Carlssons.

Arnstberg, Karl-Olov.1998. *Svenskar och zigenare*. Stockholm: Carlssons.

Arnstberg, Karl-Olov. 2005. *Typiskt svenskt: åtta essäer om det nutida Sverige*. Stockholm: Carlsson

Arnstberg, Karl- Olov. 2007. "Moralmästerskapet" in *Axess* no 8.

Arnstberg, Karl-Olov. 2008. *Sverige och invandringen*. Lund: Studentlitteratur.

Arnstberg, Karl-Olov and Sandelin, Gunnar. 2013 *Invandring och mörkläggning*. Stockholm: Debattförlaget.

Arvidsson, Claes. 1999. *Ett annat land. Sverige och det långa 70-talet*. Stockholm: Timbro.

Arvidsson, Claes. 2006. *Olof Palme. Med verkligheten som fiende*. Stockholm: Timbro.

Arvidsson, Håkan. 2008. *Vi som visste allt. Minnen från 1960-talets vänsterrörelse*. Stockholm: Atlantis.

Asp, Kent. 2012 (forthcoming). *Journalistboken. Den svenska journalistkårens partisympatier.* Kapitel 13. Göteborg: Göteborgs universitet, JMK.*

Aspelin, J 2003. *Zlatan, Caligula och ordningen i skolan*. Studentlitteratur: Lund.

Asplund, Johan. 1991. *Essä om Gemeinschaft och Gesellschaft*. Göteborg: Korpen.

Axess Blog. www.axess.se/blog.

Bahr, Jenny von. 2011. *Bidrag-* Vägen till arbete? Stockholm: Timbro*

Bahr, Jenny von. 2012. *Varför är det så svårt för utrikesfödda att få arbete i Sverige?*. Stockholm: Timbro*

Baker, Josiah. 2011. *Constructing the People's Home: The political and economic origins and early development of the "Swedish Model", 1879- 1976*. Diss. Washington, D.C.: The Catholic University of America.*

Bauhn, Per and Demirbag-Sten, Dilsa. 2010. *Till frihetens försvar. En kritik av den normativa multikulturalismen*. Stockholm: Norstedts.

Beckman, Ludvig. 2006. "The competent cabinet? Ministers in Sweden and the problem of competence and democracy" in *Scandinavian Political Studies* Vol 29: 2.

Beckman, Ludvig. 2010. *Den rimliga integrationen*. Stockholm: Institutet för framtidsstudier and Dialogos förlag.

Bengtsson, Raimond. 1972. *". . . Åt alla lycka bär?"*. Göteborg: Zindermans.

Bengtsson, Rikard (ed.) 2010. *I Europas tjänst. Sveriges ordförandeskap i EU 2009*. Stockholm: SNS.

Berggren, Henrik. 2010. *Underbara dagar framför oss. En biografi över Olof Palme*. Stockholm: Norstedts.

Berggren, Henrik and Trägårdh, Lars. 2006. Är svensken människa? Gemenskap och oberoende i det moderna Sverige. Stockholm: Norstedts.

Berggren, Henrik and Trägårdh, Lars. 2011. *The Nordic way*. Contribution from Global

Utmaning at World Economic Forum Davos.*

Bergh, Andreas. 2009. *Den kapitalistiska välfärdsstaten.* Stockholm: Norstedts.

Bergh, Andreas. 2010. *Ett nytt Sverige.* Talk at Almedalen. Stockholm: Ratio.*

Bergh, Andreas. 2011. *The rise, fall and revival of the Swedish welfare state.* IFN Working paper no. 873. Stockholm: IFN.*

Bergh, Andreas. 2012. *Från DDR-Sverige till den kapitalistiska välfärdsstaten 2030.* Wibbleföreläsningen 2012. Stockholm: Ohlininstitutet.

Bergh,, Andreas and Bjørnskov, Christian. 2011. "Historical Trust Levels Predict the Current Size of the Welfare State" in *Kyklos.* Vol 64: 1.

Bergh, Andreas and Erlingsson, Gissur. 2009. "Liberalization without Retrenchment: Understanding the Consensus on Swedish Welfare State Reforms" in *Scandinavian Political Studies.* Vol 32: 1.

Bergh, Andreas and Henrekson, Magnus. 2010. *Government size and implications for economic growth.* Washington, D.C.: American Enterprise Institute.*

Bergh, Andreas and Henrekson, Magnus. 2011a "Government size and growth: A survey and interpretation of the evidence", in *Journal of economic surveys.* Vol. 25: 5.*

Bergh, Andreas and Henrekson, Magnus. 2011b. *Varför går det bra för Sverige ?* Stockholm: Fores.

Bergkvist, Tanja. 2009-02-28. "Vetenskap eller galenskap?" in *Svenska Dagbladet.*

Berman, Sheri. 2006. *The Primacy of Politics. Social Democracy and the Making of Europe's Twentieth Century.* New York: Cambridge University Press.

Björklund, Anders et al. 2005. *The market comes to education in Sweden.* New York: Russell Sage.

Björkman, Ingrid et al. 2006. *Exit folkhemssverige.* Torsby: Cruz del Sur.*

Boekhout van Solinge, Tim. 1997. *The Swedish drug control systems.* Amsterdam: Mets/Cedro.

Borg, Henrik. 2006. *Som man frågar får man svar. Masoud Kamali, Mona Sahlin och politiseringen av kommittteväsendet.* Stockholm: Timbro.*

Boye, Karin. 2002. *Kallocain.* Madison: University of Wisconsin Press.[original 1940]

Braw, Daniel. 2009. *Bland de mest bildade folk.* Stockholm: Timbro.*

Brown. Andrew. 2009. *Fishing in utopia. Sweden and the future that disappeared.* London: Granta.

Burenstam Linder, Staffan. 2010. *Den hjärtlösa välfärdsstaten.* Stockholm: Timbro [original 1983].

BRÅ 2005. *Brottslighet bland personer födda i Sverige och i utlandet.* Report 2005:17. Stockholm: BRÅ.

Bäckman, Maria. 2009. *Miljonsvennar. Omstridda platser och identiteter* Stockholm: Makadam.

Caesar, Julia. 2010a. *Världsmästarna. När Sverige blev mångkulturellt.* Visby: Print-on-demand.

Caesar, Julia, 2010b. *Fler ministrar borde gråta.* Visby: Print-on-demand.

Cantera Carlomango, Marcos. 1995. *Ett folk av mänsklig granit. Sverige i den italienska utrikespolitiken 1932- 1936.* Lund: Historiska media.

Carlqvist, Ingrid. 2012- 04-20. "Vi vill inte gulla i er konsensusbubbla" in *Journalisten.* *
Centre for Civil Society. www.ccs.in.*

Childs, Marquis. 1947. *Sweden: The middle way.* 3rd edition New Haven: Yale University Press [1st ed 1936]

Childs, Marquis. 1980. *Sweden: The middle way on trial.* New Haven: Yale University Press.

Dagens Arena. 2010. *Arenagruppens valanalys.* *

Dagens Samhälle. 2011. *Den offentliga marknaden.* Stockholm: Dagens samhälle.*

Dahlkvist, Mats. 1975. *Staten, socialdemokratin och socialismen.* Stockholm/Uppsala: Prisma/Verdandi.

Dalrymple, Theodore. 2008. *Not with a bang but a whimper. The politics and culture of decline.* Chicago: Ivan R. Dee.

Daun, Åke. 1996. *Swedish Mentality.* Philadelphia: Pennsylvania State University Press.

Daun, Åke. 2005. *En stuga på sjätte våningen.* Stockholm/Stehag: Symposium.

Delblanc, Sven. 1987. *I Moria land.* Stockholm: Bonniers.

Demirbag- Sten, Dilsa. 2009. *Essä om Politiskt Korrekt.* Stockholm: Forum för levande historia.*

Derfler, Leslie, 2011. *The fall and rise of political leaders: Olof Palme, Olusegun Obasanjo and Indira Gandhi .* New York: Palgrave.

Diskrimineringsombudsmannen. 2010-02-15. *AF diskriminerade mannen som inte ville skaka hand med kvinnlig chef* *

Diskrimineringsombudsmannen. 2011-10-13. *Dom i Stockholms tingsrätt: Vårdcentral diskriminerade lesbisk kvinna.* *

Drugli, May Britt. 2010. *Liten i barnehagen. Forskning, teori og praxis.* Oslo: Cappelen Damm.

Eberhard, David. 2007. *I trygghetsnarkomanernas land: Sverige och det nationella paniksyndromet.* Stockholm: Månpocket.

Eberhard, David. 2009. *Ingen tar skit i de lättkränktas land.* Stockholm: Prisma.

Economist 9 June 2011, "North star" and 13 Oct 2012 "Sweden: The New Model".*

Edling, Jan. 2005. *Alla behövs.* Stockholm: Timbro.*

Edwardsson, Anders. 2010. *En annorlunda historia*. Stockholm: Timbro.

Egonsson, Dan. 2007. *Om det politiskt korrekta*. Nora: Nya Doxa.

Ehn, Billy et al. 1999. *Försvenskningen av Sverige*. Stockholm: Natur och kultur.

Ehnmark, Anders. 2000. "1789 års man. Möte med Olof Palme", in *Ord & Bild*. No 4-5.

Ehmark, Anders. 1994. *Tre essäer om frihet*. Stockholm: Norstedts.

Ehrencrona, Olof. 1999. *Nicolin. En svensk historia*. Stockholm: Timbro.

Ekberg, Jan. 2009. *Invandringen och de offentliga finanserna*. ESO Rapport 2009:3. Stockholm: Regeringskansliet.*

Ekholm Friedman, Kajsa and Friedman, Jonathan. 2006. "Sverige: Från nationalstat till pluralt samhälle" in Hedetoft et al (eds). *Bortom stereotyperna. Invandrare och integration I Danmark och Sverige*. Göteborg: Makadam förlag

Eklund, Klas, 2011. *The Nordic way*. Contribution from Global Utmaning at World Economic Forum Davos.*

Ekonomifakta. www.ekonomifakta.se

Ellis, Evelyn. 2000. "In Praise of Political Correctness" in Numhauser-Henning, Ann (ed.)*Normativa Perspektiv; Festskrift Till Anna Christensen*. Lund: Juristförlaget

Engelau, Patrik. 2011. *Från enhetlighet till mångfald eller varför politiken, särskilt socialdemokratin, har stora problem*. Manuscript. Stockholm: Den Nya Välfärden.

Engelau, Patrik and Gür, Thomas. 2010. *Låt dem inte komma undan. Tio viktiga frågor till Sveriges politiker*. Stockholm: Den Nya Välfärden.*

Engelau, Patrik and Gür, Thomas. 2012. *Den övermodiga beskyddaren - hur välfärdsstaten underminerar det civila samhället och urholkar dygderna*. Stockholm: Den Nya Välfärden

Engellau, Patrik and Rossander, Olle. 2004. *Jobbet är att mata puman – hur och varför försäkringskassorna slarvar bort 40 miljarder kronor om året av skattebetalarnas pengar*. Stockholm: Den Nya Välfärden.

Enzensberger, Hans-Magnus. 1987. *Ack Europa*. Stockholm: Norstedts. [original 1982]

Enzensberger, Hans-Magnus.1992. *Till det normalas försvar*. Stockholm: Norstedts.

Eriksson, Håkan and Rennerfeldt, Jacob. 2009. *Folkhemmets balkanisering : diskriminering- skulturens baksida*. Stockholm: Ekerlids.

Erixon, Dick. 1999. *Svaghetens moral*. Stockholm: Timbro.*

European Commission. 2011. *Awareness of home affairs. Special Eurobarometer 380*. Brussels: EU Commission.*

Familjeliv. 2010. *Sverigemamman 2010*. Familjeliv.se *

Feldt, Kjell-Olof. 1991. *Alla dessa dagar . . .* Stockholm: Norstedts

Feldt, Kjell-Olof. 2012. *En kritisk betraktelse: Om socialdemokratins seger och kris*. Stockholm: Bonniers

Findlay, Jonung and Lundahl (eds.) 2002. *Bertil Ohlin. A centennial Celebration*. Cambridge: MIT Press:

Focus. 2011. "Spionjägaren som kom hem till kylan". No 38.*

Folkhälsoinstitutet. 2009. *Child day care center or home care for children 12–40 months of age – what is best for the child?* Stockholm: Folkhälsoinstitutet.*

Freeman, Richard et al. (eds.) 2006. *NBER-rapporten 2: Att reformera välfärdsstaten – amerikanskt perspektiv på den svenska modellen*. Stockholm: SNS.*

Freeman, Richard et al. (eds.) 2010. *Reforming the welfare state; recovery and beyond in Sweden*. Chicago: University of Chicago Press.

Frenander, Anders. 1999. *Debattens vågor: om politisk-ideologiska frågor i efterkrigstidens svenska kulturdebatt*. Göteborg: Göteborgs universitet, Idéhistoriska institutionen.

Friedman, Jonathan. 1999. "Rhinoceros 2" in *Current Anthropology* vol 40: 5.

Friedman, Jonathan. (forthcoming) *PC worlds: an anthropology of political correctness*.

Futureorientation. 2006. "The Scandinavian Way". No 5.*

Fölster, Stefan. 1999. "Inkomstfördelning i välfärdsstaten" in *Ekonomisk Debatt*. Vol 26: 4.*

Fölster, Stefan. 2012a. "Framtidens välfärd blir bättre trots lägre skatter" in Almqvist, Kurt and Gröning, Lotta (eds.) *Välfärdsstatens framtid*. Stockholm: Axel och Margaret Ax:son Johnsons stiftelse.

Fölster, Stefan. 2012b. "Tuffare villkor på framtidens arbetsmarknad" in Almqvist, Kurt and Gröning, Lotta (eds.) *Framtidens arbetsmarknad*. Stockholm: Axel och Margaret Ax:son Johnsons stiftelse.

Fölster, Stefan. 2012c. *Sverige har blivit en fet katt*. Stockholm: Svenskt Näringsliv.*

Fölster, Stefan and Kreicbergs. 2011. *Framtiden väntar inte. Om världen och Sveriges välstånd*. Stockholm: Ekerlids.

Fölster, Stefan et al. 2011. *Konsten att strula till ett liv*. Stockholm: Svenskt Näringsliv.*

Fölster, Stefan and Wallén, Fabian. 2009. *Sjanghaja de som ligger - Sveriges mest missförstådda samhällsomdaning*. Stockholm: Hjalmarsson & Högberg.*

Garme, Cecilia. 2001. *Newcomers to power. Socialists conquer France in 1981, non-socialists conquer Sweden in 1976*. Diss. Uppsala: Uppsala university, Department of government.

Globaliseringsrådet, 2009. *Utvecklingskraft och omställningsförmåga. Slutrapport*. Stockholm: Regeringskansliet, Utbildningsdepartementet.*

Greider, Göran. 2011. *Ingen kommer undan Olof Palme*. Stockholm: Ordfront.

Guillou, Jan. 2010. *Ordets makt och vanmakt*. Stockholm: Piratförlaget.

Gustavsson, Gina. 2009. "Falskt om individualism" in *Axess* no 3.

Gustavsson, Gina. 2011. *Treacherous Liberties: Isaiah Berlin's Theory of Positive and Negative Freedom in Contemporary Political Culture.* Diss. Uppsala: Uppsala University, Department of government.*

Gustavsson, Gina. 2012. "Romantiska irrgångar i integrationsdebatten" in Axess no 3.

Göransson, Bengt. 2010. *Tankar om politik.* Stockholm: Ersatz.

Haage, Fredrik. 2000. *Nycklar till en modern konservatism.* Stockholm: Timbro.

Hadenius, Karin. 1990. *Frihet och jämlikhet. Politiska mål för den svenska grundskolan.* Diss. Uppsala: Uppsala universitet, Statsvetenskapliga institutionen.

Hadley-Kamptz, Isobel. 2011. *Frihet och fruktan.* Stockholm: Natur och kultur.

Hakelius- Popova, Susanna. 2006. "Viljan att flyta medströms" in *Samtida feminism.* Stockholm: Axel och Margaret Ax:son Johnsons stiftelse.

Hamilton, Carl. 2005. *Det infantila samhället och barndomens slut.* Stockholm: Prisma

Hamilton, Carl. 2012. *(S)-koden. Den socialdemokratiska utmaningen.* Stockholm: Norstedts.

Hammarberg, Daniel. 2011. *Madhouse: a critical study of Swedish society.* Print-on-demand

HARO. Riksorganisation för valfrihet, jämställdhet och föräldraskap. www.haro.se*

Hayek, Fredrick von. 2007. *The road to serfdom.* Chicago: University of Chicago Press. [original 1944]

Hayek, Fredrick von. 1960. *Why I am not a conservative.* In *The Constitution of Liberty.* Washington: Cato.*

Heberlein, Ann. 2008. *Det var inte mitt fel.* Stockholm: Forma

Heclo, Hugh. 2010. *Modern social politics in Britain and Sweden.* Rev edition. London: ECPR.

Henrekson, Magnus.1996. "Sweden's relative economic performance" in *The Economic Journal* no 106.*

Henrekson, Magnus. 2008. "Folkhem i brytningstid" in Björnsson and Berge (eds.) *Skandinaviska vägval : det framtida norsk-svenska samarbetet.* Stockholm: Atlantis.

Heritage Foundation. *2012 Economic Freedom Network.**

Hermansson, Jörgen. 2003. *Politik på upplysningens grund.* Stockholm: Liber.

Herlitz, Gillis. 2003. *Svenskar. Hur vi är och varför.* Uppsala: Uppsala Publishing House.

Himmelstrand, Jonas. 2007. *Att följa sitt hjärta – i jantelagens Sverige.* Uppsala: Happy company publishing.

Hirschfeldt, Johan. 2011. "Domstolarna som statsmakt" in *Juridisk Tidskrift.* Vol : 1.

Hirschfeldt, Johan. 2009. "Grundlagsutredningens förslag om domstolarna" in Borgeke, Martin. (ed) *Blandade uppsatser. Vänbok till Lars-Göran Engström.* Malmö: Hovrätten i Skåne och Blekinge.

Hirdman, Yvonne. 1988. *Att lägga livet tillrätta.* Stockholm: Carlssons.

Hitchens, Christopher. 2011. *Arguably. Essays.* London: Atlantic.

Holmberg and Weibull (eds.) 2007 *Det nya Sverige.* SOM-institutet. Göteborg: Gothenburg University Press.

Hultén, Gösta and Samuelsson, Jan. 1983. Mediavänstern. En närbild av den dolda åsiktsproduktionen I Sverige. Stockholm: Bonnier Fakta.

Huntford, Roland. 1971. *The new totalitarians.* London: Allen Lane.* [Swedish translation *Det blinda Sverige* 1972]

Huteau, Benjamin and Larraufie, Jean-Yves. 2009 *Le malentendu suédois.* Paris: Paris Tech.*

Hägg, Göran. 2005. *Välfärdsåren. Svensk historia 1945- 1986.* Stockholm: W&W.

Isaksson, Anders. 2006. *Den politiska adeln.* Stockholm: Bonniers.

Isaksson, Christer. 2010. *Den nya vän(S)tern.* Stockholm: Ekerlids.

Jacobsson, Kerstin (ed.) 2010. *Känslan för det allmänna. Medborgarnas relation till staten och varandra.* Umeå: Borea.

Jallai, Anders. 2011. *Landsförrädaren.* Stockholm: Lind & Co.

Jalving, Mikael. 2009. *Absolut Sverige. En rejse i tavshedens rige.* Københavnpenhagen: Jyllands-Postens forlag.

Jansson, Li. 2012. *Välståndssamhälle för alla.* Stockholm: Ekerlids.

Jeersild, PC. 1986. *Children's Island.* Lincoln: University of Nebraska Press.[original 1976]

Johansson, Lars Anders. 2012. *Hatets och illivljans kolportörer.* Stockholm: Timbro

Johansson, Fredrik. 2009. *Befria förskolan.* Stockholm: Timbro.*

Johansson, Mats. 1998. *De svarta åren. Minnen från andra sidan.* Stockholm: Timbro

Johansson Heinö, Andreas. 2011. *Integration eller assimilation? En utvärdering av svensk integrationsdebatt.* Stockholm: Timbro.*

Johnsson, Anders. 2008. *Globaliseringens tre vågor. Sveriges internationalisering under 10 år.* Globaliseringsrådet. Stockholm: Regeringskanliset, Utbildningsdepartementet.*

Jonsson, Rickard. 2007. *Blatte betyder kompis.* Diss. Stockholm: Ordfront.

Josefsson, Dennis. 2005. *Reformerna som förändrade Sverige.* The Swedish Model, rapport nr 2. Stockholm: Ratio.*

Jonung, Lars. 2002-11- 19."Kronfallet som skakade Sverige" in *Dagens Nyheter.*

Judt, Tony, 2009-12-17. "What Is Living and What Is Dead in Social Democracy?" in *New York Review of Books.* *

Judt, Tony. 2010. *Ill fares the land.* London: Penguin.

Jämställdhetsombudsmannen. 2008. *Miljongranskningen.* Stockholm: Jämo.

Karaveli, Magnus. 1997. *Blågul framtid*. Stockholm: Arena

Karlsson, Sten O. 2001. *Det intelligenta samhället: En omtolkning av den socialdemokratiska idéhistorien*. Stockholm: Carlssons

Kihlbom, Magnus et. al. 2009. *Förskola för de allra yngsta – på gott och ont?* Stockholm: Carlssons.

Kristersson, Ulf. 2011. "Bevara och förnya välfärdspolitiken", in *Axess*. No 2.*

Kågeson, Per. 2006. *Tid för barn ?* Stockholm: SNS

Kullbom, Pierre and Landin, Per (eds.) 1998. *Politisk korrekthet på svenska*. Stehag: Symposium.

Birgitta Kurtén-Lindberg. 2001. *Tokfeminismen*. Stockholm: Timbro*

Laakso, Erik and Lerulf, Philip. 2011. *Medborgare på marginalen*. Stockholm: Timbro *

Larsson, Hans-Albin. 2011. *Mot bättre vetande. En svensk skolhistoria*. Stockholm: SNS

Lagercrantz, Olof. 2011. *Vårt sekel är reserverat åt lögnen*. Stockholm: Karneval förlag.

Lambertz, Göran. 2006-10-03. "En global kris för yttrandefriheten" in *Upsala Nya Tidning*.*

Landin, Per. 2004. *Jag heter Per Landin*. Stehag: Symposium.

Larsson, Janerik. 2011. *Så förändrades Sverige*. Stockholm: Svenskt Näringsliv

Lasch, Christopher. *The revolt of the elites and the betrayal of democracy*. New York: Norton.

Lifvendahl, Tove. 2000. *Gösta Bohman. Hjälten och myten*. Stockholm: Timbro.

Lifvendahl, Tove. 2011. *Från sagoland till framtidsland. Om svensk identitet, utveckling och emigration*. Stockholm: Hjalmarsson & Högberg.

Lindbeck, Assar. 1997. "The Swedish experiment" in *Journal of Economic Literature*. Vol. XXXV: Sept.*

Lindbeck, Assar. 2003. *Välfärdstat och sociala normer*. Manuskript. Stockholm: SNS*

Lindbeck, Assar. 2008. "Sociala normer och socialförsäkringar: Teori och svenska erfarenheter" , in *Ekonomisk Debatt*, Vol. 36: 6. *

Lindbeck, Assar, Palme, Mårten and Persson, Mats. 2004. "Sjukskrivning som socialt fenomen", in *Ekonomisk Debatt*. Vol. 32: 4. *

Lindbeck, Assar.2012. *Ekonomi är att välja*. Stockholm: Bonniers.

Lindbeck, Assar. Personal website at Stockholm University http://people. su.se/~alind/

Lindbom, Anders. 2011. *Systemskifte ? Den nya svenska välfärdspolitken*. Lund: Studentlitteratur.

Linder, PJ Anders. 2006. *Ett folk i kollektiv näringsförbud*. Stockholm: Svenska Dagbladet.

Ljungberg, Carl- Johan et. al. 2009. *Betongväldet*. Stockholm: Empron.

Ljunggren, Jens. 2009. *Inget land för intellektuella: 68–revolten och svenska vänsterintellektuella.* Lund: Nordic Academic Press

Ljunggren, Stig-Björn. 1992. *Folkhemskapitalismen.* Diss. Stockholm: Tiden.

Ljunggren, Stig-Björn. 1994. *Ett visst mått av frihet.* Stockholm: Tiden.

Ljunggren, Stig-Björn. 2011-10-07. "En bitter opposition ger alliansen övertaget" in *Svenska Dagbladet.**

Löfstedt, Jan-Ingvar. 1977. *Röd och expert: utbildning för utveckling i Kina* Stockholm: W & W.

Lönegård, Claes. 2011. "Propagandaministerns plan" *in Fokus.* No 10.

Lövgren, Orvar (ed.).1988. *Hej det är från försäkringskassan.* Stockholm: Natur och kultur

Mahmood, Quisar. 2012. *Jakten på svenskheten.* Stockholm: Natur och Kultur

Magnusson, Lars. 2010. *Sveriges ekonomiska historia.* Stockholm: Norstedts.

Martinsson, Harry 1998. *Aniara. An Epic Science Fiction Poem.* Brownsville: Storyline Press. [original 1956]

Mattlar, Jörgen . 2008. *Skolbokspropaganda? – En ideologianalys av läroböcker i svenska som andraspråk (1995-2005).* Diss. Uppsala: Uppsala Universitet, Pedagogiska Institutionen.

Mattsson, Janne and Rauscher, Deanne. 2004. *Makten, männen, mörkläggningen : historien om bordellhärvan 1976.* Stockholm: Vertigo.

McKinsey. 2006. *Sweden's economic performance.**

McKinsey. 2012 *Tillväxt och förnyelse i den svenska ekonomin.**

Medborgarrättsrörelsen. 2008. *Europadomstolen är ingen-lekstuga.**

Melki, Elias. 2009. *När skatteverket anfaller.* Saltsjö-Duvnäs: Efron.

Mireja. Tankesmedja för välfärd och utveckling genom nära relationer. www.mireja. se *

Mitchell, David. 2007. *What Can the United States Learn from the Nordic Model?* Policy Analysis no. 603. Washington D.C.: CATO Institute.*

Munkhammar, Johnny. 2005. *European dawn. After the social model.* Stockholm: Timbro/Stockholm Network

Munkhammar, Johnny. 2007. *The guide to reform.* Stockholm: Timbro/IEA

Munkhammar, Johnny.2011. *Du ska bli miljonär.* Stockholm: Timbro*

Murray, Charles. 2012. *Coming apart: The state of white American 1960-2010.* New York: Crown Forum.

Myrdal, Alva. 1941 *Nation and family.* New York: Harpers.

Myrdal, Alva and Gunnar. 1997. *Kris i befolkningsfrågan.* Nora: Nya Doxa. [original 1934]

New York Times. 2008-09-22. "How Sweden solved its bank crisis".*

Nilsson, Ulf. 2005. *What Happened to Sweden? - While America Became the Only Superpower.* New Canaan: Nordstjernan-Swedish News.

Norberg, Johan. 1999a. *Fullständiga rättigheter.* Stockholm: Timbro*

Norberg, Johan. 1999b. *Den svenska liberalismens historia.* Stockholm: Timbro.

Norberg, Johan. 2010. *Fragment och argument 1990- 2010.* Stocksund: Hydra förlag.

Nordfors, Mirjam. 2006. *Vad är den svenska modellen ?* Rapport no 1. The Swedish Model Stockholm: Ratio.*

Nordin, Svante. 2008. *Humaniora i Sverige.* Stockholm: Atlantis.

Nycander, Svante. 2003-10-26. "Dragkampen om samförståndet" in *Svenska Dagbladet.*

Nycander, Svante. 2007. "What made America go to the right, Sweden to the left? On the importance of labour laws", in *American Studies in Scandinavia,* vol 39: 1.*

Nycander, Svante. 2008. "Socialdemokratin och historiens list" in *Mellan folkhem och Europa* (eds. Bennich-Björkman & Blomkvist). Stockholm: Liber.

Nycander, Svante. 2009. *Liberalismens idéhistoria.* Stockholm: SNS.

Nycander, Svante. 2010a. 2010-11-20 "Palme bröt med S-traditionen", *in Dagens Nyheter.*

Nycander, Svante. 2010b. *Sist in, först ut.* Stockholm: SNS.

Nyqvist, Anette. 2007. *Opening the Orange Envelope. Reform and Responsibility in the Remaking of the Swedish National Pension System.* Diss.,Stockholm: Stockholm University. Department of social anthropology.

OECD. 2000. *Messages from PISA.* Paris: OECD/PISA*

OECD. 2011. *Economic Survey of Sweden.* Paris: OECD.*

Oftedal Telhaug, Alfred, Asbjørn Mediås, Odd and Aasen, Petter. 2006. "The Nordic Model in Education:

Education as part of the political system in the last 50 years" in *Scandinavian Journal of Educational Research*

Vol. 50: 3.

Ohlsson, Per T. 1994. *Gudarnas ö. Om det extremt svenska.* Stockholm: Brombergs.

Ohlsson, Per T. 2006-09-28. "Sweden still the middle way?" Talk at Colombia University.*

Ohrlander, Gunnar. 2009. *Den gudarna älskar. Konsten att överleva som lärare.* Sundbyberg: Optimal förlag.

Olson, Stefan. 2011. *Handbok i modern konservatism.* Stockholm: Atlantis.

Palmer, Tom (ed.) 2011. *The Morality of Capitalism. What Your Professors Won't Tell You.* New Delhi: Centre for Civil Society.*

Persson, Leif GW. 2010. *Between summer's longing and winter's end.* New York: Pantheon.

Persson, Leif GW. 2012. *Another Time, Another Life.* New York: Pantheon.

Persson, Louise. 2010. *Klassisk feminism.* Stocksund: Hydra förlag

Psykisk hälsa. 2011. Temanummer om förskola och skola. No 3 & 4.

Rankka, Maria. 2005. *Från fristående ämbetsverk till rörelsedrivna idéfabriker.* Stockholm: Timbro.*

Rankka, Maria and Segerfeldt, Fredrik. 2006. *Makt. Om Sverige demokratiska underskott.* Stockholm: Timbro.

Rexania, Farbod. 2007. *Bortom etnicitet.* Stockholm: Svenskt Näringsliv.*

Rivière, Helena. 1998. *Bidragskulturen. Filosofin bakom socialbidraget.* Stockholm: Timbro.*

ROHUS. Riksorganisationen för hemundervisning i Sverige. www.rohus.nu *

Rojas, Mauricio. 1993. *I ensamhetens labyrint.* Stockholm: Brombergs.

Rojas, Mauricio. 1999. *Välfärd efter välfärdsstaten.* Stockholm: Timbro.*

Rojas, Mauricio. 2004. *Farväl till gemenskapen.* Stockholm: Timbro.

Rojas, Mauricio. 2005. *Sweden after the Swedish Model.* Stockholm: Timbro.*

Rojas, Mauricio. 2007. *(S)skolan.* Stockholm: Timbro.*

Rothstein, Bo. 1996. *The Social Democratic State.* Pittsburgh: Pittsburgh University Press.

Rothstein, Bo. 2005 ."Sverige – de ideologiska statsapparaternas förlovade land" in Ronit, Karsten and Rothstein, Bo (eds.). *Den politiske forvaltning. Historiske spor i nutidens bureaukrati . Festskrift till Tim Knudsen.* Köpenhamn: Systime Förlag.*

Rorty, Richard. 1998. *Achieving Our Country: Leftist Thought in Twentieth-Century America.* Cambridge: Harvard University Press.

Rothstein, Bo. 2006a. "Det moderna patriarkatet – den kausala mekanismen. En teori om asymmetriskt partnerval" in *Arkiv för studier i arbetarrörelsens historia* vol 94/95.*

Rothstein, Bo. 2006b. "Grundlagen i det mångkulturella samhället" in Blückert, Kjell and Österberg, Eva (eds.): *Gränslöst – forskning i Sverige och världen.* Festskrift till Dan Brändström. Stockholm: Natur och Kultur.*

Rothstein, Bo. 2008. *Förargelseväckande beteende: om konsten att inte sitta stilla i båten.* Stockholm: SNS.

Rothstein, Bo. 2010. "Happiness and the welfare state", in *Social Research.* Vol 77: 2.*

Rothstein, Bo. 2011a. "Social tillit, lycka, korruption och välfärdsstat" in Holmberg,Sören et al (eds.). *Lycksalighetens ö.* SOM- institutet. Göteborg: Gothenburg University Press.*

Rothstein, Bo. 2011b. *The quality of government.* Chicago: University of Chicago Press.

Rothstein, Bo. 2011c. "De dubbelt ratade" in Nielsén, Tobias and Nilsson, Sven (eds.) *Framtiden är nu: KulturSverige 2040.* Malmö: Volante QNB Publishing.*

Rönnegård, Eric. 2008. *Kris i ledningen för svensk polis: mordet på Anna Lindh inget undantag.* Stockholm: Jure.

Sahlgren, Gabriel. 2010. *Schooling for money: Swedish Education Reform and the Role of the Profit Motive. IEA Discussion paper no 33.* London: Institute for Economic Affairs.*

Sanandaji, Nima. 2011. *The Swedish model reassessed.* Libera: Helsinki.*

Sanandji, Nima . 2012. *The surprising ingredients of Swedish success.* IEA Discussion Paper no 41. London: Institute of Economic Affairs.*

Sanandaji, Nima and Nyman, Anders. 2007. *I fackföreningarnas intresse?* Stockholm: Captus.*

Sandberg, Nils-Eric. 1997. *What went wrong in Sweden?* Stockholm: Timbro.*

Sandberg, Nils-Eric. 2009. *Fritänkaren. Ett vänporträtt av Sven Rydenfelt.* Stockholm: Timbro

Sandelin, Magnus. 2012. *Jihad. Svenskarna i de islamistiska terrornätverken.* Stockholm: Reporto.

Sandelin, Gunnar. 2011-12-20. "Saklig diskussion bästa motgiftet mot rasism" in *Dagens Nyheter.*

Santeson Wilson, Peter. 2011. *Lättare sagt än gjort? En översikt av politiska svårigheter vid välfärdsstatsreformer.* Rapport no 9. The Swedish Model. Stockholm: Ratio.*

Santesson, Peter. 2011. *Kvoterad föräldraförsäkring – svagt stöd i opinionen.* Timbro: Stockholm

Santesson, Peter. 2012. *Reformpolitikens strategier.* Stockholm: Atlantis.

Saunders, Peter. 2010. *Beware False Prophets Equality, the Good Society and The Spirit Level.* London: Policy Exchange.

Schein, Harry. 1996 "Jag tror inte för fem öre på det mångkulturella samhället" in Nestius, Hans et al. *"Och vi som ville så väl . . " 19 röster om det mångkulturella Sverige.* Stockholm: Carlssons.

Schultz, Mårten. 2008. "Kritik mot kränkningsbegreppet" in *Svensk Juristtidning.* No 1.

Segerfeldt, Fredrik. 2006. *Enpartistaten – en sammanfattning.* Stockholm: Timbro.*

Segerfeldt, Fredrik. 2012. *Vad lär vi våra barn om världen?* Stockholm: Timbro.*

Segerstedt, Torgny T. (ed.). 1983. *Välfärdsstatens psykologi.* Stockholm: Ratio.

Sejerstad, Francis. 2005. *Socialdemokratins tidsålder.* Nora: Nya Doxa. [English translation 2011]

SILC. 2012. *Bistånd är politik.* Stockholm: Swedish International Liberal Center (SILC).

Sjunnesson, Jan. 1991. "Pragmatisk politik som liberalismens legitimitet" in *Zenit.* Vol 23: 2.

Sjunnesson, Jan. 1998. Chapter in *Universitetet som kulturell mötesplats.* Uppsala: Uppsala universitet.

Sjunnesson, Jan. 2002. "Filosofernas antifilosof vill återupprätta vänstern" in *Axess*. No 3.

Sjunnesson , Jan. 2008-08-21 "Hur ska invandrare ta seden dit de kommer?" in *Dagen*.*

Sjunnesson, Jan. 2012. "Arbetardöttrar, post-progressivism och den förvirrande lära-rutbildningen" in *Pedagogisk Forskning i Sverige* Vol 16: 4.

Sjunnesson, Jan 2012. *School vouchers in Sweden. Policy Review* no 5. New Delhi: Centre for Civil Society.*

Sjunnesson, Jan. (forthcoming) *Sara Sarasvati. An Indo-Swedish story.*

Sjöstedt, Erik (ed.). *FFFF: frihet, familj, flit, företagsamhet : en ny kristdemokrati*. Lidingö: Ettill förlag.

Skolverket. 2009. *Attityder till skolan*. Skolverket: Stockholm.*

Skolverket. 2011. *PM. Barn och personal i förskolan hösten 2010*. Stockholm: Skolverket.*

Skolvärlden. 2010-12-10. "Den svenska DDR skolan".*

Socialdemokratins partiprogram 1897- 1990. 2001. Stockholm: Arbetarrörelsens arkiv & bibliotek.*

Sontag, Susan. 1969. "Letter from Sweden" in *Ramparts*. July.*

Stjernfelt, Fredrik and Thomsen, Søren Ulrik Thomsen. 2007. *Kritik av den negativa uppbyggligheten*. Stockholm: Ruin förlag. [original 2005]

Ström, Per. 2007. *Mansförtryck och kvinnovälde*. Stockholm: Den Nya Välfärden.*

Ström Melin, Annika. 2010. *Persson*. Stockholm: Albert Bonniers förlag.

Svanberg, Carl. 2009. Är ungdomen individualistisk? Stockholm: Timbro.*

Svensson, Mattias. 2000. *Mindre politik, mer demokrati*. Stockholm: Timbro*

Svensson, Mattias. 2011. *Glädjedödarna*. Stockholm: Timbro.

Sveriges Offentliga Utredningar. 1976. *Sexualbrottsutredningen*. SOU 1976:9. Stockholm: Regeringskansliet.

Sveriges Offentliga Utredningar. 1993. *Nya villkor för ekonomi och politik: Ekonomikommis-sionens [Lindbeckkommissionens] förslag*. SOU 1993:16. Stockholm: Regeringskansliet.

Sveriges Offentliga Utredningar . 2000. *Steriliseringsfrågan i Sverige 1935 – 1975*. SOU 2000:20. Stockholm: Regeringskansliet.*

Sveriges Offentliga Utredningar . *Fred och säkerhet - säkerhetspolitiska utredningen*. SOU 2002:108. Stockholm: Regeringskansliet.

Sveriges Offentliga Utredningar. 2000. *Two of a kind*. SOU 2000: 83. Stockholm: Re-geringskansliet.*

Sveriges Offentliga Utredningar. 2005. *Sverige och tsunamin – granskning och förslag* SOU 2005:104. Stockholm: Regeringskansliet.*

Sveriges Offentliga Utredningar 2007. *Tsunamibanden*. SOU 2007:44. Stockholm: Regeringskansliet.*

Sveriges Offentliga Utredningar 2007. *Opinionsbildande verksamheter och små myndigheter*. SOU 2007:107. Stockholm: Regeringskansliet.*

Sveriges Offentliga Utredningar 2011. *Långtidsutredningen*. SOU 2011:11. Stockholm: Regeringskansliet.*

Sveriges Offentliga Utredningar . 2012. *Nya påföljder* SOU 2012:34. Stockholm: Regeringskansliet

Sveriges Riksdag. 1992. *Konstitutionsutskottets Granskningsbetänkande*, 1992/93. KU: 30. Del 1. Stockholm: Riksdagen.*

Sundberg- Weitman, Brita. 2008. *Sverige och rättsstaten på 2000-talet*. Vällingby: Elanders Gotab.

Sundström, Göran, 2009. "He who decides: Swedish social democratic governments from a presidentialisation perspective" in *Scandinavian Political Studies*. Vol 32: 2.

Svallfors, Stefan. 2011-01-05 "Efter arbetet" in *ETC*.*

Svallfors, Stefan. 2011. "A bedrock of support? Trends in welfare state attitudes in Sweden 1981-2010" in *Social Policy & administration*. Vol 45: 7.

Svanborg- Sjövall, Karin. 2011. *Kentucky Fried Children. Om den svenska valfrihetens rötter och dess fiender*. Stockholm: Timbro. English translation 2013.

Svenska Institutet. 2010. *Sverigebildsrapporten 2010*. Stockholm. Svenska Institutet.*

Svenska Institutet. 2012. *Sverigebilden utomlands*. Stockholm. Svenska Institutet.*

Svenska Dagbladet 2010-04-20. Debattinlägg om vårdnadsbidrag.*

Svenskt Näringsliv. 2009. *Advantage Sweden - A programme for the future of companies and jobs*. Stockholm: Svenskt Näringsliv. *

Svenskt Näringsliv och Landsorganisationen. 2011. *Faktiska konsekvenser av lagen om anställningsskydd*. Stockholm: LO and Svenskt Näringsliv.*

Sydsvenska Dagbladet. 2010-10-10."En myndighet för mycket".*

Söderbaum, Jakob E:son. 2011. *Konservatism och kapitalism. Ett omaka par*. Stockholm: Tradition och Fason.*

Söderlund, Gustaf (intro.) 1958. *Revolt mot välfärdsstaten*. Stockholm: Natur och Kultur.

The Local. Sweden's news in English. *www.thelocal.se* *

Thelin, Krister. 2000. *Sverige som rättsstat*. Stockholm: Timbro.*

Time Magazine. 1969-10-10. "Hot soup from Olof".*

Time Magazine. 1973-01- 29. Interview with Olof Palme.*

Tribell, Håkan. (ed.) 2011. *Den nya borgerligheten*. Stockholm: Timbro.

Tribell, Håkan (ed) 2012. *Den borgerlige optimisten*. Vänbok till PJ Anders Linder. Stockholm: Timbro.

Tullberg, Jan. 2011. "Invandringen och den svenska ekonomin, in *Ekonomisk Debatt*. Vol 39: 1.*

Trägårdh, Lars 2011. *Det borgerliga samhället: I tur och retur?*. Stockholm: Timbro*

Trägårdh, Lars. 2012-02-02. "The Swedish model is the opposite of the big society, David Cameron" in *The Guardian*.*

Uddhammar, Emil. 1993. *Partierna och den stora staten*. Diss. Stockholm: City University

Wager, Merit. 2012. *Inte svart eller vitt utan svart och vitt: miggor berättar*. Stockholm: Mummelförlaget.

Warnling–Nerep, Wiweka. 1995. *Kommuners lag- och domstolstrots*. Stockholm: Juristförlaget.

Washington Post. 2012-03-13. "Who created the Nordic Model trademark row rages in Europe's North".

Westholm, Carl- Johan. *Se Staten!*. Stockholm: Timbro.*

Wickman, Kurt. 2010. *Höga skatter gör staten instabil*. Stockholm: Skattebetalarna. *

Wijkström, Filip et al. 2006. *Swedish academic and public civil society debate 1995- 2005*. EFI/ CINEFOGO project. Stockholm: Stockholm school of Economics.*

Wikipedia. http://sv.wikipedia.org/wiki/Melodifestivalen_1976 .*

World Values Survey. www.worldvaluessurvey.org . *

Zaremba, Maciej. 1992. *Minken i folkhemmet*. Stockholm: Timbro

Zaremba, Maciej. 2003. *När blir Sverige europeiskt?* Wibbleföreläsningen 2003. Stockholm: Ohlinstitutet.*

Zaremba, Maciej. 2006. *Den polske rörmokaren*. Stockholm: Norstedts.

Zaremba, Maciej and Malmström, Cecilia. 2003. *Vad har Sverige i Europa att göra ?* Rapport till EUs framtidskonvent. Stockholm: Vision Europa.

Zetterberg, Hans. 2011. *Texter i urval*. Stockholm: Timbro och Hydra förlag.

Zetterberg, Hans and Ljunggren, Carl Johan. 1997. *Den svenska socialstaten*. Stockholm: City University Press.

Ådhal, Martin. 2009. *Den svenska landsbygdsliberalismens betydelse*. Stockholm: Fores.*

Ödman, Per-Johan. 1995. *Kontrasternas spel. En svensk mentalitets- och pedagogikhistoria*. Stockholm: Norstedts.

Östberg, Kjell. 2002. *1968. När allt var i rörelse*. Stockholm: Prisma.

Östberg, Kjell. 2008. *I takt med tiden. Olof Palme 1927- 1969*. Stockholm: Leopard.

Östberg, Kjell. 2009. *När vinden vände. Olof Palme 1969 – 1986*. Stockholm: Leopard.

Östergren, Petra (ed.) 2008. *F-ordet. Mot en ny feminism*. Stockholm: Pocketförlaget.